PRAISE FOR
ONE WITH THE ROAD

"Reger takes the reader on a wild ride all around the US, and we get to share in the experience of how opening our eyes to the world around us and the people we share it with can change us for the better and enrich our lives. In his refreshingly different take on the classic travelogue, the author offers us all a possible solution to one of the great miseries of modern time, the ennui of living a too 'normal' life. Put your helmet on and take it for spin!"

—Larry Olmsted, *New York Times* Best-Selling Author of *Real Food/Fake Food* and *Fans*, Award-Winning Travel Writer

"At first glance, *One with the Road* appears to be an Easy Rider fantasy. For John Reger it is a classic search for himself and the United States while driving a Harley Davidson motorcycle. John Reger, in his forties, visits forty states and meets interesting people—among these, a hitchhiking preacher, a truck-stop dentist, and many others. Taking everything into account, these people accentuate that being different is what makes life interesting. Once his pilgrimage is finished, John Reger arrives home and goes to the beach. His last line says it all: 'While the water from the ocean nipped at my feet, I fantasized about what it would be like to ride to Alaska on my motorcycle.' Seems like the road ain't through beckoning!"

—Tony Dora, Author of *A Boy, an Orphanage, a Cuban Refugee: The Road to Freedom*

"What an adventure! Well written and fast paced, Reger's brutally honest memoir chronicles his Harley-inspired journey of self-discovery, daring us to revel in the joy of spontaneity."

—Kathleen Reid, 2021 PenCraft Book Award Winner, Author of *Secrets in the Palazzo* and *Sunrise in Florence*

One with the Road

by John Reger

© Copyright 2023 John Reger

ISBN 978-1-64663-903-8

All rights reserved. No part of this publication
may be reproduced, stored in a retrieval system,
or transmitted in any form or by any means—
electronic, mechanical, photocopy, recording, or any other—
except for brief quotations in printed reviews, without the prior
written permission of the author.

Published by

köehlerbooks™

3705 Shore Drive
Virginia Beach, VA 23455
800-435-4811
www.koehlerbooks.com

ONE WITH THE ROAD

BY JOHN REGER

VIRGINIA BEACH
CAPE CHARLES

★ Sunset Beach

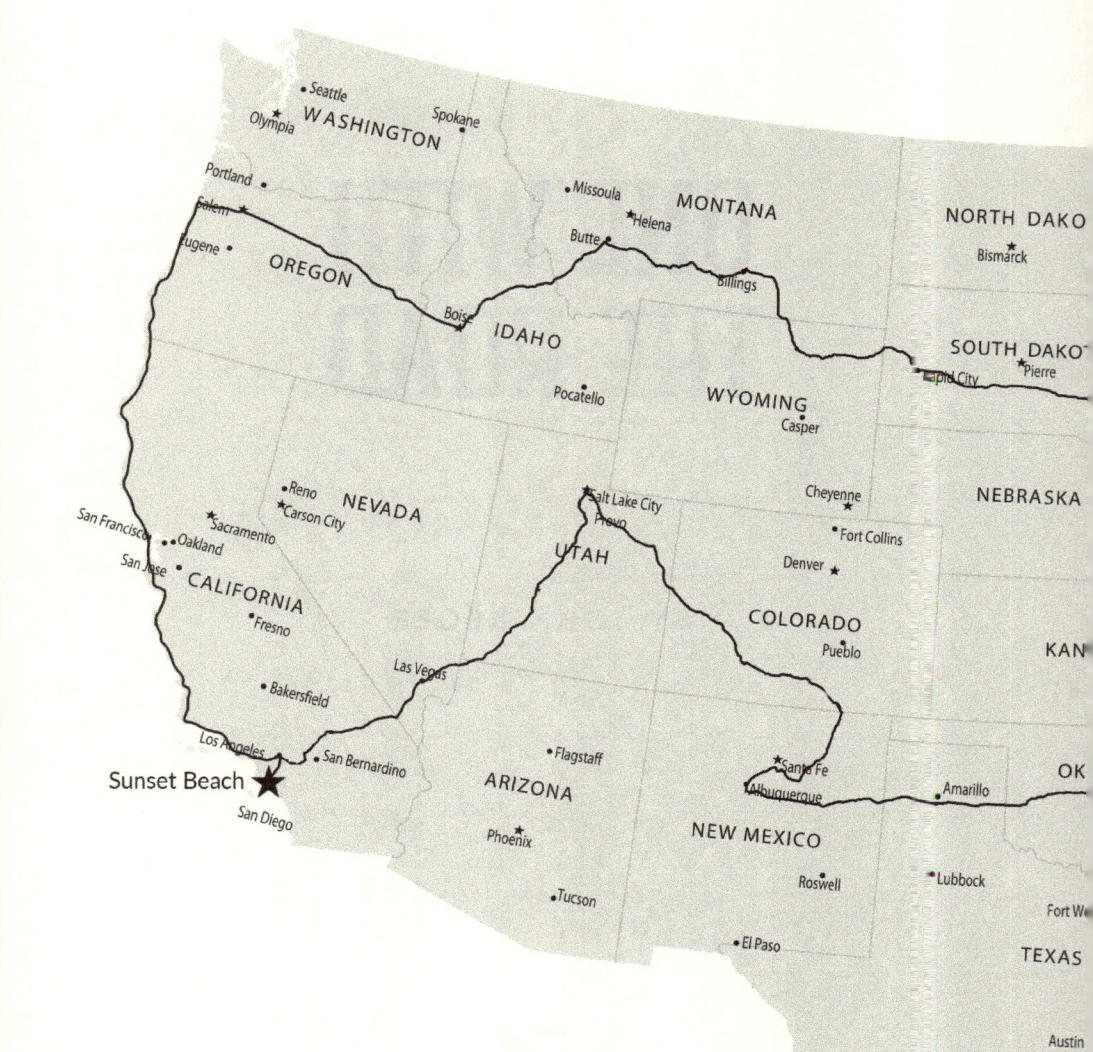

MAINE
Bangor
Augusta
Portland
Montpelier
Burlington
VERMONT
NEW HAMPSHIRE
Concord
MASSACHUSETTS
Boston
Providence
Syracuse
NEW YORK
Albany
Springfield
Hartford
RHODE ISLAND
Buffalo
Scranton
New York
CONNECTICUT
Trenton
NEW JERSEY
PENNSYLVANIA
Harrisburg
Pittsburgh
Philadelphia
Baltimore
Annapolis
Dover
DELAWARE
Washington
DC
MARYLAND
WEST VIRGINIA
Charleston
VIRGINIA
Richmond
Norfolk
Virginia Beach
Cleveland
Toledo
Detroit
Grand Rapids
MICHIGAN
Chicago
Fort Wayne
INDIANA
Indianapolis
Columbus
Cincinnati
Frankfort
Evansville
Duluth
Minneapolis
St Paul
Madison
Cedar Rapids
IOWA
Des Moines
Kansas City
MISSOURI
Jefferson City
St Louis
Springfield
Knoxville
Winston-Salem
Greensboro
Raleigh
NORTH CAROLINA
Charlotte
Wilmington
Greenville
Columbia
SOUTH CAROLINA
Charleston
Atlanta
GEORGIA
Macon
Columbus
Savannah
Birmingham
Meridian
Jackson
Fort Smith
ARKANSAS
Little Rock
Shreveport
LOUISIANA
Baton Rouge
Biloxi
Mobile
Valdosta
Jacksonville
Tallahassee
Orlando
Tampa
FLORIDA
Miami

To Heather,

we did it.

CHAPTER

1

Misguided was the direction that never seemed to get me lost. It was a well-worn path, traveled frequently and with great obstinacy masked as a conviction. It was the route I always took, despite the advice of others, who traversed more ordinary roads in life and thought it was best for me if I followed. They knew their words were wasted. The straight and narrow never appealed to me.

Still, they tried, hoping they could persuade me into conformity. They wanted me there with them. Maybe it was good intentions, but I suspected it was more to validate their own choices, give comfort to decisions they questioned, and erase some doubt and regret.

What they didn't realize—and I never divulged—was that the banality of life petrified me. I abhorred it and fought it constantly. Often, I won temporary victories in the battle, but the war seemed to be lost, unnoticeable until I was firmly in the clutches of the mundane, and then the crushing defeat was apparent, though there was not a formal surrender on my part. Stubborn German genes would never allow that. I had constructed an impenetrable wall built with pride and denial that I hid behind, convinced I was safe from all that terrified me.

My angst was triggered by events most would embrace with extreme satisfaction: a job that reached a milestone anniversary; a relationship headed toward marriage; hell, even staying in an apartment too long was enough to trigger my anxiety. All were a signal it was time to go. Run, run anywhere but where I was, anywhere that gave the appearance of security and roots. It seemed impulsive, but I was frighteningly predictable and repeatedly ran. Deserting responsibility seemed sensible. It felt correct. This was my normal. I knew no other way, nor did I have the tools to find an alternative.

My upbringing wasn't the culprit—or maybe it was. I grew up in La Crescenta, California, a middle-class neighborhood in the hills above Los Angeles, never needing anything but always wanting more than what was provided. I should have been happy; the security of the suburbs kept my spirit satisfied. Instead, it choked me with panic. I wasn't a wandering soul. I was a fleeing refugee.

Being parents wasn't high on either my mom or dad's list. It was a sense of duty they felt they had to perform as a married couple. My mom admitted later that if they had to do it over again, they would have been childless. This wasn't said to hurt me; it was just the blunt, matter-of-fact communication method both my parents used with their children when they chose to talk to us at all.

My parents had one of the greatest relationships I had ever seen. My mother's mom died during her birth, and her father didn't know how to be a parent, much less a single father. Her formative years were spent with an abusive stepmother, and when she was a teenager fresh out of high school, the roles reversed and she was taking care of my divorced grandfather. He chased dreams and get-rich-quick schemes that never seemed to pan out. She worked and paid the bills. When they couldn't pay the rent, they moved to another apartment.

My father grew up in a lower-class neighborhood in suburban Buffalo, New York, raised by two stern parents who instilled stability. He graduated from a Catholic high school and briefly went to college, but work appealed more to his blue-collar nature.

He met my mom in a bar and took her away from her troubled world. They married and moved to Hollywood, California, trading snow and bone-chilling cold for sunshine and palm trees. They had nothing but each other and it was more than either could have dreamed of possessing. They were totally in love, and when my mom died after forty-four years of marriage, my dad followed fourteen months later, the victim of a broken heart.

That love came at the expense of my brother and me, and while they worked diligently on their marriage, my sibling and I suffered from the lack of attention.

The neglect gave us a lot of time to ourselves, an opportunity to be free spirits. While I embraced it, my brother rebelled, acting out in a fruitless attempt to get any attention, even if it was negative.

Rather than stay and fight, as my brother vainly did, I chose the coward's way out. I took off whenever possible. Initially, my bicycle provided the escape peddling to other neighborhoods, not coming home until well after dark.

The sleepy little town I grew up in was a safe place for a kid mostly on his own. There was no fear of abduction or assault, so common today, and I reveled in the oasis. I left the house early, often at first light, and rarely got home before dark. There was a loose rule about coming home when the streetlights came on, but I frequently tested it and rarely suffered any consequences.

I began with the mountains behind my house, where there was a former sanitarium that had been washed out during a flood. Its cement buildings and a few old rusted-out Packards and DeSotos were at the bottom of the canyon. I caught crawdads in the riverbeds and hunted crows with a BB gun. When I got bored with the mountains, I peddled to the main drag venturing into the stores and back alleys. These were limited journeys, and I soon outgrew them.

When I could afford it, around age fourteen, I bought a used moped and rode the fifteen miles from my home to downtown Los Angeles and investigated the enclaves. I avoided the highways, one, because my vehicle wasn't freeway legal, and two, the streets were always infinitely more interesting.

I saw merchants in Chinatown slaughter ducks in the alleyways and hang them in storefront windows. I talked to the homeless on Skid Row in downtown Los Angeles and to prostitutes who strolled up and down the main streets of Hollywood. I ate next to undocumented Mexicans at taco trucks in East Los Angeles. I went to the Watts Towers before I was fifteen, naively parking my unlocked scooter in an area that had seen riots when I was a newborn. It was now a gang-infested area White people ignored, and if they did go down there, they went in the safety of packs. Not me; I felt oddly secure alone.

My first car was a hand-me-down 1965 Volkswagen Beetle my father had bought off the showroom floor, after accomplishing planned milestones of purchasing a new house and having his first child the year before. His German heritage instilled precision, and his family was complete a year later when my younger brother was born in 1966.

The VW was the first new car he had ever owned, and when I turned sixteen, he gave me the keys in one of the few father-son moments I remember from this detached, mostly emotionless man. He thought he passed down a life lesson by instilling the same structure he so coveted, but it was more like handing me the keys to my freedom.

That car and I went everywhere. I drove it when I should have been in school, and when the other kids were going to dances or football games, I was somewhere else, far away. I was the only one of my high school friends who didn't go to my senior prom. While others were celebrating a memory, they would fondly recall at future reunions, I drove past the host hotel wondering why I had no interest in attending. I was rambling around the city late into the night, searching for an answer that never came.

All I knew was that I was most comfortable mobile. I covered every inch of Los Angeles County and beyond. I could end up anywhere in the area and know where I was and how to get home.

My love was the long north and south streets like Alameda and Figueroa and Avalon Boulevard, and I could take them all the way down to the port of San Pedro to watch cruise ships or cargo tankers ease into the bay, imagining their point of origin.

A favorite east-west route was Century Boulevard. It started at Los Angeles International Airport and ended at the Jordan Downs Housing Project where the Grape Street Crips gang claimed ownership.

I discovered the canals in Venice and played basketball on the city's public courts, eating pizza and drinking cokes between games. I located every entrance in and out of Dodger Stadium. There were seven of them, eight if I counted the service road from the police academy I utilized on my motorcycle when I didn't want to pay for parking.

Towns that people had never heard of or had forgotten, I discovered: Rosewood, Bassett, Avocado Heights, Athens, City Terrace, Elftman, El Sereno, and Mount Washington were some of the cities I stumbled upon.

My favorite drive, though, was Sunset Boulevard. The road was as diverse as the city. I started with a French-dipped sandwich at Philippes, a place my parents brought me to once when relatives came from out of town. The iconic restaurant was on Alameda Street, a block from Sunset Boulevard. After a ham dip with macaroni salad and a slice of banana cream pie, I drove a block south, making a right on the famous street, the section of road to be named after Cesar Chavez, the union leader and civil rights activist. Then for the next twenty miles or so, I would stay on the boulevard made famous by Billy Wilder's 1950 movie.

Sunset Boulevard tickled the underbelly of Dodger Stadium and Echo Park on Route 66 before entering the artist community of Silver Lake and the old money neighborhood of Los Feliz. When it reached East Hollywood, I passed the hospital I was born in, my father waiting at a diner across the street, drinking coffee and smoking cigarettes with other soon-to-be fathers.

A popular section for me was a stretch from Western Avenue to Doheny Drive. Movie and television studios with high walls, restaurants, and nightclubs where celebrities ducked into back doors. Also, there was the iconic Sunset Strip, where heavy metal music was born at clubs like The Roxy, Gazzarri's, and Whisky a Go Go. Sometimes I parked and looked around, but most of the time I kept on driving.

The walls got higher when I reached Bel-Air and Beverly Hills. I knew houses were behind the concrete and trees, and as I passed, I wondered who lived there. Pacific Palisades always signaled the road's coming conclusion. The temperature dropped, as did the road, and when I saw the ocean at Pacific Coast Highway, it was a gratifying end to the day's adventure. I would park by the side of the road next to a curb of sand and stare at the water with the pride of a Magellan or da Gama.

The drive home always felt like defeat. I would take different routes—Olympic, Pico, or Santa Monica boulevards, and though I would see different sites, the direction I traveled couldn't fool me; I was headed back to a home where I didn't want to be.

College in Long Beach felt like an escape, even if it was only thirty minutes from my parents' house. It felt far enough away, but I was there not to drift but to earn a degree and begin what millions did. I got my first job in my junior year and quit twelve credits away from my bachelor's degree in journalism. I went there to prepare for a job, and the piece of paper the university held didn't seem necessary to me. The position as a reporter at a small newspaper in my hometown felt like a success, but it was short-lived. I was poor, alone, and miserable. I left after a couple of years for a road trip that confounded everyone around me. They thought I was throwing away a promising newspaper career. I was convinced I had avoided a tightening noose.

Three months later, I believed them. I didn't see much more of the country than a tourist would have. I made it to the East Coast before running out of money. I came back to Southern California feeling like I hadn't answered a calling but survived a poorly planned vacation. I was still broke but back in the arms of the love of my life whom I had met a month before my trip in California. Her name was Michelle. Like my parents, we met at a bar. She was a Puerto Rican from the Bronx who, when I told her I was a writer, replied, "I'm a reader." She was beautiful; dark hair, soft brown eyes, hourglass figure, and a smile instantly made me fall in love with her. She was sassy and ballsy, the rough New York City upbringing coming out if she felt threatened or insulted, which resulted in her telling you where to go and what bus to take to get there. Her personality was exotic to someone from such a vanilla upbringing, and, having never seen anything like it I was immediately attracted to it. I only knew I wanted her and thought I would do anything to keep her.

I got another newspaper job and worked my way up. We moved in together to a cramped studio apartment in the overpopulated San Fernando Valley. We happily sweltered through the summer with a broken air conditioner the landlord refused to fix, staying up late dreaming of moving to a better neighborhood. It was a charmed life. We moved to a beach town an hour south in Orange County, two days before the studio apartment was heavily damaged by the 1994 Northridge Earthquake.

The foundation for our relationship was built, and almost as soon as its completion, I thought of tearing it down. We were young and petrified at the possibility of a joyous life together. That level of happiness was foreign to both of us.

With tears in my eyes, I broke off the engagement. I didn't know why; I was just convinced it had to be done. It was a decision that haunts me to this day, and I frequently wonder why and what could have been. Maybe as a self-imposed punishment, I married a horrible woman a few years later. She was soulless, filled with hate, empty of passion, and got joy from the misery of others. She beat out whatever dreams I had left, and after three years, which felt like a hundred, I happily divorced her.

Like a rudderless ship, I floated around Southern California for a couple more years. The only constant was working at what many considered a dream job, covering professional golf at a major metropolitan newspaper. Though it never brought me the happiness others thought I should have, it was a job, and, yes, it was better than emptying septic tanks, but it was still just a job. I always saw work as a way to make money so that I could do what I cared about. As I approached ten years at this newspaper, I took a leave of absence and started planning a trip across the country.

As expected, my colleagues thought I was insane, to which I replied, "I'd be crazy not to go." Someone whom I didn't care for flippantly accused me of having a midlife crisis. "If that was the case," I said, "I've been having it since I was twelve years old."

But when enough people whispered in your ear, it became a roar. There were several nights spent lying in bed, trying to shout down the self-doubts. The reflections did allow me to ask pointed questions I might have otherwise avoided. I had to figure out how this trip was going to be any different from the East Coast sojourn that ended so pointlessly.

It seemed people left on these trips to discover America. I didn't need to find this country; I needed to find myself. Why did I have such a craving to eschew the trappings of life so many coveted? Why couldn't I conform? It was a puzzle I hadn't solved on the previous attempt. I marched to a different beat and figured there had to be people like me out there. Instead of trying to be like everyone else, I needed to stop apologizing for who I was and embrace myself.

It took a month, but I finally convinced myself that this trip was necessary. Instantly, it didn't feel like running. I wanted to go.

This time, I would do it right. Or so I thought.

CHAPTER 2

In the wee hours of the morning, doubts came calling, the type of sudden panic-stricken thoughts that bolted me out of a deep slumber and left me unsettled for the next hour as I attempted to calm myself enough to fall back asleep. It never worked. I tried to extinguish these newfound terrors, but they were stronger than ever. My sleep pattern provided a stage to easily entertain irrational scenarios.

Insomnia had affected me since my late teens. I tried to go to bed by midnight and could count on being awake two hours later. This continued until five or seven o'clock, and after just a couple hours of rest, I would rise for good by nine. The precision was impressive, always awake at the top of the hour and back to bed sixty minutes later.

Darkness was the enemy, and I countered this fear by leaving the lights on and the television blaring. The argument could be made that was what kept me up, but that scenario was the only thing that calmed me enough to make even the lightest sleep possible.

In college, I had a roommate in the dormitory who demanded absolute blackness and quiet, so I wasn't able to utilize my coping mechanism. I was up at least three to four times a night and spent a lot of time in the common area watching television. When the resident assistant banned me from late-night, small-screen entertainment, I wandered the campus, coming across the college radio station. Surprisingly, the door was unlocked, and I walked in, nearly giving the disc jockey a heart attack. Relieved I wasn't a serial killer, we talked while he spun jazz records per the station's format and gave me quite an education on artists such as Dinah Washington, Miles Davis, and Dexter Gordon.

The lack of sleep got worse as I got older, and when I was awake in the dark, all I could think about was what illness I had, convincing myself I was suffering from a pending heart attack, or cancer, tumors, exotic fevers indigenous to countries I had never been to, and aches and pains that I imagined as more serious than they were. There wasn't much else to do at 2 a.m. than let my hypochondriasis run wild, and it became sort of a twisted parlor game.

Now I had put aside my hobby of self-diagnosis to agonize about this trip. The list of senseless reasons that would doom the adventure was multiplying by the day. What if I crashed the motorcycle? It was possible. I had three previous accidents, though not one was my fault. The random drunk driver could slam into me, or an inattentive motorist sideswipes me changing lanes. The road was full of peril, and I had envisioned every possibility.

The most prevalent doubt was the fear of failure, and my subconscious was all too willing to point out the precedent that had been set years earlier. Try as I did to quell this fear, there was nothing I could say to refute it. I had failed and had a pretty good time lying in the black of night beating myself up over it. The question was always the same. Would this be another vain attempt that ultimately sees history repeat itself? Sure, why not? It wasn't like I had a rich résumé of following through on anything. I didn't graduate from college, my longest relationship was three years, and I began books only to quit reading them before the midway point.

All those inadequacies were trumpeted in my head, and no matter how hard I tried, I could offer no solution to dispel them. Right when I was convinced I was defeated, a friend and fellow author gave me some fatherly advice I wished I had gotten as a kid.

"I would rather fail spectacularly than succeed mundanely," he said. "If you don't go, it will haunt you for the rest of your life."

It was the verbal slap upside the head I needed. All those phobias disappeared, and I embraced the feeling of having nothing to lose. I could taste the freedom, and my trepidation was replaced with tangible excitement.

With the groundless reasons finally conquered, I had to confront two far more valid issues, and I was not looking forward to addressing either one.

Both my mother and my best friend Heather were suffering from terminal cancer. The thought was to be away from them for three months, but if either one said she needed me, the trip was done before it began. I needed a clear mind for this; I didn't want to be in Michigan and get a phone call that they were in trouble. Neither would admit it, but I was a lifeline for each of them for different reasons.

With my mother, I had to take over the role of caretaker and decision-maker because my father was incapable. He was facing the fact that he was going to lose his wife and wasn't handling it particularly well. He had gone into a shell and let his health deteriorate. I believed he was trying to beat my mother to the grave.

It made me furious that he was shirking his responsibility to the woman he had taken a vow to care for, and I felt a duty to do what he would not. I still remember the befuddled look on his face when we sat in the house and talked about her diagnosis. I knew then I would be making a lot of decisions.

The cough my mother developed around Thanksgiving wasn't going away, and she refused to go to the doctor. Two months later, she bent to tie her shoes and couldn't get back up. She went to the same hospital I was born at and sat in the ER room for a day and a half before they finally admitted her. The doctor came in and coldly told her she had stage-four liver and lung cancer and could expect about six months of life. He then abruptly left the room.

Fortunately, I had a friend who was an administrator at a much better facility, and she got my mom into a renowned cancer hospital.

Their prognosis was much better. She was still going to die, but it wasn't going to be in less than a year.

So I wasn't that concerned she was going to quash my trip. She looked and felt great and was back working at the travel agency she owned. The medicine extended her life for four more years, and she and my father left Southern California and retired to North Carolina.

I told her of my idea but also asked permission to take the trip. She had to say yes unequivocally, and if I saw the slightest hesitation, I would know she wanted me nearby.

Going to my parents' house was rarely enjoyable. It was not the house I had grown up in, and I always felt like an unwelcome guest. I was never encouraged to visit, and the only time I went there was for holidays out of duty rather than celebration. My parents sensed it as well, and one year they told me two weeks before Christmas that they were going to Hawaii. In some ways, it was a relief. I spent that Christmas day feeding the homeless, and it was one of the best holidays I had ever experienced.

She and I were more alike than either of us wanted to admit. I reminded her of her father, a dreamer of a man who shunned responsibility, and the likeness angered and frustrated her.

The difference was that my dreams didn't affect her as her father's had. That allowed me to pursue them, and as long as I didn't drag her down with me, she remained apathetic.

We sat at the dining room table across from each other and I began the sales pitch I had recited on the hour-long car ride from my apartment.

"I am going across country for three or four months," I began. "I want to discover—"

She cut me off.

"Didn't you do this once before?" she said, her nose wrinkled like she smelled something rotten. Being immediately on the defensive was something I was used to and expected. Unfazed, I continued.

"I want to discover myself and this country," I said. "I don't feel like I did that the last time."

"You aren't going to need money like last time, are you?"

"No, and it's not like you gave me any," I retorted, agitated. I caught the rage and lowered my voice a few decibels. "I will be fine. The reason I am telling you is I want to know if you'll be okay while I'm gone."

She didn't even flinch and looked at me like I was bothering her.

"I'll be fine," she snapped.

"Are you sure?"

"Of course, I'm sure. You go. It's not like I could stop you."

"You could, that's why I'm asking."

The annoying glance returned. I believed her. I had no reason not to.

That left Heather. It was a phone call I dreaded and had put off for a couple of weeks. I must have picked up my phone twenty times with every intention of calling but couldn't find the strength to do it. I even called her number a few times, hanging up before she could answer.

Over our fifteen-year friendship, we had faced turmoil, but nothing like this. At first, we never talked about her cancer, though it was on both of our minds. She got sick before my mom, and her prognosis was far more dire. Most people diagnosed with pancreatic cancer lived less than a year, and fewer than 8 percent survived more than five. With a will I had never seen before, she was already at eighteen months and looked healthy. Still, I wanted her to tell me that she felt good, and that was going to require her to talk about something uncomfortable for both of us.

We had met in college, and I knew we would be good friends. She had transferred from UCLA to Long Beach State where I already had one drunken year under my belt. I was a journalism major, and she had enough experience to be immediately named sports editor of the university's newspaper. I managed to grab one of the spots on her staff.

In our newsroom, she was the master of stealing gulps of my

Diet Coke and nibbles of my French fries. I was thankful she didn't eat red meat, so at least my cheeseburger was safe.

When she was not committing culinary petty theft, she showed me what a great editor she was. With an intense love of the language, her talent impressed me. On occasion, it also hurt me. I had several pinch marks on my arm and pulled chest hairs as punishment for any egregious errors she discovered while proofreading my work.

Another bond we shared was that we both drank heavily. We weren't like typical college students gathering around a keg and imbibing cheap beer at parties. We were professionals. We went to dive bars and drank massive quantities of vodka or rum or whiskey, and that misguided bond brought us even closer together. We spent most nights drinking until neither one of us could feel the pain. But before slurred words and blurred vision, we would talk about everything—school, literature, travel, the world, dreams, heartbreaks, the past, the future.

Through these discussions, not only was she teaching me to be a better writer but also how to be a better person. Not that all her advice resonated; some lessons had to be learned on my own, painfully.

People were convinced we were in a relationship, and we were, just not a romantic one. We never entertained it. Not once. What we had ran deeper. I knew she and I would always be friends and no more, which was more than enough.

It wasn't that I wasn't attracted to her. I thought she was beautiful. She was petite, with luxurious blond hair and a smile that melted every man's heart. She had the biggest blue eyes that let some in who were invited and, conversely, could protect her against anyone perceived as a threat. She was perfect in so many ways, which was why I knew it could never be. With proclivity for self-destruction, it would have ended badly. What we had was unique, and I didn't want to destroy it.

Before I met Heather, I never had a close relationship with anyone, and it was she who taught me how to love a friend. I remember the first time she told me she loved me. Surprisingly, we were both sober, and I never had friends or family tell me that. I was so uncomfortable that it showed, but she stuck with me, and, every time we said those words, it got easier.

After college, we still hung out, and often it was at a bar. She grew tired of that life before I did, and my resentment cooled our friendship. I missed her wedding and the birth of her son, and though I wallowed in a stew of anger and self-pity, she never gave up on me. She could have stopped calling or carried a grudge or let me fade away like so many do when there are tough times. She didn't, and eventually, I put the brakes on my descent to oblivion.

We enjoyed that special bond once again, and I got to see her son Connor grow up, hold her when she got divorced, and proudly include her in my wedding party. When I got the call from another friend that she was in the hospital, I got on my motorcycle and drove as fast as I could the forty-five miles to the hospital.

She had been wheeled into a room from surgery where they removed cancer from her pancreas. Everyone knew it was serious; we just didn't know how bad. I knocked on the closed door and Heather's mom asked who it was. "John," I answered.

"Who?"

"John," I said again, this time a little louder.

"Who?"

In my fog, I forgot that Heather never called me by my first name; she called me Reger. So, everyone who knew her knew me only by my last name.

"Reger!" I yelled like I had solved the puzzle on *Wheel of Fortune.*

The door swung open and Heather's mom, Jordan, hugged me immediately. I looked over her shoulder during the embrace and saw her daughter in bed, asleep, helpless, with an IV in one arm and a Demerol drip in the other. Still, she remained angelic looking, as she always did when she slept, and her face had such a look of peaceful contentment like it was the only time the demons couldn't touch her. It always made me smile. My smile vanished when I realized why she was there.

Her boyfriend du jour was in the corner with a scowl that never seemed to leave. He didn't like me, and the feeling was mutual. Most of Heather's boyfriends, I didn't care for, but I never told her. Neither did she on my countless questionable concubines. It was an unwritten agreement we had, though we were always there for the other when the relationship derailed.

I resisted the temptation to throw daggers with my eyes at Mr. Scowling. I said hello and he ignored me.

Heather awoke and scanned the room, locking onto my face, and a sweet smile flashed.

"Reger, I'm so thirsty," she murmured.

"Here, baby, have some water," I replied, putting the straw up to her lips while she sipped from the plastic cup.

This didn't please the boyfriend, who concluded he was the third most important person in that room, behind her mom and me. He brusquely ordered me out, saying there was too much commotion and Heather needed her rest. I agreed and asked him to come out in the hall so I could get his phone number and call for updates.

As soon as the door closed, and the only witness was a passing nurse, I grabbed him by the shirt with both hands and threw him up against the wall.

"I was here before you, and I'll be here after," I snarled.

I released my grip, he dropped to the floor, and I went back into the room as if nothing had happened.

I prided myself on being the big brother she never had, and I joked that she was like the little sister I never wanted. It wasn't a perfect relationship, but it was the most genuine and consistent one I ever experienced. Emotions I spent a lifetime suppressing, as I had been taught as a child, couldn't run away from her. Heather wouldn't allow it, and I never fought that hard against her.

This phone call, though, was different, the toughest one I had ever made. I stared at the phone like it was a foreign object. What was I going to say? "Hey, I know you are fighting for your life, but can I abandon you for three months so I can selfishly traipse across the country and live out my *Easy Rider* fantasy?"

A phone seemed cowardly. This had to be done in person so I could see her reaction. I had to be certain she approved and would be all right, or I wasn't going. I would never forgive myself if something happened to her and I was 3,000 miles away.

The distance from my apartment to hers was seven miles, and as I drove, I rehearsed. None of it sounded right. It came off as selfish, and I felt guilty even going over to ask. The knot in my stomach tightened as I pulled up to her address. I turned off the car and sat for about ten minutes, my body paralyzed, and I found it difficult to breathe. Short hiccups were all I could manage, certain I was hyperventilating.

Boy Scout training from thirty years earlier kicked in, and I pushed the seat back and put my head between my knees. It took a minute, but I regained a normal breathing pattern.

When I thought I could get out of the car and not fall over, I opened the door and methodically swung my left leg out as if this was the first time I had exited a vehicle. Foot planted firmly on the asphalt, I dragged my right leg and placed it next to my left. I then used the door for leverage and thrust my torso upward, my arms gripping the metal atop the open window. The first few steps were shaky, but muscle memory trumped my anxiety.

Heather's door was open, her window blinds drawn, so she saw me from the living room, which was good because I seriously doubted I could have mustered the courage to knock. That golden smile filled my eyes. It was the same expression I had seen a thousand times; it always seemed as fresh and new as the first time I saw it fifteen years earlier. This time, however, my facial response was unusual. I didn't greet her smile with my own, and Heather immediately noticed.

"What's wrong?" she asked. She was intuitive and perceptive, and most of the time, I admired it. Not today.

"Nothing, I'm fine."

"Bullshit," she fired back.

Bluntness was another quality she abundantly possessed.

"Now tell me what's wrong," she ordered.

I sat next to her on the couch, and all the practice for my speech was for naught.

"I was thinking about taking a trip across country," I began. "But I want to make sure it's okay with you."

"Of course, why wouldn't it be?"

"I don't want to abandon you if you need me. I did that once, and I'm not doing it again."

"You aren't abandoning me. You're going on a trip that you should have taken five years ago."

Heather knew I should have left the newspaper job. It was killing my creativity. We had talked about this trip, and she was my biggest advocate. I knew she wanted me to go.

My uneasiness evaporated, but I still wasn't convinced about leaving.

"What if you need me while I'm gone?"

"I won't."

"Well, that makes me feel loved."

"You know you need to do this. You've talked about it for years. Now's the time. If you don't go, you'll regret it the rest of your life. You're not leaving forever, and I'll be here when you get back."

She leaned across the couch and hugged me tight to reassure me and signal her approval. I held onto her and slowly began to surrender to the fatigue of the moment. I stretched out on the couch, Heather next to me, and soon I drifted off to sleep.

When I awoke, Heather was next to me, sleeping with her head on my chest. Content, I lay there as one of the few people in this world who truly loved me was giving me yet another gift I could never, ever, repay.

CHAPTER 3

From my apartment door, I walked eighty-five steps to the sand, then trudged in my motorcycle boots another fifty or so yards across the light-brown soft grains that separated the city of Sunset Beach from the Pacific Ocean.

It was a hard city to leave. The beach community was located on a two-mile strip with houses and apartments on each side of the Pacific Coast Highway and a scant number of businesses sprinkled throughout. Four massage parlors, several bars, a few restaurants, a couple of tarot card readers, and four hotels that never seemed full, even in the summer.

The quirkiness was what attracted people like me, and we took pride that the town wasn't like every other cookie-cutter suburb in Southern California. The residents fiercely protected the city's uniqueness and had a healthy distaste for outsiders, whom they called inlanders.

The town, however, was beginning to lose its appeal. The larger neighbor of Huntington Beach was winning its decades-long war to annex Sunset Beach. New residents, who cared more about replacing quaint cottage-style houses with large three-story blocks of cement that obscured others' views and alienated second-generation property owners, favored bastardizing paradise in the dubious name of progress.

It was a war the old timers weren't going to win. They never did. As I looked out at the cool brownish-blue surf crashing into the land that spit out a white foam before it retreated to the water, I wondered how much my town would change during my absence.

At that moment, it hit me that it wasn't my town anymore. The newbies didn't want me. In their eyes, I took more than I gave, and my opinion of the new guard was considered heresy. As I watched the oil platforms that would certainly soon multiply and creep closer to shore, I realized I had little use for them as well.

My time on the beach was brief, the goodbye even quicker. I turned my back to the sea and returned to my garage and the fully packed motorcycle. I started her up and pulled out, looking straight ahead, careful not to make eye contact with anything in town. I was on the freeway headed north before the Harley was fully warmed up.

We ran together, the motorcycle and I, sprinting away from troubles I spent a lifetime collecting, certain they couldn't catch me if I rode fast and far enough. When life became too real, it made the most sense to try to outrun it. Nothing stuck as long as I was in motion. There was a sense of invincibility while riding. The only time my existence ever made sense was when I was on a motorcycle discovering some new road, eagerly wondering where it would lead me. Riding solo across the United States seemed perfectly logical to me. A trip across the country on a motorcycle had always been in my head, and now it settled in my soul.

For this trip, there was no real itinerary, just a basic idea. Any wandering soul will declare the best journeys were never thought out, the most memorable treks made spontaneously. I spent more time picking out a shirt to wear in the morning than I did figuring logistics of this trip.

Impulsiveness, I inherited from my mother. Structure, I got from my father, and the two tried to coexist in a yin-yang pattern, but it was a rocky relationship. I always tried to balance them and choose my battles, but the war constantly simmered. An urge bought the bike, but meticulous research decided which one I ultimately selected.

This one was my first Harley and not easily acquired. I walked into my local dealership often and looked at the models on the showroom floor. I talked to countless salesmen who would tell me all about the features and specifications of each model. I openly gushed as they described each bike, the same spiel most of the time, but I never got tired of hearing it. Then I would ask questions as any interested buyer would. "Why is the Road King better than an Electra?" "Is the Fat Boy a good cruising bike?" "Why is a Heritage Softail so popular?" After exhausting their knowledge, I would take a business card and tell them I had to talk it over with my wife.

I never had enough money to buy one, but I kept thinking someday I would. In the meantime, I would dream about where I would go on my Harley and all the adventures I would find riding across the country with all the clichés that come with it, wind in my hair, men in minivans glancing over in envy, young women in cars honking and waving. It was all out there, I knew it was, and all I had to do was come up with the cash to make it happen.

Ironically, it took me getting married for that day to arrive. One condition I laid out to Marianne was that I was going to get another motorcycle—a Harley. If she had a problem with that, then we shouldn't get married. She agreed, and I think it was probably because she never thought I would be able to do it. Can't say that I blamed her; my record of not following through on declarations was well established.

Then I got some extra money from a book I wrote and was ready to buy a Harley. I thought she would share in my excitement. She didn't. Instead, Marianne balked at our arrangement and said she never agreed to it. I guess I shouldn't have been surprised, her being an attorney. Also, the motorcycle represented everything she feared. I would have freedom, which, of course, would lead to choices, and ultimately in Marianne's mind, divorce.

One evening, she vehemently started to object, using her lawyer skills. She threw down the gauntlet and told me that I was not ever getting a motorcycle. After listening to enough of her rehashed arguments, I said, "Don't make me choose you or the Harley because you won't like the choice." Not shockingly, the marriage ended soon after, barely surviving three years. That wasn't the main reason for its demise, but it was indicative of other issues.

I owned a house I didn't want, surrounded by people I didn't like, who didn't acknowledge me when I greeted them. We all had our fences and walls, living paranoid behind them. We shopped at the same stores, and bought identical groceries, clothes, furniture, and cars. We ate the same food at the same chain restaurants and drank the same drinks. We complained about the same trivial issues we saw in the same newspaper and marveled at the most mundane moments.

I was at the tail end of this disastrous period of my life when I walked into a Harley-Davidson dealer and bought a 2003 Dyna Wide Glide. The gas tank and fenders were midnight blue, and I fell in love instantly. I pulled out of the parking lot with tears of joy. I took the long way home, riding along the Southern California coastline, the tears only getting more intense. They gave way to a euphoria I had never experienced. I didn't want that sensation to end. For the first time in what seemed like forever, I felt alive.

I named my Harley *Libertad,* the Spanish word for liberty. It was fitting given what I endured to get her. The freedom she gave me was immeasurable.

It was those moments that darted back in my mind as I navigated the Los Angeles freeways to begin the latest journey. Getting out of Southern California was never easy, and I slogged through stop-and-go traffic. I went about seventy miles to Thousand Oaks and pulled off the freeway to visit my old friend Jeff for a late breakfast at a local diner.

We had known each other since fifth grade, and it was his motorcycle I borrowed when we were teenagers until I could afford my own.

Two wheels stuck with me, but not with him. That was the last motorcycle he ever owned. I tried to persuade him to get another, but his heart wasn't in it. It would have been nice to have somebody to ride with, but one either loved two wheels or didn't. I soon discovered he did me a favor. One saw more when riding alone.

We lingered over bacon and eggs, talking about my trip. I detected a hint of envy, but he knew deep down he couldn't take a trip like this for several reasons. Still, the curiosity was there, and his engineer mind wanted to know everything. He peppered me with questions about the route I would be taking, where I would sleep, what equipment I would bring, and how much money I thought it would cost. It was a scene that replayed itself several times on the trip, asked by both friendly and envious strangers.

Jeff would have stayed and talked more, but I was feeling anxious to get on the road. I started to get uncomfortable as the conversation got deeper. People, even good friends, were better at a distance.

Because I dawdled, I wasn't going to get as far as I had hoped. I planned to go on Highway 1; the entrance was at the Central California town of San Luis Obispo. I didn't want to rush the experience of one of the most scenic roads in the world, so I found a cheap motel nearby, right before San Luis Obispo, and figured I would start fresh in the morning.

CHAPTER 4

Lunchtime approached when I finally rolled out of bed after the maid had knocked for the second time. When I opened the door, I noticed my motorcycle was the only vehicle in what had been a full parking lot the night before, thus confirming my successful procrastination.

It was the first time I had ridden any distance, and the 200-plus miles had taken more out of me than I expected. My goal of arriving at Highway 1 in the morning was blown, but I wasn't that disappointed about the missed deadline.

A small, chubby Hispanic woman, with her hair in a bun and a clipboard in her hand, walked toward me with purpose.

"You check out now," she said in broken English.

I told her fifteen minutes, but we both knew it would be closer to half an hour.

After a shower, I dressed and packed the Harley. The large duffel bag was secured on the back seat with black rubber straps and provided a nice backrest. My sleeping bag was held by bungee cords on the ape hanger handlebars and helped keep some of the wind and bugs off me.

As I wrapped the last of the six black straps to secure the duffel bag to the motorcycle, the motel owner walked toward me. I braced, expecting an argument for being well past the 11 a.m. checkout time, but his body language was nonthreatening as he approached sheepishly.

"Nice machine you got there," he said while coming within reach of me. "I had an old Shovelhead when I was younger. What type of Harley is that?"

When I told him it was a 2003 Wide Glide, he looked over the front end carefully, inspecting all the chrome I had added. His right hand traced the shiny forks up to the steel braided cables and stopped at the top of the left side of the handlebars and mirror.

"How much did it cost you?" he asked nonchalantly, not even concerned at the possible rudeness of the question.

"It cost me a really bad marriage, and it was worth every penny," I answered. "She made me choose between her and the Harley, and you see what won."

I thought the blunt answer would end the conversation, but instead, it seemed to invigorate him, so I loosened up.

He told me he had owned the motel since the 1980s, moving to the central coast of California from Los Angeles when he was in his forties. He was ahead of his time in a way. He was tired of all the people and the traffic and decided to slow down. He couldn't have picked a better place to achieve that objective. His wife had checked me in the night before while he watched television in the back room. His white skin had a tinge of a tan. He was shorter than average, balding on top with gray hair on the sides. He walked cautiously and methodically, seeming to inspect all around him with every step.

During the day, he made repairs he deemed necessary, which meant he had plenty of time to visit with guests. He asked me what name I had given my bike. He said he had named his after an old girlfriend and then told me how he and that girlfriend got as far as Bakersfield one summer, spending the afternoon fooling around in an oil field before heading back the two hours to Los Angeles.

"Mine's named Libertad," I told him. "It's the Spanish word for liberty."

He looked puzzled. I explained that Libertad provided me total freedom and it seemed like the perfect name.

"Where you headed?"

"Not really sure," I said. "But I got three months to get there."

"Three months on a motorcycle? That's a long time."

"Yeah, I guess it is, but it doesn't seem like nearly enough."

"What are you going to do out there?"

"See if everything is the same as it appears."

"You must not have a job to go back to."

"Not much of anything to go back to."

"Well, I wish you well," he said with a smile. I always wanted to take a trip like that. I hope you find what you're looking for."

"So do I," I said, starting up the Harley. I pulled away and waved to him as I pointed Libertad to the ocean.

Of all the numerous paths I have traveled in my life, few compared to Highway 1. It was the best stretch of road I have ever experienced. It was the first long trip I took when I bought the Harley three years before this journey. There was no place I would have rather gone to break in my new motorcycle.

The highway was the perfect combination of scenery and asphalt with the two constantly vying for my attention. Get lulled by the Pacific Ocean to the west and a sharp curve would throw me into a hillside ditch. There were rolling hills and grassland to the east. Cows stared at me with indifference, but I still couldn't help but be mesmerized by them and the land they grazed upon. The cliffs leading to the sea also demanded further inspection and as much attention as I could provide while trying to avoid meeting them up close.

All those pleasant memories of past excursions filled my head as I reached the beginning of Highway 1, five minutes past two in the afternoon.

From San Luis Obispo, it was 127 miles to Monterey, but with the stops I had scheduled, and the winding road, it was going to take much longer than the two hours I had initially estimated.

About ten miles on Highway 1, past the rural farms, was a small incline on the four-lane highway that presented the city of Morro Bay. Visible at the top of the hill was the gigantic Morro Rock, a 576-foot-tall boulder named by Spanish explorer Juan Cabrillo, who first saw it in 1542. This was the town's focal point, nicknamed the Gibraltar of the Pacific, and was well beyond the shoreline.

The road kept vehicles at a distance from the water, but as I left town, the ocean came nearer, the crash of the waves audible, the shoreline detectable and its features distinct.

About twenty miles into the ride, the road shrank from four lanes to two. The single lane made passing difficult, especially on a summer day filled with tourists. The rugged coastline jutted in and out and when I thought I'd seen the most spectacular view, I turned the corner and another one appeared better than the last. This road demanded attention. It requested I slow down, admire it, study it, and enjoy it. Most travelers don't. They speed, tailgate, and pass dangerously, making the same moves they would during the morning commute, oblivious to the scenery and the road's mystique.

The first town past Morrow Bay was Harmony, population eighteen, then Cambria shortly after. Hearst Castle was eight miles beyond Cambria. The estate built by newspaper magnate William Randolph Hearst perched on a hill about two miles from the coast, retreating from view, much like the man who lived there.

The road undulated quite severely after Hearst Castle, and the first dip lifted my body while my stomach stayed put. It was alarming at first, coming off the seat of the motorcycle ever so slightly, but I maintained my speed, the sensation outweighing the risk.

The vista five miles north of San Simeon at Piedras Blancas had been a favorite stop of mine. I parked and walked to a vista to watch elephant seals on the beach. The massive mammals fascinated me, and I spent a good hour watching them do a whole lot of nothing.

Occasionally, two of them would squabble and belch at each other, and that kept me there long enough to wait for another skirmish. I watched hawks, crows, and sparrows share the tops of fence posts. Buzzards, though, continuously hovered above, never seeming to rest.

I pulled out onto the highway and, without warning, the road tightened. The speed limit signs went from forty miles per hour to thirty to twenty as the road rose and the turn further tightened. Giant boulders resting near the shoreline added to the beauty of the ocean. The waves crashed into them, spraying water dramatically as they exploded onto the rocks.

Small towns dotted the landscape, and I wondered how Gorda, Plaskett, and Lucia got their names, something to ponder as I inched my way to one of my favorite towns.

The artist colony of Big Sur was thirty miles south of Monterey. It was a small, quaint inspirational setting that artists had been coming to for years. The Henry Miller Library was there, as well as several art galleries. The road dipped, and the water was invisible before popping out again on three expansive bridges. There were houses I would never be able to afford, but it was a nice daydream as I wondered what it must be like to live in one of them.

By the time I reached Monterey four hours after I began my day, I was ready to get off the road. I wanted to continue through to San Francisco, but the traffic made it impossible.

Staying in Monterey wasn't an option either. It would have been far more convenient to stay at a hotel there, but my budget wasn't going to allow a room that cost north of a hundred dollars. I was looking to spend less than half that, so I got on Highway 68 and rode twenty miles inland to Salinas, where I knew cheap motels were abundant in this farming community made famous by the one-time resident, author John Steinbeck.

This town was the antithesis of Monterey—gritty, blue collar, and genuine, just like the people, who, despite their roughness, were usually friendly. I felt akin to them. I had been there a few times and had stumbled on a semi-legal poker game. I had profited, so I thought maybe I could add some funds for my trip.

Fields on both sides of me framed the entrance of Salinas, and, as I got closer to downtown, I saw the faces of the new labor force. They were small and brown, with big eyes that scanned the road for work trucks they hoped would pick them up for any type of menial labor. The day was done for them, the sun soon to retreat, and these poor souls who didn't get work picked up small backpacks and headed back to a run-down apartment building where they lived in wretched conditions.

They were the Chinese of the late 1800s, the Irish of the 1920s, and the Okies of the 1940s. They sat and talked on street corners of Steinbeck's hometown and wanted nothing more than a better way of life, having risked death crossing an international border to get it.

They were treated poorly and routinely taken advantage of, often by people of their own race. They came back, though. Back to the empty parking lots near hardware stores, eager to volunteer for jobs legal residents won't do. They worked for half the pay they deserved and smiled the entire time.

I ate an early dinner at a favorite Mexican restaurant a couple of blocks from the Steinbeck Museum. I was torn about the shrine to one of my favorite novelists. Chronicling the history of one of the greatest American writers was something I was fully in favor of, and I learned a lot about him when I went there on previous trips. But it bothered me greatly that the town that had ostracized him while he was alive now treated him like a favorite son, seizing the opportunity to make a buck off his corpse. I guess it was inevitable, and at least his memory was being kept alive, even if it was for the wrong reason.

The poker room was in full swing, two tables in operation when I walked in the door a shade past seven o'clock. I bought in for a hundred dollars and parked myself at one of the two remaining seats, waiting for my opportunity to fleece the suckers and dream chasers.

The table was full of them, and I had analyzed every player who was my foe. It was a skill taught to me when I started playing in college. It's like the old saying goes, "If you sit at a table and can't spot the sucker in five minutes, the sucker was you." Most of the people there were degenerate gamblers, those who don't know how to play holding too many losing hands. One guy could play, and I steered clear of him for most of the night, though I did fool him on a hand for a big pot.

Three hours later, I doubled my money and cashed out. I made sure no one followed me out the door, hopped on the motorcycle, and took off, looking for a bar where I could safely imbibe and celebrate.

I found a dive near my motel and sat at the bar next to two Mexicans. By the way they were spending money, I knew they found work that day. Tony and his cousin Hector were enjoying their evening. Tony was younger, smarter, and more personable. Hector was graying, mistrusting of gringos, and had seen way too much pain. They drank tequila shots with beer chasers. Tony cut pickled eggs in half and shook salt on them, enjoying this self-perceived delicacy.

Tony told me the two came across the border five years ago when he was twenty. They both wanted to make money to send to relatives back home in Chihuahua. They hitchhiked to Tijuana and spent the night in a riverbed by the border. In the middle of the night, with a rush of about thirty others, they crossed through a hole in the fence and scattered like roaches in the light. Some were caught, but Tony and Hector were lucky. It wouldn't have mattered. They would have been bused back across the border, but they would have tried again the next chance they got.

They heard from a guy they crossed with that there were jobs in Salinas, mostly farming country. The two liked the idea of working outdoors, but they didn't realize the heat of the summer was as oppressive as at home; that detail was conveniently left out from the job description. So was the fact that jobs in the fields weren't as plentiful as they were led to believe.

The parking lot was near the one-bedroom apartment they shared.

Hector had the bedroom, Tony the living room. They both slept on the floor until they earned enough money for a used bed and a couch.

Hours passed slowly for them in the parking lot when the trucks didn't come by. The wait for work was excruciatingly slow. When a vehicle appeared, the men swarmed like jackals on a gazelle carcass.

There was a strategy for getting picked up, but Tony was reluctant to share it, especially when Hector shot him a look that said he had already told me too much. When Hector went to the bathroom, Tony told me the secret was to sit with smaller men so you look stronger, but you can't look threatening. Hector usually stood behind Tony when the trucks came.

The relatives got about two hundred each a month from the men, and that went a long way in the little shack that housed numerous brothers, sisters, in-laws, cousins, grandparents, aunts, and uncles.

Work would be calling in the morning, and the two mutually agreed to stay in the bar until midnight. They got picked up on Saturday and worked a job digging up a lawn in the backyard of some rich White guy's house. Paying forty dollars apiece for Tony and Hector was cheaper than hiring a landscaper and only slightly more expensive than renting a rototiller.

There was some money left over from Saturday's celebration, and Tony insisted on buying me a drink, even though he wouldn't remember me in the morning. Hector stopped scowling at me, and I took that as a sign of guarded acceptance.

I asked them what they wanted in life, and Tony told me they already had most of what they needed. Money was good, the rent got paid, and they had more food than they ever did in Mexico. A television would be nice at some point, Tony said. I tried to buy them a round, but Tony wouldn't allow it.

"You are my guest tonight," he said.

I attempted the offer later, but it was again refused.

It was late, and I was tired from the first full day of riding. It would take a couple of days for my body to get accustomed to the motorcycle and the road. My hands were tingling from being on the high handlebars, and my legs were sore.

Midnight arrived, and Tony and Hector's deadline had passed. They wouldn't leave until the bar closed two hours later. They wanted me to stay, but I convinced them I had to be up earlier than they did and politely excused myself for the evening. As I walked toward the door, I got the bartender's attention and gave her a twenty-dollar bill. I told her to buy Tony and Hector a couple of rounds on me.

CHAPTER 5

It was early morning, but the heat embraced me the instant I opened the motel door. The air-conditioning in my room had kept me cocooned from the ninety-five degrees that would accompany me for most of the day's ride.

Fortunately, my travel was short. It was less than two hours to San Francisco and would be cooler there. I found a motel in the city and would see friends before I headed north. It would be the last contact with anyone I knew until I reached the East Coast.

Before I arrived a debate raged in my mind. Part of my brain believed a short 106-mile ride was ludicrous. It wouldn't even be noon when I quit, and the urge to drive through San Francisco tempted me. I could ride another 250 miles and be that much closer to Oregon.

When I bought the Harley, I pledged never to be in a hurry. Initially it was for safety reasons, but here it fit another purpose. There was supposed to be no schedule. I had nowhere to go and all day to get there. I had recently left a job that revolved around deadlines, and I wanted to meander.

Newspapers wouldn't have been my ideal job choice. I knew I could write but didn't know what sort of writing I wanted to do. I began in newspapers because it was easy. Covering a high school football game seemed mindless, but at the same time, it was writing, so I did it.

I dabbled in news reporting for a while, but that was too

depressing. I couldn't stand the tragedy and the drama. Once, I had to go to a house where a suspected drunk driver had killed two mothers and two daughters while they were out on a summer walk after dinner. The police informed the first husband/father that his family had been decimated, and I apparently was to ask the father for his reaction. There was no way I could do it. His pain to me was unfathomable and the last person he wanted to see would be some news vulture asking him how he felt. I stood silent while the police told him the news. His anguish was gut-wrenchingly painful to witness. I went back to the office, not able to bring myself to go to the home of the second family.

I covered the Los Angeles Riots in 1992, but after getting hit in the head with a bottle the first night, and shot at by gang members the second, I decided to go back to covering sports. Being a sportswriter for a large Southern California newspaper had been a goal and I thought, *What other job could be better than watching sports and getting paid for it?* Unfortunately, I missed the part of the job description about the long hours for insultingly low pay, spoiled and surly athletes who lashed out at sportswriters for fun, grueling travel, bitter coworkers, and vindictive bosses.

What I experienced in that job didn't make up for all the negatives, but I did enjoy it. I was fortunate enough to have a relationship with golfer Tiger Woods and had a front-row seat as he marched toward history. It was incredible what I saw him do on a golf course.

I interviewed famous athletes and celebrities, but for me, the job was just that, a job. For fifteen years, though, it was all I knew and all I thought I was qualified to do. Leaving was terrifying, but staying would have been worse.

Even though I had gotten out of the newspaper business, it hadn't entirely left me and was an unwelcome companion on this trip. I constantly felt I needed to know what time it was. I looked at maps incessantly, calculating mileage and the time it would take to go from one point to another. I choked down meals with the thought of needing to be somewhere. That sense of angst would ruin this trip if I didn't quash it.

"The journey was better than the inn," Spanish novelist Miguel Cervantes wrote in *La Numancia*. I would repeat that phrase many times, and it became a mantra. As I got on the freeway, my anxiety level lowered enough to enjoy my surroundings.

Besides, if I kept going and didn't stop in San Francisco, I would have disappointed my friends, and I had done that too much in the past. There were countless missed get-togethers with no phone call or lame excuses when I managed to contact them. There was always the promise of gathering, but I never followed through. I would sit in my house thinking about the offers I had, then drive around and wonder why I couldn't enjoy time with family and friends.

As I drove up Highway 101, I thought about how I could improve my relationships. I pondered about what I should do and then questioned whether I could. It was not an easy topic for someone who had spent a lifetime avoiding it. I wasn't even sure I knew how to start. I read somewhere you make most of your lasting relationships when you are a teenager, and new friendships, now that I was in my forties, always served a purpose. I thought I had made friends when I was at the newspaper, but when I quit, they stopped calling me. They worked with athletes or did public relations for golf companies or tournaments I covered, and when I couldn't do anything more for them, they didn't have the time to meet.

It was depressing to think about, and I eagerly let the garlic fields break my concentration. Ninety minutes from San Francisco was Gilroy, a town known for the sweet pungent scent of the bulbous flowering plant. The annual festival had been the previous weekend, so the smell surrounded me for several miles.

The aroma was evidence of why motorcycles were better for travel. My feet were ten inches above the asphalt, the sounds had no barriers to my ears, and the smells had no obstructions to my nose. There was no windshield to hinder my eyes. It was there before me, ready for me and me for it. As the pavement flew beneath the bike, everything else around seemed still.

On the freeway, I let the topic of relationships creep back into my brain. It bothered me that I didn't reach out more to people, and I couldn't figure out why. Was it fear of rejection? It was true that I cut people out of my life for the smallest indiscretion. You only got one chance to burn me, and if you did, that was it. I never called you again. This stubbornness was a fault I needed to correct, but I couldn't quash the anger and hurt I felt when someone wronged me.

As I got closer to San Francisco, I remembered a friend who lived in the city, and, when I settled into my motel, I called him for lunch. He, too, wrote, worked for a competing California newspaper, and had always been gracious to me.

The profession of journalism was built on jealousy, enemies, and low pay. When I left the business, some were dismissive because I had left the fold. Not Tommy. He recognized it was only a job. A good bottle of wine and a thick steak were vastly more crucial than a story on some golfer who most people would forget about the next day. As we ate, he glowed about how genuinely happy he was for me.

I was equally delighted that he had found a way to live in one of the best cities in the country. San Francisco had always been one of my favorites and one of two places I would move to. New York City would be the other. They both provided continuous energy. There was always something happening, and when you were there, anything was possible.

That was what made San Francisco so appealing. It was different. It wasn't people who walked as one, moved from the car to the office, creeping along a freeway to a job they didn't want to go to, and then returned to a home that looked like all the others

Tommy and I laughed about the job, reminisced about the good times we had working and the tournaments we covered, and talked about the future. His life seemed so well-thought-out, so organized, so inspiring. I probably should have taken notes.

After lunch, I wanted to see the water. Down at Fisherman's Wharf, I watched some visitors as I fed the remaining pieces of my clam chowder bread bowl to the seagulls. It was sixty degrees and windy, and one family's vacation was in peril. They wore shorts and freshly bought sweatshirts, the telltale sign of tourists who read a brochure instead of Mark Twain's attributed quote that, "The coldest winter I ever spent was a summer in San Francisco." He never said that, and whoever did had remained a mystery, but the quote is accurate.

The family bickered with one another; the father yelled at the kids to stay close, the mom chided her husband not to raise his voice to the kids, and the kids complained that they wanted to go back to the hotel and swim in the pool. It was hard to watch. I winced as the voices got shriller, and the two little boys started crying in frustration and protest. I left as one of the boys was getting spanked.

I got on a public bus to go across town to meet another friend for dinner and was startled by a woman smiling at me. It meant nothing more than hello, but it disturbed me. I wasn't used to it. I smiled back, though it took a moment to do so.

Many years in a big city had taught me to scowl. No one smiled in Southern California unless a camera was present. It was the most insincere area in the country. I don't even believe people in Los Angeles wanted to smile or say hello. They only did what was required. If avoiding contact with others was possible, most did.

Haight-Asbury was the opposite of LA in that regard. My friend Damin had lived there for years and, like me, was a product of the city's sprawling suburbs. Unlike me, he wisely got out, landing where the hippie movement of the 1960s was born. A lot of those tenets—loving your brother and social consciousness—still applied in Haight-Asbury. All appeared to be the same, except for the free love, much to my dismay.

I was sitting in a café, drinking hot chocolate and people-watching when I was rewarded with a kid in his twenties with long blond dreadlocks wearing a headless chicken suit. It wasn't a work uniform; it was his apparel of choice, and he didn't seem bothered by it. Neither did anyone else in the café. It seemed I was the only one who noticed and immediately became self-conscious. If he didn't mind wearing the outfit, why should I judge him?

He reminded me I was late to see my friend, who probably had the same outfit hanging in his closet. I had privately admired Damin since we met. He had a sense of humor stranger than mine. Many thought of him as immature, but I found Damin's personality refreshing, and I could always count on an evening spent with him to be memorable or infamous.

This night was no different. He insisted we go to a bar he said I would enjoy. This was an immediate red flag. Damin reveled in shocking me, so I tried to play it cool when we walked into Divas. The bartender was a stunningly beautiful platinum blond, who I would have sworn was a woman, had not his large, man-size hands revealed his true gender.

It took two minutes to ascertain that most of the clientele was also born male but had taken great care to mask their true genetic identity. Damin laughed as my eyes grew wider, satisfied he had shocked me yet again.

The main attraction for the transgendered was the unity they shared and their nonjudgment of others in the bar. The second benefit was the karaoke, which, for them, was as serious as attention to their femininity.

Listening to popular song titles sung an octave or two lower than they should be was very entertaining, and I resisted the urge to serenade the crowd with the Aerosmith song, "Dude Looks Like a Lady." Thankfully I didn't mention the idea to Damin, who would have done it in a heartbeat, and then we would have had to fight our way out of there. I was running a solid streak of not getting a stiletto heel in my eye and wanted to keep it that way.

I had one more obligation the next morning before I could leave San Francisco. My friend Susan and her husband, Dan, were about forty-five minutes north of the city, and I wanted to visit them for lunch before I imposed myself on strangers rather than friends.

I packed up the Harley and began to head toward their house. We were to meet at noon, and I felt the pressure to be on time. I took a scenic route from my motel to the Golden Gate Bridge, and on the way, I parked Libertad in front of the Buena Vista, a restaurant my father once told me he had been in when he concluded he wanted to start a family.

An iconic pub near the last stop of one of the cable car lines, its first owners claimed to be the inventors of Irish coffee in the United States. The owner and a travel writer spent a night in 1952 trying to perfect the concoction they both had tasted at the Shannon Airport in Ireland. They were successful in recreating the mixture of coffee, Irish whiskey, and whipped cream. The drink went down smooth, and I had imbibed too many on several prior visits. I have always wondered if my father's consuming several of the beverages had anything to do with influencing his decision to want children.

I was going to enjoy one of those famous cocktails and could already taste it as I pulled up outside the place. As I got off the Harley, a woman approached me and asked if I could help her with her motorcycle. She had a Suzuki with a dead battery.

If you lived as a true biker, one of the codes was that if someone had broken down, you helped. Whenever I drove by a motorcyclist on the side of the road, I slowed and gave a thumb's up, then a thumb's down, questioning if all was well, and then I awaited the person's answer. Sometimes, they had no idea what I was inquiring about, so I pulled over and asked them. Most of the time, they were fine. Cell phones had eliminated the need for most assistance. No one seemed to be in the middle of nowhere any longer, and help was usually a phone call away.

But assistance wasn't a phone call away for Elaine. She was happy for my aid, and it was something I was all too glad to do. Her machine wasn't going anywhere. The four-year-old battery had no pulse, and jump-starting it wasn't going to bring it back to life. We tried to quick charge it, but that didn't help either. She needed a new battery. My problem was that I was supposed to be at my friend's at noon, and the time was creeping toward my appointment. I hadn't seen Susan in quite some time, and she had to leave for work at two, so already, the visit wasn't going to be as long as either of us would have liked.

It was going to be even shorter if I didn't get going. Elaine, though, was stuck. Her friend wasn't coming for a couple of hours, and she would be forced to sit around and wait.

If not for meeting Susan and Dan, I could have run over, bought Elaine a battery, and put it in, and she could have been on her way. I apologized for having to leave. Elaine was very gracious about it, but still, it bothered me.

The moment stuck with me as I went up Highway 101. Through the fog off the Northern California coast, I wrestled with my own cloudy mind. I was beating myself up for not following the biker's code, and I felt like I had abandoned someone who needed my help. I realized assistance was coming, but I could have saved her a couple of hours. I vowed visiting Susan would be the last deadline I would have on this trip.

The fog was still present as I left Susan and Dan's and it kept the temperatures low, going from the mid-nineties to low sixties in a day, and I spent the ride trying to block out the cold. I remembered a story I had read about Tibetan monks in the Himalayas, wearing only their robes and sleeping on a mat. Their power of concentration and meditation was so great that they blocked out the freezing temperatures. I channeled my mind to do the same and failed miserably. My powers of mediation lasted about seventeen seconds, and all I thought about was why it was so bloody cold in August.

I would have warmed up if I stayed inland on Highway 101, but I was constantly drawn to the water, and, if there's a choice, it doesn't take me long to make my decision. I cut back over to Highway 1 at Manzanita and headed toward Muir Beach.

This part of Highway 1 was far less traveled, but just as scenic, and, in parts, more accessible. I parked at Muir Beach and walked on the trail looking at wild mustards, pine trees, and bull thistles. The overlook onto the beach was about a quarter mile from the parking lot, and it was a great place to stop and take a break from the ride.

Hugging the rugged coastline for the six miles, I found the views incredible and, again, I fought drifting into the opposing lane while I was gawking at the ocean.

Disappointment that the road was heading inland soon turned to elation, as I was soon upon a road that bikers dreamed of discovering. It was past Stinson Beach, the Bolinas Lagoon to my left. I braced for miles of boredom but soon saw I was mistaken. The road began to twist, and with no one in front of me, I was able to goose the throttle. The brush on the right met the road, except for the occasional gravel driveway.

Highway 1 became Shoreline Highway and continued with gentle turns with the topography much the same for several miles. Soon I was treated to huge oak and pine trees that outlined the road and provided a tunnel-like path for a couple of miles before spitting me out to a couple of rural homes. Another twenty miles, and I arrived at Point Reyes Station. I wanted to check out the lighthouse there, so I pulled off the road into the small town and took a brief rest. The lighthouse was one of forty-eight similar structures in California, and even though it was a drive from the highway, I figured it would be worth it. There was a little fog, and as I was about to start the Harley and proceed when someone told me that fog had closed the facility for the day.

With Tomales Bay on my left, I continued up Highway 1 through more farmland until I reached Bodega Bay, the fog riding along with me for the forty miles.

Even with the cloud cover, the views were spectacular. Bodega

Bay, where they filmed Alfred Hitchcock's horror movie *The Birds*, was a beautiful little resort town, and I forced myself to stop and take in the scenery. I sat at the wharf and, through the thick air, watched some fishing boats return from a day's work.

My respite was brief. I wanted to get to Fort Bragg and still had a hundred miles remaining. It felt like I was never going to get out of California. I hadn't realized how long this state was, and I wanted to get into Oregon so I could feel like I had accomplished something.

Going north on Highway 1 were redwood trees on the right and, again, the ocean on the left. Cypress pines sprang up as well, and there were many turnouts on the left to sit and watch seagulls and pelicans fly by. Several of the towns along the way looked like they depended on tourist dollars that just weren't there. Stewarts Point, Elk, and Albion were all stops that if you blinked, you missed, but still desperately attempted to lure the road-weary to stop with colorful signs outside of the businesses.

This highway took a lot out of me, the twists and turns numerous, and the temptation to quit constantly there. I reached the former military town as the sun set. I stopped and found a motel that had a hot tub, soaked my weary bones, and fell asleep soon after, skipping dinner.

CHAPTER 6

Twenty miles north of Fort Bragg was a turnout next to Juan Creek on Highway 1, the last chance to see the ocean before the road turned inland into the forest of pines and sequoias, and I wanted to take one last look.

I pulled off the highway, and Libertad wasn't very pleased, since we had just started riding. I parked at the dirt turnout and was the only person there.

Sitting on the cliff's edge, I stared at the blue sea crashing onto the rocks below and, for the first time, actually listened to the water. It amazed me all times I had been at the beach and never heard the ocean. I thought I had but hadn't. The sea was a backdrop for me, an extra in a movie of distraction. My beach strolls with someone were usually used for seduction, and my walks alone were often in worried thought. This was different. There was no other matter taking up space in my head. I was free to enjoy the rhythm of the water and the symphony it made.

There was the obvious crashing sound, but, in addition, there was an almost guttural growl as the water pulled back from the shore, like an old man with arthritic knees, wheezing as he got up from a recliner. It was a bass tone of feigned misery. Then the noise crescendoed as the water regained its strength and slammed back to land.

I thought I was alone, but out in the water, a seal popped his head up and was looking back at me. I didn't think he could see me because I was perched up about a hundred feet on the cliff. He would duck into the water and then emerge again, looking at me before going back under. He appeared to be searching for fish but seemed more interested, at least temporarily, in staring at me. When I moved to the left or right, so would he. Then he went in the other direction, and I followed him. We played this silly game for a few minutes, and I was sure it was amusing more to me than to him. He dove back into the water and vanished. It did make me smile as I scanned the ocean for my new friend.

The appearance of water always calmed me, though I was terrified to immerse myself in the ocean. I walked alongside the shore and went out to a certain point, but swimming past the waves never happened. My greatest fear was being in the middle of it. It was a carefree feeling others enjoyed but petrified me because I had no control.

My desire had been to live at the beach, but I ignored the beauty, despite its closeness. I made promises, but my visits were infrequent, and something usually deterred me. The ocean was there, but I wondered how long it would wait for me.

I thought about calling the girlfriend. It had been several days since I left, and I hadn't talked to her, though I had promised I would. I knew how the conversation would go and didn't want to hear it. She was against my leaving, though she didn't have a vote. She barely had a boyfriend. I met her a month before the trip. She was one of many women since my divorce. I waited for them to love me, and then I stopped calling.

This relationship was close to the end. The trip postponed the inevitable. It was reassuring that someone was waiting for me at home even if I didn't want her there when I returned. I removed my cell from the saddlebag and dialed her number. Before she answered, I hung up. The phone was ringing as I put it back in the saddlebag. I started the Harley and pulled back onto the highway, leaving the ocean behind.

I immediately missed it. The temperature was cooler at the coast and the scenery infinitely more interesting. I remembered I was with my dad once and we were going to my new apartment in Dana Point, a coastal town in Orange County. As we exited the freeway, the view of the ocean jumped out at us. I said, "What do you think of the view?" He replied, "You can only look at the ocean for so long." I shot back, "Like the rest of your life." It was one of many subjects we held opposing viewpoints on.

We were just different people. He grew up in a blue-collar area of Buffalo and moved out to California with my mother shortly after they were married. He hated the snow—that much, we had in common. But I could never relate to him on anything else, no matter how hard I tried. He saw the world differently and had a hard time understanding my choices.

One night, the two of us went to dinner without my mother, who usually served as the buffer to any possibly tense conversations. He was telling me a story about famed New York City columnist Jimmy Breslin, who was about to undergo surgery to remove a brain aneurysm. He asked the doctor if this was going to affect his writing, and the doctor asked why. Breslin said that if it did, he wanted the doctor to kill him. I told my dad I understood where Breslin was coming from, and my dad exploded. He said, "You could do anything for work. You could sell cars." I calmly said, "Man, you don't get it. I don't want to sell cars." The rest of dinner was eaten in silence, and my angst to get out of the restaurant and go home intensified.

The last forty miles on Highway 1, before it merged with Highway 101, turned away from the water and headed inland. The road was twisty and had steep inclines and declines. The temperature rose about ten degrees, and the fog was gone, but the shade from the enormous sequoias kept me cool.

The contortions of Highway 1 disappeared once I entered Highway 101 and made it much more receptive to speeding, which, in turn, made Libertad quite happy. Although I never went faster than fifty miles per hour on Highway 1, I never went slower than sixty-five the rest of the way to Crescent City. That was fine with Libertad. She liked to ride fast and was comfortable right around 75 mph.

I had spent more time in California than I had intended but did not regret it. I had never seen the coast above San Francisco and now was twenty-five miles from the California-Oregon border.

Following a night's rest in Crescent City, I was ready to cross into Oregon after six days in one state. The road was two lanes, and I enjoyed the last spell of coolness before the late morning heat arrived. It was that point in the day when you hold on to the weather as long as it let you. The temperature would soon jump, and the afternoon would be uncomfortable.

As I contemplated my arrival time into Oregon, a deer bounced in front of me onto the highway. Fortunately, I wasn't going that fast. I let off the throttle and hit the brakes, the animal harmlessly passing before me. Still, it woke me up better than any cup of coffee.

Control on a motorcycle is tenuous, but most situations can be identified and managed. The danger happened, and I dealt with it. A piece of tire in the road could be easily sidestepped. I avoided getting behind pickups in case something fell out of the bed. Any driver on a cell phone, and I moved over two lanes.

Deer were different. Only cars have downed more bikers. Deer were completely illogical animals. They came out of nowhere and froze in front of a vehicle instead of eluding it.

They were my worst fear on this trip, and I had a healthy contempt for them. I was not a murderer of animals, but I was fully in favor of mounting a machine gun onto my handlebars and taking out as many of these stupid creatures as I could. Since animal homicide was not an option, I tried to cut down the risk of any interaction with them. I know they generally came out early in the morning and around sunset when they wandered across roads in search of food or water, so I avoided riding at those times. Also, highways with trees on both sides had to be carefully perused and my speed lowered. If I was alone, I beeped my horn to tell them I was there.

Deer encounters had happened all too frequently to me. I was in Idaho once driving across the country in a car and missed a deer by inches, nearly swerving off the road. I pulled into a gas station afterward and was trying to calm down when this trucker asked if I was all right.

He noticed how shaken up I was, and I told him what had happened. He then told me a story about when he was a teenager and he hit a deer with his pickup. He clipped it and the deer was hurt, unable to move. He stayed with it, giving it water and putting a blanket over it. His father came down the street looking for his son at two in the morning and told his boy to go home; he would look after the deer. In the morning, he walked into the kitchen and asked his father what happened to the deer. The patriarch told him he had to shoot the deer because it was suffering. He told me about how he cried when his dad told him. I couldn't believe this stranger told me this story in the middle of a gas station and teared up while doing so.

The trucker was on my mind as I continued up Highway 101, and I wondered what he was doing these days when I saw a sign for Pelican Bay Prison.

Prisons have always fascinated me. I don't know why. I had known somebody who was a guard at Corcoran Prison in central California, and she gave me a tour one time. Corcoran was the prison that housed Charles Manson. The tour was incredible. I got to go into a cell and talk to a couple of inmates. It was extremely scary and instantly gave me a sense of claustrophobia. I could almost touch the walls if I spread my arms outward. A bunk bed, a metal toilet, a desk, and two shelves on the wall—that was it. It amazed me how these guys lived like that.

Pelican Bay Prison was built in 1989, designed to be a better alternative to the notorious but aging facilities at Folsom and San Quentin. It was a super maximum-security prison designed to hold the worst of the worst.

It was surprising when I drove up to the entrance and there was no one at the guard shack. I rode onto the grounds and down to a parking lot. I parked Libertad, and some inmates were out in an exercise yard. They immediately noticed me and started staring. There was a fence with razor wire on top, and we were probably one hundred feet apart, but I could feel their eyes.

They walked or ran around the track, but I never left their sight. A trio stopped when they got close and came over to the fence. Then another two wandered over. There were twenty-five guys on the field, and soon, about all of them were by the fence.

Some glared in hatred while others gazed with curiosity. I wanted to talk to them but didn't dare. I knew I was being watched by the guards and was already in trouble for riding onto the property. Besides, I was wearing jeans, which was a huge problem since that was part of the inmate's uniform.

All I could do was look back. Those who cared tried to figure out what I was doing. I reclined on the bike, my feet on the handlebars, and some of the guys checked out the bike. The smallest guy in the group gave my machine the thumbs up, and pretty soon, this interruption in their day became a refreshing intrusion.

The employees certainly didn't appreciate it. That became apparent when a white van pulled up alongside me and three guards got out. They asked why I was on prison grounds, and I didn't have a good excuse.

They demanded identification and put on quite a show for the inmates. One guard was to my right, another to my left, and the third directly behind me. Their arms were crossed, their feet wide apart, and their bodies tense. It was their training to expect confrontation, and I couldn't blame them.

After a couple of minutes, they were satisfied I wasn't an escaped convict and told me to leave. I resisted the urge to tell them that if I was an escaped convict, I wouldn't be hanging out in the parking lot of the prison I had fled. They probably surmised that as well.

I started the Harley, gave it a few revs for the guys behind the fence, and motored out onto the main road. I was in Oregon in ten minutes, escaping California after what seemed like a month.

CHAPTER 7

Though I was out of my home state, it was not out of me. When you were born and raised in an area as impersonal as Southern California, mistrust grows as plentifully as the palm trees. There was an angle to everything. The only truth was that no one told it. The hustle was what kept the town flowing. It was easy for me to get caught up in that world and even harder to leave it. It had certainly enveloped me. It was all I knew, and changing now was going to be difficult.

Part of this trip was to see if there was another part of the country I could tolerate. Living in a place with perfect weather is hard to leave. Those of us who lived at the beach were big babies, and I might have been the biggest. If the temperature got below fifty degrees, I was ready to petition the governor to declare a state of emergency. In the summer, there was always a stretch of three or four days when it was ninety degrees, and my friends wouldn't even take my calls because they knew I was going to whine and complain. I didn't get much sympathy from them, especially the ones in the South who were dealing with the same temperature but oppressive humidity as well. Hard to lend a caring ear to a Southern Californian when it feels like you were living in a sauna for three months.

The weather was why so many people endured the otherwise ludicrous conditions in Southern California. If any other area had overpopulation, overregulation by the government, a higher cost of living, daily work commutes of two hours or more, and unfriendly neighbors, they would have left in droves. But the sunny skies and mild temperatures hypnotized people and kept them anchored to this paradise.

Oregon was a nice place so far and was on the list of states I could have considered moving to. The weather was hot, but there was no humidity, and the coast provided some relief from the heat. I had no idea how I would react to as much rain as they received annually, but it had to be better than snow.

With 285 miles under my belt, I reached Salem, Oregon, and pulled into a small motel. I continued the drill I had executed in California. I used motel coupon books that I found at diners and gas stations but realized they were nothing more than a scam.

The first motel owner I presented a coupon to in California told me they had sold out of the coupon rooms despite a near-empty parking lot. I expressed extreme skepticism about their occupancy rate, and the owner assured me they were sold out but had other rooms available for twenty dollars more a night.

I made my argument more persuasively, and when a tired, scowling, six-foot, 250-pound goateed guy who looked like an extra from a bad motorcycle movie requested the coupon room a second time, he got it. I know that my dress, my manner, and the motorcycle all made me pretty intimidating. I decided using that tactic was more effective than calling the Better Business Bureau.

But rather than run into the one motel owner who would actually make me fulfill my promise to break up his establishment, I instituted a more passive strategy. About thirty miles from my nightly destination, I would look at the available motels and call one of them. I would cheerfully engage the desk clerk in a conversation about occupancy rates and ask if he had plenty of rooms. If he said yes, then I would tell him I wanted a room and would be there within the hour. When I arrived, I sprang the coupon on him. If he protested, I reminded him we had talked on the phone where he had assured me he had plenty of rooms. At that point, I usually didn't have any problems.

I still braced for confrontation, and my strategy at this motel was no different. I walked slowly and purposefully through the front door and made sure each step was measured, like I was preparing for a shoot-out at high noon. I opened the door slowly, glaring menacingly at the guy behind the desk. Then I lowered my voice a couple of octaves and conserved words, selecting grunts as appropriate replies.

This motel owner was different. He gladly accepted my coupon and welcomed me to Salem. He was curious as to how long I was staying and suggested a nearby place for dinner. At first, I thought it was fear, but he was genuinely nice. It was disarming. I truly didn't know how to handle it, and my uneasiness was apparent. The middle-aged man of Iranian descent wasn't alarmed by my social ills and engaged me in conversation. We talked awhile about what I was doing and where I was going, and I couldn't help but think he was casing me so his friends could steal the motorcycle while I slept. He proved to be most hospitable, and I felt a little guilty about the way I treated him and my suspicions.

The interaction gnawed at me during dinner. As I ate, I couldn't help but replay the incident in my mind. It was a lifetime of conditioning not to trust anyone and be skeptical of the most innocent people.

That was certainly how I felt about Charlotte King. I had read about her before I left and instantly thought she was insane. I had arranged to see her before I left California and wanted to prove my suspicions. We got together in a park, sitting at a picnic table. King had claimed for years that she could predict earthquakes in different regions of the world by the type of pain her body felt and the sounds she heard. That assertion had earned her skeptical reactions from the public, some of whom have questioned her mental faculties, including her own aunt, who wondered why her niece was stopping suddenly and staring off into the distance, looking for the source of a sound that no one else heard.

Sitting across from King, it was hard to envision someone with a mental problem. When we had lunch, she was three weeks shy of her fifty-ninth birthday. Rubenesque, with porcelain skin, soft hands, and warm blue eyes that complimented her infectious smile, she looked like a grandmother right out of a 1950's television show. Her life, though, had been anything but ordinary.

Her condition began in 1976 when King was reading a book and heard something that sounded like a foghorn. She asked around, and no one else noticed the sound. Oregon State University came out and did tests and verified a low-frequency sound. King's hearing was examined, and she heard sounds well below what most humans and some animals could hear. King also noticed that every time the sound changed, there was an earthquake.

"I didn't know where," King stated. "I just knew there was one."

King called the local television station, but they weren't interested. She persisted, and one of the editors started keeping track of her claims. When she made sixty correct predictions, the station listened. So did scientists and doctors, who tested King to see if there was any validity to her declarations. "Prediction" was a word King shied away from, preferring "forecast" instead.

In 1980, King experienced excruciating migraines and projected they were associated with Mt. St. Helens. She called the television station to tell them and, twelve hours later, the mountain fully erupted.

"I was watching television and got up to turn the station," King recalled. "I walked across the room into the fireplace. I had no control of where I was walking. That was scary."

It had taken several years to define her pains and what they meant. The process had not only been painful but tedious.

"Part of my body pertains to a certain geographical location," King explained. "Every time that part of the body was in pain, that was the area that will be affected. The window was always between twelve and seventy-two hours."

It had long been known that animals have this ability, so why was it not possible for a human to have the same gift? The only difference was that King was able to communicate it, but that doesn't mean people wanted to believe the message.

"Absolutely, people looked at me funny. They still do sometimes," King noted. "I went to the hospital once by ambulance, and I was telling them it was due to solar flares, and they put on my chart, 'delusional.' That was what the emergency room treated me as. I told them to give me something for the pain and let me go home."

Even her own family didn't want to believe her.

"Let's put it this way," King said, "it ended an eighteen-year marriage. I lost my kids, my home, my job. I lost my health. There was no doubt in my mind this could kill me."

King set up a website and now had a network of people who experienced the same pain and suffered the same doubts from the public. She had been in the media several times, and slowly, the public started to believe her.

"We found that everyone was having the same symptom at the same time, no matter where they lived," King remarked. "There are several people that email or call me."

King said the official agencies hadn't been very receptive to her claims.

"The government said it wasn't possible to make earthquake predictions, and now the USGS [United States Geographical Survey] has a site predicting earthquakes," King shared. "They aren't all that accurate."

King, who had a stable of doctors and scientists validating her condition, slowly convinced governmental agencies. Scientists who noticed the correlation between her picking up changes in sound and seismic activity coined it "The Charlotte King Effect." King's website helps people become more prepared by predicting seismic activity. She honed her gift and worked with a biologist on "Project Migraine." The two put together a comprehensive list of her symptoms and corresponding locations of seismic activity.

By the end of our two-hour-long chat, King had made me a believer. Her claims gave me something to mull over as I left Salem and made my way to the Willamette National Forest. I hoped the higher elevation would provide a break from the triple-digit heat and boring farmland setting surrounding me. I was right about the scenery change but not about the heat. There was a slight temperature drop, but not as much as I expected, and I was on the lookout for a shady place to stop.

Fortunately, I found one shortly after I entered the Cascade Mountain Range. Three guys were fly-fishing in a spot off Highway 22 near Detroit Lake, and I pulled over to watch them.

The pleasure of fishing had always escaped me. I never enjoyed it, though that was due to my incredible lack of patience. My world was results oriented in as quick a manner as accurately possible. I once wrote a story that contained six hundred words in twenty minutes to make a newspaper's deadline. There was no editing, no spell check, and no quality control whatsoever. It was typed like a third grader let loose on a computer keyboard, and I hoped there was nothing defamatory.

The deadline was everything. It was the only thing. Miss it and life apparently ended, at least it did for my bosses, who in turn made the deadline offender's life equally miserable. I long suspected that the words from a reporter didn't necessarily have to be coherent as long as they were timely. People don't operate newspapers, clocks do, and when the bell tolls for the presses to run, there had better be pictures and words to spit out onto the paper. The advertisements were already on the page, the stories wrapped around them to fill it out. When I didn't care about the deadline anymore, I knew it was over. I didn't miss any, but they didn't seem as crucial as when I started the job. When the deadline wasn't vital, neither was the job.

I tried to break free from this world, but old habits always haunted me. With fishing, I demanded a fish be hooked within five minutes of casting my line or I was ready to abandon the pursuit and move on to something else more exciting. While I didn't like the activity, strangely, I enjoyed watching others perform it. The three men I saw on this day looked to be relishing the opportunity to fish. I yelled out to them, asking what they were fishing for, and the three snapped their heads back in annoyance with me. I had committed a fishing *faux pas* of talking loudly, thus potentially frightening the fish. I have been underwater several times in my life and never heard anything above the surface, but I didn't debate them, instead apologizing.

One of them told me they were going after rainbow trout and that the water was flush with them. The three had already had some success. What puzzled me, however, was that they weren't keeping what they caught; they opted for hooking them and then releasing them back in the water. I also had a hard time trying to figure out how they were catching anything with all the rocks in the stream, and I marveled at the skill they displayed.

As I sat on the bank, I watched as they stood there, the river up to their thighs, not talking, just repetitiously sending the line out, only to bring it back with nothing. Then I noticed the rhythm their wrist made as the line hit the water, danced for a second, and came back out, then repeated with an identical, perfect tempo. It was artistry, a motion symbiotic with the river. The water connected to where the fly hit it on the end of the line that ran to the hand of the conductor. It seemed as one. It was one. One fluid motion, all connected, moving like a machine, precise, efficient, the goal secondary but an inevitable conclusion. A fish would find that line because it had no other choice. It was destiny.

I waited until one of the guys got a bite and then watched him reel in a decent-sized trout. He admired it for a moment, showed his two friends, then unhooked the fish and placed it back in the water.

My payoff was complete; I got back on the Harley and took off east down the highway, though I didn't get very far. I found a motel, surrendering to the extremely warm conditions, a defeat that bothered me for most of the night.

CHAPTER 8

After traveling so little the day before, guilt gripped me, so I decided to make up for it.

Riding 106 miles should have given me a sense of accomplishment, but I felt like a failure. That night, I thought about how little I had traveled and spent a good portion of the evening beating myself up about it. Self-criticism had always been one of my most dominant character flaws, and even though I had people around me to point out my faults straight away, I was there to pile on as well. Self-loathing became a part of me, and I could never seem to shake it, though I tried to lessen the blows. The origin began in junior high school, when, as a smaller, hyperactive teenager, I was a noticeable and easy target of bullies. Walks to and from school were filled with older sadistic classmates lurking behind cars, waiting to pounce on the younger, weaker prey.

Recess was a time for roughhousing. At least that was how the adults who were monitoring the outdoor areas saw it. In classrooms, it started as verbal insults, then moved to throwing pens or using rubber bands to propel paperclips into the back of my head. It got so bad, I stopped going to class. My mom and dad knew I was a truant, but penalties were rarely meted out, so I kept skipping class.

In a way, it was a blessing because it was where I began my wandering ways. I had to fill the time away from school, and I would walk around town looking in stores or playing in the park. There were mountains surrounding my neighborhood, so I often went there and got lost among the trees.

When I got to my second year of high school, I had grown, and the bullying stopped. I punished some of the kids who had picked on me, which was greatly satisfying.

Though I stopped the beatings by others, I was still doing it to myself. If I wrote a story I didn't like, I would obsess about it for days, pondering how I could have made it better. It seemed like nothing I did in any part of my life was good enough.

The previous day's ride was no different. Just when I thought I had put it out of my mind, drifting off to sleep, I had a dream that I was riding on a road that went in a circle, and no matter how hard I tried, I couldn't exit. I woke up in the middle of the night panicked from not knowing where I was. It took me a minute to remember that I was in a motel, and then I set out trying to calm myself. I stayed awake for the next hour trying to think of how to make up the miles I was convinced I needed to gain until exhaustion finally knocked me out.

I don't know why the feeling was there, but it was. I had no set place to be, but it was still that conditioning of having to produce results that worked on my mind. It was a hard habit to break. Routines, good or bad, were never easy to discard, and I felt myself lapsing into my old life. Fortunately, the Harley forced me to get off the road to fuel up every 120 miles. In a car, I could drive for miles, cross a couple of states, and never have to leave the air-conditioned comfort. Libertad, though, demanded a respite every two hours, and, though I won't admit this, I wanted the rest just as badly. So, whenever I saw something that looked interesting, I pulled off to the side of the road. It was a great way to break the obsession with completing miles and believing that I had to be somewhere I didn't.

The route I took on this day didn't have much to look at. All the views I would get this morning were more rangeland, dirty yellow grass, burnt areas, and some hills sprinkled about, with the occasional tree. When I approached the town of Bend, Oregon, I was eager to see buildings and immediately exited the freeway. There was nothing spectacular about Bend, which was in the middle of the state. It followed a city planning outline I had seen in many smaller towns along the way.

Exiting off Highway 20 dumped me into the far end of town, which was being built up. Big-box stores had invaded communities like Bend. Home Depot, Dick's Sporting Goods, Target, Walmart, and the like had proliferated in areas like this. Chain restaurants, too: Olive Garden, Outback Steak House, Chili's, and others, littered the streets. It broke my heart. The soul of a town got ripped out and replaced with corporate mega-companies. I guess they provided jobs, but it tended to knock out any mom-and-pop businesses.

Bend had exploded. I passed through it about twelve years before, when it was small. One of the people I talked to told me the town was one of the fastest growing in the country. That was said with the usual scornful look when talking about change touted as progress.

"This used to be a nice city," the middle-aged woman told me. "There are too many people here now."

There was a 154-percent population increase from the 1990 census to the 2000 one. I could totally understand the angst if I was a resident and saw the population grow from 20,469 to 52,029 in a decade. More people came in the following ten years, increasing the population to 76,639 Most newcomers migrated from bigger towns, thinking Bend was quaint. Of course, they were accustomed to all the amenities of a bigger city, which was why the chain stores followed.

I wanted to eat but couldn't find a diner. My preference for restaurants on the road was small joints for two reasons. The first was that the food was distinct and often better than in chain restaurants. Secondly, the people were friendly and often knowledgeable about their town. I learned something while I was eating, and it made the experience that much more enjoyable.

Still searching for lunch, I left Bend around eleven in the

morning with the heat of the day upon me. The upcoming miles were going to be long, hot, and relatively boring.

I stopped forty-five miles east in Brothers. The town had one place that provided gas, a market, and a café. It was still the only sign of humanity in the last hour, so I pulled in and topped off the bike. Inside, there was a resident sitting at the counter, waiting for his lunch, an older man in his sixties with a hard face and a gap between his front teeth. He was in overalls and a red baseball cap. I sat next to him and mentioned that I was coming from Bend. He lamented the growth in that city.

"It's one of the fastest-growing cities in the country," the man said. "There are too many people here now. It was a pleasant place to live before."

The temptation to engage him in an argument appealed to me, since I was bored, even though I mostly agreed with his position. His mind was locked, and I had long since learned that debating with someone whose mind was made up was futile. It was best to nod your head and move along. Plus, I learned more when I listened than when I talked.

It was another ninety miles to Burns, which gave me time to debate whether growth was good for a city. I was of a moderate political leaning even though I was a registered Libertarian.

My initial thought was that growth was necessary. The population was increasing, so why shouldn't the space? It created jobs, revitalized the local economy, and often improved the quality of life. But, admittedly, something is lost in that transition, things like quaintness or even a town's culture.

In this country's disposable culture, change is what we do. We tear down buildings the minute they show any sign of wear. Our sports stadiums have a shelf life of about thirty years, with only a handful of them designated as icons. I was glad I got to see the old stadiums that the Detroit Tigers, New York Yankees, and San Francisco Giants played in before they were razed.

It wasn't just ball fields that faced the wrecking ball. Las Vegas casinos are in a constant state of flux. The old joints from the 1960s were leveled to make room for even more opulent resorts.

There was no tangible link to our past in this country. Nostalgia is better served in our memories than our streets.

I was in London once and saw a wall that had a bunch of holes in it. Someone told me it was from an old building that was attacked by German warplanes in World War II. They left it up as a reminder of the war so the younger generation would know what the city endured seventy years prior.

As I continued down Highway 20, I came across an American oddity. The shoe tree seemed to crop up in the most remote places. This one was no different. Twenty miles outside of Juntura, a lone mesquite tree and some of the shoes started coming into view. These quirky decorated pieces of nature had been around for decades, but their origins were unknown. They were all over the country. Nebraska, California, Arkansas, Michigan, and Nevada all had shoe trees. Apparently, area youths started flinging pairs of old shoes with the laces tied together so they snagged on a limb and dangled. Over the years, other people in town continued the tradition. Some who traveled this route, often from other areas, brought old shoes to add to the tree. I had been following Gold Creek, watching the stream run alongside the road, when I saw people parked to the side. The tree was left of the turnout and hanging from it were hundreds of shoes. Most on the tree looked in pretty good shape. I guess the custom could be considered harmless, but I wondered how many of those shoes could be on the feet of children who walked barefoot.

We waste in this country, though we deny it. We throw away good food, buy more clothes than could be worn in a year, cast aside toys to make way for newer ones, and hang shoes from trees. I would rather see a tree hung with the names of the people who gratefully received the shoes, but that wouldn't be as fun.

Heading east, I reached the Oregon-Idaho border at sunset, and

I found a room in a little motel in Ontario, Idaho, with a friendly cat patrolling the courtyard. The cat pushed open my door, which was ajar, and decided to inspect the room while I wrote a letter. She didn't want to be in the heat any more than I did. I had some cheese and broke off a tiny piece for her. She barely acknowledged it. The air-conditioning and new leg to rub against contented her. A nice shower and a soft bed did so for me. Seems like the cat and I weren't too difficult to please.

CHAPTER 9

No matter how long you ride a motorcycle, the day will come. On a beautiful summer afternoon in the Idaho Hills, my number got called.

My mid-morning departure should have been warmer, but cloud cover made it much more comfortable than it had been on previous days. I looked up to the sky before starting Libertad, thanked the gods for the pleasant weather, and thought about what a great day it was going to be.

My destination was Salmon, Idaho, making it necessary to take the interstate, despite my contempt for it. I wanted to get there before sunset, but my morning procrastination put my estimated arrival in jeopardy, so I chose expediency over principle. I justified it by convincing myself that fifty-nine miles wasn't too long to be on that type of thoroughfare.

I had been on meandering coastal byways and two-lane country roads, so whizzing along at eighty-five miles per hour got me where I needed to be in less than an hour. I didn't know what to do, so I stalled with breakfast.

Finding independent, mom-and-pop restaurants, especially right off the highway, was becoming increasingly difficult, and the chain restaurants dominating the roadside held zero interest for me. I found a mom-and-pop, and a hostess there took an interest in where I had come from and asked where I was headed. I wanted a waitress with sass, one who called me "honey" or "sweetie." One of my biggest pet peeves with servers was when they came to the table and said, "Hi, folks, I'll be taking care of you." Yeah, you want to take care of me? Why don't you make my house payment or nurse my sick aunt? I loathed such insincerity, even if it was benign.

If I had uttered those words when I was a waiter, my manager and friend to this day, Billy, would have grabbed a metal-slotted spoon and beat me with it. We had a guy who came from a chain restaurant to our dinner house, and Billy drove him to the unemployment office in less than a week.

So, I always searched a little longer until I found a place that didn't serve the same bland food and conversation. In Boise, it was more difficult, but when, off a service road, I found a place that had character, I felt triumphant. The waitress provided a copious amount of attitude, and we engaged in a spirited contest of verbal jousting. It felt like an Italian family meal in New York City. My eggs and sausage with hash browns and a side of rye toast tasted that much better.

Full in both belly and spirit, I told her I was leaving and to try not to cry. She fired back that she had already forgotten me. I smiled for the next ten minutes as I replayed the repartee.

Route 21 was seven miles from Boise, and I found it rather easily. The road led to a large recreation area called Lucky Peak State Park at the bottom of Lucky Peak Dam, which was built in 1955 and was twenty miles from the middle of the city. Speedboats mostly took up the space on the lake, but farther north, I could see people pulled off to the side of the road, swimming in the creek that fed the lake. The road began to climb into the Boise National Forest, and I had thirty miles of tree-lined highway until I would reach Idaho City, and another 200 miles until my day's final destination of Salmon. I reached the summit of the mountain, which was about 6,000 feet, and headed toward the tiny town of Lowman. Everything was going well, and I enjoyed the shade of the giant pines.

The descent from any peak increased my speed, but I made sure the incline didn't rule my miles per hour. Traffic was light, and the area so peaceful and serene that I was in no hurry to get through it. I was about ten minutes from Lowman when I saw rocks on the road. I wasn't going very fast, probably about forty miles per hour, but was entering a turn. I slowed, but the rocks forced me wide right. I knew I wasn't going to hold the curve, so I bailed out into a turnout area.

Unfortunately, its surface was soft sand, and the bike's front tire sank, dropping the front end and sending me sliding with it, though not pitching me over the handlebars. It only took an instant, but there I was, lying underneath the motorcycle, my left foot pinned and my boot getting burned by the transmission case.

A guy in a truck saw what had happened and pulled into the turnout. He lifted my 650-pound machine off me. Together, we pulled the Harley back upright.

Now it was time to assess the damage to both me and Libertad. My wounds were limited. I had road rash on my left arm, a sore foot, and nothing else. Libertad's injuries were more serious. The apehanger handlebars were bent, and the gearshift linkage and metal housing were turned inward, rendering them useless. This was a huge problem. Not being able to shift made the Harley inoperable, and getting a tow truck was going to be almost impossible. It took me a minute, but I came up with an idea. I took a crescent wrench from my saddlebag and bent the metal housing back, and then forced the shifter into third gear. By doing a little roadside patch up, I would be able to nurse it slowly back to Boise. There was a Harley dealership there, and the mechanics could provide a more permanent repair.

Backtracking, as my friend Warren said, was a dirty word, and he couldn't be more right. I was seventy miles away from Boise, but backtracking was my only option. I rode back to Boise, not able to do more than thirty miles per hour and avoiding stops because then I would have to burn the clutch to get her going again. It was a tedious process, taking about three hours. I found a motel near the dealer, parked my battered Libertad, and went in to tend to my wounds. The worst thing about road rash was picking the tiny pebbles out of the raw, affected area.

When I was in my twenties, and much dumber, I rode a scooter in shorts and sandals and got run down by a Station Wagon. I had road rash from my ankle up to my ass, and I had never felt such agony. Anyone who has had a large area of skin scraped off would say they would rather break a bone. The pain was intense and only got worse. I didn't have medical insurance, so I went home to fix myself. Taking off my shorts was a logistical nightmare. I managed to do it after about thirty minutes. My mom had prepared a bath with Epsom salt, and I limped into the tub, the warm water acting like a million needles jabbing my leg. The water instantly turned black from the dirt and asphalt as I sat there trying not to cry. I soaked as long as I could take it and then got out to begin phase two of self-treatment. It took me an hour of picking out the debris remaining in my leg, flicking pebbles and asphalt, wincing with every motion. I had one step remaining, and it required the assistance of my father. I sat on the closed toilet as he pulled the top off the hydrogen peroxide.

"Just put it on a little at a time," I pleaded.

My father, being German, didn't think that was logical. So, he poured that antiseptic liquid down my entire wound. I pulled the towel bar out of the wall and yelled at the pain I had never experienced before.

"You would have never made it if I did it your way," he reasoned.

Grudgingly, I agreed.

I had crawled into bed with a bottle of cheap vodka and drank until I passed out. *A prudent treatment*, I thought. That was until the following morning, when I awoke and realized the bed sheet was stuck to my leg. I spent the morning gathering the courage to rip it off my leg. After an hour, I finally did, and whatever scab was developing stuck to the sheet that I then threw in the trash. That might have hurt as much as the crash, but I toughed it out. It was a trait I learned from my mother. I wanted to help her now, but she wouldn't let me. I knew the stubborn pride that ran through her. It shut you down and was hard to let someone who loved you get close enough to admit vulnerability. You don't want to ask for assistance, at least not me. I once was doubled over in pain with what I thought was an ulcer and had a roommate who was so horrified that she was going to call 911, but I drove myself to the hospital. Maybe that characteristic will leave me someday. Maybe it will soften. Maybe I'll reach out to someone close before it was too late.

The injury in Idaho, too, was going to be dealt with in solitude. I was in a motel room, alone, but fortunately, this scrape wasn't nearly as bad as the scooter accident. It covered an area on the underside of my forearm about two inches wide by ten inches long, but not deep. The skin was only minimally affected. Still, it had to be dealt with, or infection was certain. I sat on the edge of the bed, took a deep breath, and started pulling off my dirt-stained clothes. I turned on the shower, got in, and picked up the little bar of soap provided by the motel. I took a few deep breaths as the water beaded off my chest. I lifted my arm, took the soap, and began to rub the bar up and down the affected area. Surprisingly, it didn't hurt as bad as anticipated. I guess when you slide down a street in shorts on a scooter, other pain becomes relatively small in comparison.

Although I was in little physical pain, I was ailing mentally. I was about a month into the trip, and, for the first time, I wasn't sure I wanted to continue. There was nothing like a dingy motel room to cause the mind to imagine scenarios I didn't want to confront. The loneliness of the road was getting to me, and knowing I was going to be stuck for at least a day did nothing to ease my sense of solitude.

When I moved, I felt connected. People in passing cars waved as I rode by. The landscape seemed to be there for me, and looking at farmhouses or ranches always made me wonder who lived there and if their lives were more satisfying than mine. I was sure they had everything they needed, and I imagined they had a satisfaction that few people ever attained.

Animals appealed most to me. I put sugar cubes in my saddlebags for horses I would see along the country roads. Most of the time, they would take them and allow me to pet their noses. The cows, however, wanted nothing to do with me. They were perfectly content and didn't need any socializing. Goats and sheep were equally aloof. When I stopped the Harley on the side of the road, they would retreat from the fence line, moving a safe distance away. All my novice tongue clicks and soft whistles failed to lure them. Even that snub made me feel like I was part of the land, that livestock wasn't shunning me, that they just liked their personal space.

People tended to be more hospitable. Merchants at gas stations took an interest in my travels, as did those filling up at the pump next to me. More times than not, they asked where I was headed and where I would end up. I would tell them I wasn't certain of the destination, and that seemed to intrigue them even more. Some had a hard time wrapping their brain around my itinerary that didn't have a point A to point B. It was nice to see locals tell me of places to go and take pride in their hometowns. They also recounted past trips with vigor and a smile, no matter how long ago they had gone. That whole "cautiousness of a stranger" washed away as they dropped their guards to ask me more questions. One answer would lead to four more inquiries, and suddenly, they were like a five-year-old at the zoo. It comforted me to see humanity interact without trepidation, and, in some way, however brief, we connected. These fleeting exchanges injected the days with normalcy. I convinced myself that I belonged, that the world wasn't as isolated as it felt when I went to sleep alone in a town I had never been to.

This night was different, though. The walls closed in, and I needed to get out, if for no other reason than to distract myself from the thought I had of giving up and going home. With no transportation, I would be walking wherever I went, which aided in pushing out the negativity that was packed into my mind. It was a good stroll. I passed businesses that were mostly closed, but the open ones, I popped my head in and said hello, did a little browsing, and talked to the person behind the counter. Thirty minutes into my jaunt, I came upon a little dinner house, deciding to exceed my usual meal budget and treat myself to some shrimp scampi and a Caesar salad. By dessert, I had had my fill of food and conversation, and I deemed it safe to return to the motel. My mind was clearer, and sleep was much easier to attain than I thought.

In the morning, I took Libertad into the Harley dealership, hoping against hope they could fix her and not gouge me, though they had every right to, for as quickly as I wanted her back.

One of Harley-Davidson's rules was that if you were on the road and broke down, that machine got fixed first. It was a great philosophy, and one that I was ready to take full advantage of, despite the back lifts filled with other Harleys. Kevin looked at the motorcycle and assured me they would get her looked at. The handlebars were twisted, as was the gear shifter, and I was looking at several hundred dollars and at least two days, and that was if they had the parts in stock. For some reason, though, I wasn't upset or even worried. Kevin's demeanor was so soothing, I figured it would get done when it got done. I was ready to hike back to the motel when he asked another customer, a local, to give me a ride. I thanked him for the lift, and after a quick shower, searched for breakfast.

I found a place and, over my meal, talked with the waitress about the town and how it had grown, and I didn't get the usual *progress was evil* spiel. She was glad the town had gotten bigger.

I strolled around downtown for a while, and it seemed friendlier than most bigger cities I had visited. Boise moved at a quick pace but didn't have the faceless energy a lot of them possessed. People walked, but not hurriedly, and they smiled when they passed.

By the time I got back to the motel, it was late afternoon, and Kevin had called to tell me the Harley was ready. They were able to bend back the metal housing and the handlebars, which saved me a bunch of money. The general manager of the store picked me up at the motel. I paid for the repairs and noticed they had washed it for free. I was reeling.

In such a good mood, I took Libertad out for a little spin around town. As I motored down the street, I noticed a bar that had a Texas hold 'em tournament that began in an hour. I walked in and found that the tournament was free. No entry fee, you got some chips, and you played until they were gone. First place was dinner for two at a nice restaurant.

Among the forty people playing was a woman named Diane. She was in her early thirties, fit, with a touch of masculinity. Having lived in Los Angeles my whole life, it wasn't difficult to guess that she was gay, but I didn't have to. She and her partner were fairly open, holding hands during breaks and acting like a couple. She told me that Boise had definitely changed. She had lived here most of her life and said that people were far more accepting than five years earlier.

"Then I wouldn't have been able to be myself in a place like this," Diane beamed. "Now there are a couple of places I know I can't go to, but it's a lot better."

She was a regular in this neighborhood bar, and no one seemed to care about her sexual orientation. When she was knocked out of the tournament, she got a conciliatory hug and kiss from her partner. No one recoiled in horror, which made me smile. Love was always a welcome sight, and I wished I saw more of it.

While it made me happy for them, it also brought sadness to my situation. In forty-two years on this earth, I had had one loving relationship, and that was in my late twenties. It had been a good thing, and we somehow managed to screw it up. Now, back in my motel room, I lay on the bed and rewound my life, wondering why I couldn't have what Diane and her girlfriend had. Did love scare me? Did I even know what love is? I concluded that, since Michelle, I was pretty bad at picking girlfriends. It wasn't for lack of trying, but it was certainly a matter of quantity over quality. The meaningless unions stacked up like jets on the runway of a busy airport, and I decided now was a good time to start recounting the last fifteen years of my personal life. There were so many train wrecks that I thought it best to go chronologically, instead of by severity of disaster. When you're grasping for happiness, you will clutch at anything, even if you know there were thorns.

In most cases, it wasn't any fault of the women. They loved me—or tried to—but I never let them get close enough. I remembered a female coworker saying to me once, "You are the worst type of guy out there. You get a woman to love you and then you walk away." It was a valid, though painful, point.

Relationships were about what I needed, what I wanted, and I didn't consider anything or anyone else. I didn't care about their feelings or interests or desires. The women were an accessory, something to turn on and off as needed, and when it got too complicated or cumbersome, I traded them in for a new model.

This 2 a.m. epiphany was as unwelcome as a telemarketer's phone call, but it was necessary, a long overdue introspection. I mulled it over for a couple of hours with more questions than answers. Finally, exhaustion wouldn't let me ponder it any longer, and I drifted off to sleep.

CHAPTER 10

When late morning came, I did my usual routine of packing the Harley and checking it over. I wasn't much of a gearhead. I routinely ignored monitoring tire pressure, checking the lights and signals, as well as pulling out the oil dipstick.

This morning was no different, but there had also been a hesitancy to leave.

At first, I attributed it to my self-reflection in the wee hours of the morning. Something else, though, was nagging me, and it wasn't my come-to-Jesus moment in the middle of the night. I went into the motel room and sat on the edge of the bed, paralyzed. I couldn't move from that spot, and, if someone had seen me, they might have surmised I was having a stroke. In a way, I was. It finally hit me what was going on. For the first time, I was afraid to get on a motorcycle, and that was scarier than the accident I had been in two days before.

It was not my first crash. There had been three ones prior, and they were a lot more serious than this one.

My first was the scooter mishap, which took about three months for the road rash to fully heal. My next was a couple of years later in Long Beach. I had come from a restaurant near the Queen Mary and was on a one-lane road leading back to my house. A car came at me with no lights, and I swerved to avoid it. When I did, I lost control of the old Honda Nighthawk and went flying over the handlebars onto a dirt lot. I separated my right clavicle and still have the bump on my shoulder as a souvenir. The third incident was the scariest Same Honda, but this time I was at an intersection letting a guy cross the street. I heard the screech from behind me, and the pedestrian's eyes got as big as silver dollars. The police figured the car hit me at about thirty miles per hour. I went flying down the street and busted up my knee, my totaled motorcycle fifty yards behind me, pinned under the car.

Every time, though, I got back on, no problem. And the first thing I did was drive by where the crash occurred to get rid of the bad karma.

This accident was different. I had never had this apprehension. I don't know why, but I didn't want to get on Libertad. I sat on the edge of the bed and thought this was it. I was packing the Harley and abandoning the trip. I sat and thought about what a failure I would be if I came home. How could I quit now? What would I tell everyone, that I was afraid and had given up instead of pursuing this odyssey? If I couldn't get over this, the whole effort would be wasted. I had quit enough stuff in my life, a pattern easily repeated.

My self-pep talk was falling on deaf ears. I chided, cajoled, and chastised myself, but nothing was moving me from where I had sat for the last hour. It took some time and a lot of self-convincing, but I slowly persuaded myself that I had to continue. I remembered a saying that I had packed in my bag and was also on the wall in my apartment. It was from the Dalai Lama, and it read, "Take into account that great love and great achievements involve great risk."

That was two epiphanies in less than twenty-four hours. This trip was something I had wanted to do for years, and I couldn't let one setback deter me. I packed my bag, hopped in the shower, and soon greeted Libertad with a smile. She fired right up and sounded as good as new. In a way, so did I.

The first part of the road was traveled territory. Highway 21 was where I rode on Sunday, and I thought the familiarity would be settling, but it wasn't. It acted as a reminder of me dropping the motorcycle in the soft gravel. A sense of anxiety ran through me as I kept replaying the crash in my mind. It didn't help that the blacktop was stained with early morning rain.

At the first tight turn I approached, I almost stopped, going so slow that the car behind me honked. That startled me and made me even jumpier. I hit the brakes again, and, despite the successive blasts of the guy's horn, I blocked out all distractions and cautiously negotiated the curve. This made Mr. Road Rage go ballistic, and he started to tailgate me. There was no place to pull over, and even if there had been, I probably would have stayed where I was. Since the mountain road was twisty, there was a constant double yellow line, and passing was not only illegal but unsafe. Of course, this didn't deter the middle-aged man in the gray sedan. He tried a couple of times to go around me and was thwarted by cars and twice by a semi-truck, one of which almost hit him.

I thought this would be an opportune time to show him my fourteen-inch crescent wrench I keep in my saddlebag for such occasions. I bought it in rural Colorado at a flea market on the side of the road. My friend Mark, who had owned motorcycles most of his life, had one and said it was an effective deterrent for tailgaters and aggressive drivers. I called it my "attitude adjuster" and had only used it once in five years. I was in Wisconsin on my way from Madison to Milwaukee on Interstate 94. Traffic was jammed, and I could tell by the blue and red lights about a mile ahead that we had an accident. All the cars had stopped, and I began to ride between them in a common maneuver used by motorcycles called lane splitting. A woman in a van, a self-appointed road monitor, swung her vehicle to the left, blocking my path. I clutched the right brake lever and jammed my foot on the brake pedal; both the front and back brake engaged as I swerved the Harley to the left to avoid hitting her. When traffic moved, I waited for her to inch forward, which she did, still blocking the space between me and the car in the left lane. I was behind her now, so I started to move to her right to split that lane, but she was having none of it and performed the same maneuver on the opposite side. I went to her left, but she kept swinging the van in whatever direction I was trying to pass her. On about the fourth time of her using her car as a weapon, I grew tired of her trying to knock me off the motorcycle. I took out the wrench and swung at her side-view mirror, breaking the glass and leaving the housing dangling by the side of her van. She rolled down her window and started screaming at me, and I calmly informed her that the next swing would be at her head. She promptly rolled up the window and straightened out her van, allowing me to pass.

Fortunately, in my current situation, all this guy had to see was me pull the tool out of the saddlebag. He decided it was in his best interest to drop back a few hundred feet. Once the road provided a passing lane, I moved to the right, and he sheepishly went around me and soon disappeared from view. On my own now, I was able to continue my leisurely pace, accompanied by a medium level of angst. It didn't take long before I was near the turnout of my mishap, and I took my hand off the throttle, coasting to the scene of the crash. Libertad sputtered like she knew where it was and didn't want to relive that moment any more than I did. I could now see the soft gravel, my tire impression still visible. When I was parallel to it, I spit on it in contempt and hit the gas, not looking back.

Route 21 turned much softer after the town of Lowman, the tight twists lengthening out. I had climbed a thousand feet from Boise, and the lower fork of the Payette River soon was on my right. The river ran alongside me on the road, named the Ponderosa Pine Scenic Route. It was one of those paths that instantly gave comfort. It's benign but scenic, and the water cascades downstream as you go upstream. The forty-one miles from Kirkham Hot Springs to the entrance of the Salmon/Challis National Forest had water most of the way. Even when it wasn't in sight, I took comfort knowing it was nearby.

I gradually climbed another 3,000 feet, stopping a couple of times to marvel at the river that was my copilot. The highway had gentle curves that allowed me to flow with its bends, giving the sensation that I was one with the surface. Libertad and I burst to the right and then snapped back left, and at one point, I didn't even feel like I needed to control the motorcycle. I was just a passenger, and I embraced a consciousness that I had no control over, giving my power and trust to the highway, which, in turn, cradled me up through the hills and allowed me to sense my surroundings.

When I reached Banner Creek Summit, I was at 7,000 feet. It was still summer, so the air was staler than it would be in a couple of months, where a tinge of cool would make it crisper. My descent through the forest was similarly peaceful, and, in a little more than twenty miles, I reached Highway 75 in the town of Stanley. There, I was introduced to the Salmon River that would accompany me for the rest of my ride. It was as picturesque, though its current wasn't as strong as the Payette. Fishermen dotted the stream, waist-high in the current, fly-fishing for trout. Other sportsmen took a more relaxed approach to their pursuit of fish and cast out from the shore.

The Salmon River was discovered by Lewis and Clark in 1805. I felt like the explorers, although I was in no way comparing myself to them. It was still nice to know that I was traveling the same route, albeit far more comfortably. I watched the water grow more restless the further into the national forest I proceeded. In some spots, the flow was aggressive, even treacherous. It was raging in one place, and I was certain this was where it earned its nickname "The River of No Return." Still, it looked inviting, water crashing over rocks as it made its way south, while I, going north, marveled at it.

I glided up the road with the water. Its serenity further lulled me into that Zen-like state. I welcomed the feeling for miles, even as I exited out of the national forest and headed twenty miles to Challis, catching Highway 93, which isn't an interstate, but it stretches 1,300 miles, beginning at Wickenburg, Arizona, and traveling north to the Canadian border, passing through Arizona, Nevada, Idaho, and Montana.

Idaho was where its beauty bloomed. After cutting through the desert of the Southwest, the road split through the Sawtooth National Forest. After I passed through Challis, I was twenty miles from Elk Bend when I hit construction. The signs warned me about the impending work three miles away: "ROAD WORK AHEAD." "LEFT LANE ENDS." "SINGLE LANE AHEAD." "FLAGMAN AHEAD."

A woman who I surmised was in her early fifties was manning the traffic flow from the south. With great authority yet a grandmotherly demeanor, she held the sign on a pole with STOP on one side and SLOW on the other. She had the opposite problem I had. While I had to melt the fear and intimidation strangers thought I greeted them with because of my biker attire and their preconceived notions, she had to inflict her power upon people reluctant to bend to her will. The job of flagman was the lowest position on a road crew's hierarchy, yet it holds much power, and with that comes the fury of others.

The flag person on Highway 93 was no exception. Truckers, vacationers, and commuters all had schedules she disrupted. When they approached the familiar orange and diamond-shaped sign that showed a figure with a flag, you could almost hear the sighs of frustration and imposition. Rest areas, meal breaks, gas fill-ups, and even historical stops were accounted for in a wayfarer's schedule, but not two lanes turning into one to accommodate road improvements. That, in the traveler's mind, was an unnecessary evil and one they were in denial over, much like when a dentist finds a cavity during an annual checkup. One knows it's possible, but we convince ourselves it always happened to someone else.

I was second in line; a local driving a pickup was in front, in conversation with Betty, who waited for word on the walkie-talkie that it was clear for us to proceed. It was going to be at least a ten-minute delay. They were widening Highway 93 to make more room and clearing out some rock on the side of the hill. It was a good point to take a break. I turned off the motorcycle and took a stretch. I was talking to Betty in between leg and back stretches and told her I was on my way to visit with Dugout Dick and asked if she knew him.

"Of course, I know Dugout Dick," Betty exclaimed. "Everyone around here does. He was our local celebrity. He's very nice."

There was a good chance I might even run into him on the road, she informed me. It was noon, and he might be headed into Salmon, eighteen miles north of his place, to get supplies.

He drives an old blue Dodge pickup, Betty told me, adding that there would be no way I could miss him if he was on the road.

"He goes pretty slow," Betty stated. "Don't ever try and get him to move over. He was going to do 35 mph. He'll let you pass, but he isn't going to speed up."

When I asked how to find his place, Betty smiled at the local in the truck.

"You can't miss it," she instructed. "It's up the highway on the left."

When we got moving again, I went around the pickup so I would be certain I would be able to see Dugout Dick's place. It turned out I didn't need to. As I was looking along the hillside for the sign, I almost rear-ended him. He was plodding along Highway 93, as Betty had promised, going no more than forty miles an hour on a road where some doubled that speed. His estate was visible from the highway. On the hillside, a sign with missing letters proclaimed, "Dugout Dick's Ice Caves." The caves that were bored into the hillside dotted the otherwise untouched landscape. I shadowed his vehicle, much to the disgust of the drivers behind me, who beat on their horns and flicked their high beams to get both of us to pull over. At one point, I counted eleven cars visible in my rearview mirror as we inched up the road. Either he didn't hear the horns or notice the headlights, or he didn't care.

When he reached his place, he signaled left and went across the yellow dividing line to a row of mailboxes. I followed the illegal and semi-dangerous maneuver and pulled alongside him, experiencing the wrath of an oncoming motorist I cut off to perform the identical maneuver.

He picked up mail formally addressed to Richard Zimmerman, but sometimes carries no other posting than "Dugout Dick, Salmon, Idaho." He was startled he had company, but my calm introduction, complete with an outstretched hand, seemed to put him at ease. He welcomed me and invited me over to his home, but first had to check the mail to see if his government check had come.

Dugout Dick was diminutive and couldn't have been taller than five-feet, six-inches tall. He was wearing blue jeans, a flannel shirt, and a red miner's helmet. The mail had no money but included a fair number of letters from fans who wanted to know more about his unique attraction. The letters had postmarks from Britain, Spain, Australia, and various states in the US, all wanting to stay at his famous caves. He put the correspondence in the truck, then motioned for me to follow him. We crossed a one-lane bridge he built in the fifties after the previous one washed away. Before the bridge, for seven years, the only method of traversing the current was by a pulley he had constructed, using it to get himself and building materials across the water until work on the wooden passage was completed. As we sat on a bench seat from an old Station Wagon outside one of his caves, he told me about his unique life.

Zimmerman found this patch of Idaho in a roundabout way. He hitchhiked from Nebraska after running from his Milford, Indiana, home when he was a teenager. He didn't have much use for school, but his dad gave him a choice of the classroom or a belt across the backside. He chose neither, instead leaving and getting an education by traveling the country. Salmon, Idaho, wasn't an ideal location, but the weather was too cold to roam, and he figured he had to stop at some point. Plus, there was work. A local farmer needed help, and Zimmerman came cheap. It was a pretty good life for a teenager, and it gave him time to explore. One place he found was a nearby stretch of land that was bisected by the beautiful Salmon River. The serene landscape touched him, despite being eighteen miles from town, which, back in the late 1930s, was an eternity when you walked everywhere you needed to go. It was a place he continued to think of frequently but couldn't determine why. His mind was soon consumed with World War II. He was drafted by the Army and shipped off to the South Pacific to protect the islands from the Japanese. There was more lounging on the beach than fighting the enemy. Fresh fruit picked off the trees, warm tropical weather, and beaches with clear blue water all appealed to Zimmerman. His paradise was interrupted by his former employer in Salmon, who needed him back on the farm.

"Back in those days, they had a rule that if you were needed on a farm, the Army could send you back home," Zimmerman recalled. "I was needed by my boss. I didn't want to go back, though. I loved it in the South Pacific."

The farmer who called him back from the war had no place for him to live, but Zimmerman knew exactly where he wanted to reside. The first year, he lived in a tent by the Salmon River on the property he had discovered a decade earlier. The Idaho winter convinced him he needed more permanent shelter. Using a pick, a shovel, and a crowbar to excavate the cave, he carved a home into the hillside, approximately twenty feet long by six feet wide. Scrap lumber helped fortify the ceiling and walls. There was no electricity, no phone, and no gas, but it was his.

Well, not exactly. Technically, Dugout Dick was squatting on federal land managed by the Grazing Service, created in 1934 to manage cattle and other livestock feeding on public lands. That agency would be merged with the General Land Office in 1946 as the Bureau of Land Management. Zimmerman put in four mining claims on an approximate two acres in 1948.

"I wanted to buy it, but they couldn't figure out why." Zimmerman chuckled. "They wondered what I wanted with that piece of ground. 'You couldn't give it to an Indian,' they said."

So, Zimmerman, rebuffed from purchasing his dream site, decided to live there anyway. No one was going to care if he set up his home there. He was right. He lived a peaceful, solitary existence for decades. Somewhere along the line, he's not sure when, he decided to expand his estate. He had already remodeled his first cave, adding a window from an old camper shell and bringing in a wood-burning stove. In the far corner of the cave was an icebox, which, because of the cave's depth, provided natural refrigeration. Now he started digging more into the hillside. He added fourteen more caves over the years, some dating back to the fifties. He used materials he got from a junkyard or what people threw away. Many knew him and gave him old building materials.

Zimmerman lived a quarter mile down the road from the original cave he constructed. He said he pays property taxes of $125 a month and gave up two of the four plots he had put mining claims on. The Bureau of Land Management, after several unsuccessful attempts to evict him, agreed that he could have the land until he passed away. It was an arrangement that suited the ninety-year-old just fine.

On this day, he was canning apricots, using old mason jars he collected over the years. In two pots on the stove, he heated the apricots, then scooped them into the jars.

"I'll eat some of them," Zimmerman noted. "I might sell some too." It was a simple life, and over the years, Dugout Dick had survived with odd jobs, social security, and checks from the government for his service in the Army. He also earned income by renting out the caves to vacationers, who came from all over the world, especially after the British Broadcasting Corporation did a documentary on him in the mid-eighties.

"I've had people from Germany stay here," said Zimmerman, who charged five dollars a night. "I have water leaking into one of them, and it stinks, but they still rent it. They don't seem to mind."

A full-time tenant, a cross-dresser named LeAnn, occupied one of the caves near the entrance and paid twenty-five dollars a month in rent.

"It is beautiful here," said LeAnn, adorned with blue high heel shoes, a cobalt blue dress, and red lipstick. "At night, the deer walk down the road outside the house to drink from the river."

Zimmerman got a couple of neighbors about ten years ago. There were two sprawling ranch-style houses on the other side of the river that clouded his view.

"I used to fire my gun across the river, but I can't do that anymore," Zimmerman sighed.

Walking with the aid of a cane because of arthritis, Zimmerman still enjoyed writing and listening to music but was unable to play the guitar any longer because of sore hands.

"Why would I want to live anywhere else?" Zimmerman observed. "This place has all I need."

We talked for about an hour, and I was so engrossed in the conversation that I didn't notice the dark clouds gathering like people gawking at an accident scene. The sky was black, and a couple of drops fell on my face. I put on the rainsuit and headed north.

I got to Salmon and had a decision to make. The clouds were behind me but gaining. I could remain in Salmon and call it an early day or try to outrace the storm to Montana. I needed to make up some time so I could get to Sturgis, South Dakota, to see my friends who were going to be at the annual motorcycle rally. I looked back at the clouds, then at the time on my cell phone. It was 2:30 p.m., and I had at least 200 more miles to go with about five hours of patchy daylight remaining.

Being a gambler, I started Libertad up and headed toward the Continental Divide, reaching 7,000 feet when I turned right onto

Highway 43. As I arrived at the small town of Wisdom, the thunder was in my ear. I gassed up and jetted toward the town of Divide. That was where Interstate 15 was, and then I would make good time to Bozeman. The rain got me a little, but my rainsuit kept it mostly off, and by the time I reached Bozeman, it was late; the sun had set an hour earlier. I wanted to get to Sturgis by the next day, so I got to bed early, another 400-plus-mile drive awaiting me in the morning.

CHAPTER 11

When I awoke, I had every intention of driving the 470 miles from Bozeman to Sturgis. I had timed the trip to arrive in the little town at the same time as the largest motorcycle rally in the country, but the crash in Boise had put me behind my informal schedule. Today was supposed to be the first day in town, buying T-shirts and hanging out with the other members of my motorcycle club. We'd spend the afternoon telling lies in some bar, laughing, and busting each other's chops. At some point, we'd get dinner, then a nightcap or five before we walked back to wherever we were staying.

Instead, I was going to have to go on what bikers called a "balls-out run." That meant interstates and high rates of speed, all while hoping not to crash or get pulled over by a state trooper. It wasn't going to be enjoyable at all. I was going to be flying by areas I would rather have ambled through. This was a part of the country I had never seen, so I felt like I was cheating myself by blowing by it.

I would be lucky to get to Sturgis by nightfall, even if I left early in the morning. Riding close to 500 miles takes a lot out of you. I would try to break it up as much as possible, but between the ninety-plus-degree heat and the overabundance of Montana law enforcement, I couldn't go nearly as fast as I desired. I ended up taking a break about every forty-five miles. I had left by eight in the morning and knocked out 150 miles before noon, reaching Billings, dehydrated. Even in the mid-morning hours, the heat had beaten me up. I went into a little diner and immediately guzzled water while I waited for my lunch to be prepared.

After I ate, I spent more time in the diner than I probably should have, but I couldn't motivate myself to get back on the motorcycle. By the time I did, it was past one o'clock. The afternoon sun, especially in the summer, sucked the life out of me, and I wasn't looking forward to going back out in it and warring with the elements. After noon, my head felt like it was baking in that helmet. I could take off my T-shirt and soak it, but it was usually dry by the time I got four exits down the interstate.

I reached Crow Agency, Montana, ninety minutes later. I had stopped twice prior despite it only being sixty miles from Billings. Exiting the freeway gave me a much-needed rest, though it was hard to get back on the motorcycle and continue. I found myself lollygagging at the rest stops after getting gas. I read magazines or looked at all the crazy merchandise that those places sold. It was easy to lose myself in there and procrastinate, all the while knowing I had three more hours to go.

I forced myself back to it, though, mentally, I wasn't ready for the battle, and I found a convenient excuse to pull off the interstate. Just before Wyoming in Crow Agency, there was a sign for the Little Bighorn Casino. I pulled off to investigate. This was not the type of establishment I was used to seeing on my trips to Las Vegas. There were no neon signs announcing the name of the place, instead a crudely painted sign above a one-room module building with two teepees sitting in front and a speaker playing Native American chants as I pulled into the drab parking lot. Inside was even bleaker. There were no gaming tables, no poker room, no buffet restaurant, and no glitzy showroom. There wasn't even a hotel connected to the casino. Several poker and slot machines and locals sitting at them, that was it.

When the establishment was built, the goal was to help those on this reservation, but it appeared only residents were gambling. Out of the thirty-six people I saw in front of a machine, thirty of them were Native Americans. It made me think of the lottery. The very people it was supposed to help were the ones playing it. It basically came down to a tax on the poor. They didn't seem to mind. Their faces lit up when a television crew would show up at a liquor store to interview those waiting in a two-hour line for a ticket. The reporter would ask the obligatory question, "What will you do if you win?" and the answers were equally foreseeable. "I'll quit my job," or "I'll buy a new house," or "I'll travel." But they don't win. They never do. Even if they did, the money would overwhelm them, and there were so many stories about people squandering their winnings and having nothing to show for it.

There was a happiness in the procession of people purchasing Powerball tickets, and if that got them through the day and made them forget the troubles that plagued their lives, then who was I to judge?

In the Quonset hut that housed the slot machines at Little Bighorn Casino, I didn't see the same hopeful faces. I saw despair. I saw emotionless women pushing a button almost with the expectation of losing. The look didn't change, even if by some small chance the machine paid off for them. They kept robotically pushing the button, taking a drag on a cigarette, and repeating the process until the money they couldn't afford to gamble with was gone. It was both eerie and sad.

I left after an hour, returning to the Harley with a feeling of depression. I couldn't seem to shake what I had witnessed. I got on Libertad but didn't start her up. Instead, I sat in the parking lot trying to process the scene with little success.

The best course of action, I thought, was to try to outrun the emotion. While I was zooming down Interstate 90, a new issue arose. I had wasted so much time dawdling that I had put myself well behind schedule. As town after town whizzed by me, I wasn't sure I was going to make my destination. About two hours into the ride, I looked east and saw nothing but a dark horizon. There were no clouds, just a wall of bluish-black sky, and that was never good. With clouds, you had a chance that they would break up, or at the worst, spit out a temporary seasonal thunderstorm. That was manageable. This was not. This was "get ready to get soaked." This wasn't going to last for an hour; this was going to drench me with sheets of water for the rest of the day.

I had been on the road enough times to know what was ahead. The biggest question was when I was going to get hit and how bad it was going to be. Those questions were answered about two hours later, near Sheridan, Wyoming. I thought I was going to get lucky, dropping down south on Interstate 90, but it seemed this storm wanted to welcome me to the Cowboy State. Even though I had daylight remaining, I ducked into the overhang of a Best Western Hotel as the first claps of thunder rumbled in the distance. Soon I saw the lightning appear in little squiggles across the sky. Some ran vertical, others horizontal, but it seemed, with each one, they announced the storm's imminent arrival.

I knew my day of riding was over. The storm jumped me like a mugger. I went inside and paid too much for a hotel room. I was in no position to haggle for a better rate or go down the street and bargain hunt. Usually, I would cruise up and down the main street of a town, stopping at three or four motels, price checking, using coupons, bartering with the person behind the desk like I was buying a Berber rug in a Moroccan bazaar. Often, I told the poor proprietor that there was no way he could charge such an outrageous sum for such inadequate accommodations. Some of my retorts to innkeepers when they told me the nightly rate had been:

"I must have missed the sign outside that said 'Four Seasons.'"

"Do you have a fever?"

"Is that in US dollars?"

"Do you tuck me in at night and read me a story for that price?"

"You know that price-gouging in this state is illegal."

Some of the time, the sarcasm was lost because of a language barrier. There were a few times when I got a couple of bucks taken off the rate. Most of the time, however, they gave me a look that said, "Go pound sand." I then moved on to the next establishment.

This night, I figured I had about twenty minutes to check in, pay, and unpack the Harley before I could expect what I predicted would be a Biblical tempest. Of course, when you live in Southern California, and rain is measured by the thimble, three drops of water classifies as a deluge. Unfortunately, I was not wrong with this one, though I did overestimate its arrival. As I unpacked the duffel bag from the motorcycle, a thunderous boom rocked above my head, followed by a bolt of lightning that set off a car alarm in the parking lot. I moved a lot quicker, got my bag, and hustled off to the safety of the room as rain reigned.

Watching out the window, I was happy that I had enough sense to stop riding for the day, even though it was going to set me back even further in my reunion with my biker friends.

CHAPTER 12

The ride from Sheridan to Sturgis was a brief 215 miles, and I left earlier than I normally would to make sure I got to my destination with plenty of time left in the day to enjoy as much time with the guys as I could. When I got closer to town right before noon, I could already tell the circus was in full swing.

The Sturgis Motorcycle Rally has been around since 1938 but had grown from a small group of dedicated motorcyclists coming together for a day of racing to a festival that attracts nearly a half-million people. I probably would have enjoyed the earlier years when there were only a couple hundred people, but, as I have often suspected, I was born in the wrong decade.

Nowadays, Main Street was full of Harleys and their owners, as well as those gawking at the motorcycles and amateur exhibitionists flashing their boobs whenever police weren't around. Gift shops, tattoo parlors, T-shirt vendors, and bars all made more money in this one week than they did all year. It had become a commercialized spectacle that was far more about selling souvenirs and drinking than the lifestyle of riding a motorcycle.

True bikers called the hundreds of weekend warriors that descended on Sturgis and similar motorcycle rallies RUBs, an acronym for "rich urban biker." RUBs usually had more money than sense. Most had minimal riding skills and had fallen in love with the idea of living untethered for a week. Funny thing was, most of these middle-management types put their motorcycle on a trailer and towed it with their $100,000 motorhome, parked outside of town, and then rode in like they had completed the journey of a lifetime. You could spot them a mile away. Their Harleys are unblemished, lacking the nicks or scratches inevitable if you rode. Also, RUBs were usually adorned with the latest trends that Harley-Davidson Genuine MotorClothes were pushing; they looked as spotless as their machines.

I was outside a biker bar by my house once when a wannabe showed up on a nice, polished Harley. He probably had fewer than five hundred miles on it, pulling up as if he had ridden across the country. He looked at me and said, "Your bike's pretty dirty." I replied, "That's what happens when you ride them."

Not that I couldn't find a way to enjoy the Sturgis Motorcycle Rally. I had been there before, and even though my drinking days had long since passed, I could find other ways to amuse myself without the liver damage. I figured that, with the boozing I had done in my twenties and thirties, I had drunk enough for two lifetimes.

All my heroes were drunks with a writing problem: Ernest Hemingway, Dylan Thomas, and Charles Bukowski. I aspired to be them, so I went to the bar every night and drank and wrote. But let's be honest, I did far more boozing than writing. I would bring a yellow legal pad and some pens, sit at the bar, and put myself under the illusion that I was practicing my craft. By the seventh or eighth vodka and 7UP, the pages were the rants of a babbling alcoholic. That went on for years until it finally dawned on me that my writing was awful, and my health was being destroyed. I substituted cigars for alcohol and led a much more peaceful existence.

The guys I hoped to meet would more than make up for my semi-teetotaling. They belonged to a motorcycle club I had joined called the Orange County Assholes. This was a great group of guys. Membership was mostly made up of middle-class, blue-collar males from the Orange County, California, area. Butthead was the president, and other associates included Fang, Tattoo Tom, Torchy,

Chooch, One Beer Mike, Panhead Jimmy, Speed, Corky, Aussie Glen, and Biker Bob.

This was not a one-percenter club like the Hells Angels, who got that moniker after a group of outlaw bikers descended on the small town of Hollister, California, in 1947 and created a night of mayhem. The American Motorcyclist Association said that 99 percent of motorcyclists were law-abiding, and that only 1 percent were outlaws. We didn't fit the outlaw characterization. It was a lifestyle, but it didn't define who we were. I didn't have that level of commitment. Being an outlaw biker was your life, twenty-four-seven. If the president of the club called at three in the morning and said he needed you, the request could not be denied. I admired such dedication, but I was much more comfortable with my group of misfits.

George Reiter, my neighbor across the street, was a founding member, and while I was mired in a bad marriage, I would flee to his house in the early evening, sit outside, sip Jack Daniels and Coca-Cola, and talk about motorcycles. He had three of them. I had none, but Crazy George, as he was called, gave me the encouragement and motivation to get one. He would talk, and I would listen, each story better than the last. It provided me with two hours of escape before I had to take that dreaded walk across the street and pretend I loved my wife.

Crazy was my kind of guy. We shared the same birthday, but he was twenty-two years older. Crazy was born on Alcatraz Island, back when families resided there, and his dad was a prison guard. Crazy had worked as an electrician but was retired. In those evenings, he taught me about Harleys. My resolve to ride bolstered after every evening with him.

He also showed me the world of philanthropy. Most bikers were giving people, whether it was helping a fellow rider broken down on the side of the road or giving a few bucks to a guy in need of a meal. George had organized the group's annual ride to Skid Row in Los Angeles two weeks before Christmas. We collected toys throughout the year and then brought them to the kids, who had been waiting in line since the previous day, trying to avoid the prostitutes, drug addicts, and mentally ill. These kids were only getting one toy, so they got there early to make sure it was a good one.

The first year I went, it crushed me to see these little boys and girls with ripped clothes and dirty faces, clapping and cheering when we pulled up. I tried to hug every one of them. The following year, I brought candy canes and handed them out. One three-year-old girl was too shy to come up and get one, so I put one in my pocket and walked up to her. She already had a lollipop in her mouth. I bent down to give her the treat, and she took the lollipop out of her mouth to give to me. It was the only possession she had in this world, and she wanted me to have it. I picked her up and put her on Libertad, letting her play on the Harley. I thought that I couldn't make her life better forever, but I could for one day, and maybe the next day, someone else would help. That lesson I learned from Crazy George was one of many that I've never forgotten.

When he told me earlier in the year that he was going to Sturgis with some of the guys, I wanted to meet them. They wouldn't be hard to find. I just had to go to the loudest bar in town. Chances are, they would be there, making the most noise. When I pulled onto Main Street, there was nothing but two wheelers parked side by side in two tidy rows that stretched five or six blocks in the middle of the main drag. A parade of motorcycles did loops around them, getting to one end and then flipping a U-turn so they could go back to the other side of the street. That was one of the main activities during the day. I loved riding up and down Main Street, watching all the people, then finding a parking space and walking up and down the sidewalk. Today, though, I was on a quest. I had to find Crazy George.

I had encountered strangers on this trip by design. I was ready, though, for some familiar faces. The road was getting lonely. I needed to talk to someone I knew, dig a little deeper into a conversation. I enjoyed small talk with strangers, learning about their lives and the towns where they lived, but it was tiring at times. Often, they wanted to quiz me about my life. "Why did you go?" "When you going back home?" After the tenth identical encounter, showing enthusiasm became difficult.

It was understandable why they did it. I was a shiny bauble in lives where little sparkled. They saw me as the intriguing mysterious outsider, the renegade showing up on the big, grumbling steed. It was a sight few had seen and the most excitement they had experienced. I did realize that. But when you hit a town and want more in the way of human interaction, it was a challenge to stay cheery. I was proud that I never dismissed anyone on the entire trip. I answered every question they asked of me and always seemed engaged. I acted like it was the first time I had heard the conversation.

Still I longed to hear Crazy's voice. I had envisioned walking into some watering hole and he would shout out, "Hey, Fat Boy, what took you so long?" It was then I would know I was among friends.

Finding a parking space after only one pass up and down Main Street was a miracle. I parked and headed to One-Eyed Jack's Saloon. I had on my black Assholes T-shirt, and someone instantly recognized it as I entered.

"Hey, you one of them Assholes?" a guy exclaimed.

"Yes, you seen the guys today?" I replied.

"No, they left. Said they were riding back home."

I couldn't believe it. I went up to the bartender, a striking woman in her forties with a shock of braided red hair and a tank top that barely held her large breasts. She saw my shirt and said, "Hey, another Asshole. I thought I got rid of you guys last night?"

She laughed, and I thought I might as well continue the ribbing the guys gave her last night.

"No, I came to see the prettiest bartender in Sturgis." I smiled.

"Aw, how sweet," she cooed.

I shot back, "She must have the day off."

The patrons, who heard my playful jab, laughed. Fortunately, so did Cassandra, who flipped me off. I knew I had made a new friend.

I ordered a beer and asked her where my friends were.

"Oh, you missed them, sweetie," Cassandra said. "They said last night they were leaving first thing in the morning."

Her confirmation floored me. They had informed me they were staying until this night, but I guess they changed their minds. Had I known, I would have made sure to have gotten there in time.

While I nursed my beer, I beat myself up over missing them, the disappointment of not seeing them palpable. The more I thought about it, the more depressed I got.

One day, one lousy day. Cassandra wasn't making me feel any better when she described their antics from the previous evening. I knew I had missed out on something truly special. As the end of my beer got nearer, I had to figure out where I was going to stay that night. I chugged the last of my drink, bid farewell to Cassandra, and headed out the door.

I walked around Main Street for a while, kind of in a daze, while processing the fact that I wouldn't get to see the guys. The subject was still on my mind when I was eating dinner. I thought about what I could have done differently to make sure that I met up with them. I would have loved to hear about their ride up to Sturgis, and I was sure they would have enjoyed hearing how my trip was progressing. Crazy would have had at least two stories from their travels and at least three joking insults regarding mine.

The waitress asked me where I was staying, and I told her I didn't have a place yet. She said she had a friend who had a house around the corner that had an empty bedroom. I jumped at the offer, and she made a phone call.

In my quest for spontaneity on this trip, I didn't think about reaching out to the guys in the club to see if their itinerary had changed. I knew now I probably should have called one of them.

My last thought as I fell asleep that night was, *Well, I will see Crazy when I get home.*

CHAPTER 13

I tried to make the best of my day in Sturgis, but my heart wasn't in it. I wandered around Main Street looking at merchandise, staring into shop windows and checking out the hundreds of parked motorcycles. It was weird; I was surrounded by thousands of people, and I had never felt more alone. It was a spiraling sensation that I couldn't shake. The more I thought about Crazy and the boys, the more depressed I got. It was unusual for me. I knew the guys would be there when I get back. So, why was I so maudlin? I couldn't figure it out, so I thought maybe I could get answers on the road. I went back to the place I was staying, packed my bag, and left.

Speeding was a good way to knock me out of my funk. It had worked before, so I thought I would try it on Highway 90, leaving out of Sturgis. It didn't take long for me to start feeling better. *Wow, this really does work*, I thought. Unfortunately, an employee of the South Dakota Highway Patrol disagreed with my therapy. The lights and siren hit me about twenty miles outside of town. The officer decided it was time he and I met. He clocked me at eighty-five miles per hour, but it was closer to ninety. I sat on the motorcycle and waited for him to come up and introduce himself.

I've been pulled over plenty. It was one of the byproducts of my speeding habit. Most of the time, the routine was the same. The cop took his time, came out of the car, then asked me how fast I was going. My pat answer was, "The speed limit, sir." Said cop went back to his car, wrote me a ticket, and I got to spend a future weekend at traffic school.

This encounter with Trooper Koenig of the South Dakota Highway Patrol was the strangest one I had ever experienced. He made me sit in the front seat of his car while he wrote the ticket. He didn't even cite me for speeding. Instead, I got a twenty-dollar ticket for my handlebars being too high.

California, where I have lived my entire life, doesn't have a cooperation pact with other states. That meant I had to pay the ticket on the spot, which was smart on South Dakota's part since I would have never honored my commitment. I asked the trooper if he took a two-person, out-of-state check. Like most in law enforcement, his sense of humor was surgically removed when he entered the police academy. I handed over a twenty-dollar bill before he could find an excuse to arrest me.

I got some gas and got back on the interstate, once again revving up the Harley to 90 mph. As I immersed myself in thought of missing the guys, the first billboard came into view. It was an advertisement for one of South Dakota's biggest tourist attractions. Wall Drug Store was located fifty-five miles from Rapid City. That first billboard was the beginning of a barrage of advertising for Wall Drug. On the hour-long ride, I counted sixty-seven signs for the drug store, though I was certain I missed a couple.

The ads were crude, with no thought to design and with phrases that would make a first-year marketing major cringe. Bumper stickers said, *Where the Heck was Wall Drug?* and *Have you Dug Wall Drug?* The ads had been on farmlands for years, grandfathered in after a state law was passed in the '80s allowing advertising only in commercial zones. The company said it spent a few hundred thousand dollars a year on marketing, and the signs were all over the world, including countries like Vietnam and the Netherlands. They were even signs on double-decker buses in London.

The billboards were effective in South Dakota, where they had a captive audience on the edge of the Badlands, and they relentlessly worked on you, much like a bully poking you in the chest. None of the individual jabs brought discomfort, but collectively, they provided bruising pain.

Wall Drug began the advertising campaign during World War II. A friend of owner Ted and Dorothy Hustead put bumper stickers up overseas, and soon GIs were requesting the stickers and putting them up all over Europe. It was Dorothy who began the ad campaign in this country. The drug store she and her husband bought in 1931 was struggling, and one day, after being awakened from a nap by cars going by the house, she put out a sign advertising soda and offering free water. The idea worked. Tourists on their way to Mt. Rushmore pulled off the highway, and business began to blossom.

Now the store was a ten-million-dollar operation and received more than two-million tourists every year. It had grown from a small drugstore to a huge complex, complete with a restaurant, gift store, outdoor recreation area, and art gallery, all in a 75,000-square-foot facility.

The attraction pulled many off what was a boring stretch of interstate, breaking up the monotony of a 400-mile drive between Sturgis and Sioux Falls. An eighty-foot dinosaur greeted patrons and the Main Street, and stores replicated an old Western town. It had been my experience that the more signs an attraction offered, the more of a tourist trap it was, and often, it was disappointing.

Wall Drug, though, was harmless fun if you don't go in expecting a lot. Ted Hustead, who died in 1999, had a saying that he didn't want to make a lot of money from a few people, but a little money from a lot of people.

It appeared he succeeded. On this day, he got eight dollars from me for a cheeseburger, fries, and a soda. It was food, so I ate it, and it gave me enough energy to continue down the interstate until I reached Sioux Falls. I had been on this highway before, and I knew there was little to see, but there was one spot that was breathtakingly out of the ordinary. There was a huge concrete bridge that connected the towns of Chamberlain and Oacoma, which were divided by the Missouri River.

The Missouri wasn't doing much, but that didn't matter to me. I stopped on the concrete bridge, pulling as close to the wall as I could, and risked getting plowed by a semi just to watch the slow but powerful current move from north to south. Amongst the cars and trucks whizzing by, some honking their displeasure at me, I sat mesmerized by the water. As I saw a boat coming up from the south, I turned to watch it go under the bridge. I saw another older bridge up the river and thought I should go investigate.

I'm glad I did. The Chamberlain Bridge was on King Road, about a mile from the newer concrete overpass. This bridge was steel and had supports that encased me while I was on it but were still open enough to see out. It was also closer to the river than the newer bridge, but it was too narrow for anyone to stop. I went up and back a couple of times, slowly, so I could enjoy the Missouri River.

The bridge had been around since 1925 and became obsolete twenty-eight years later when the newer bridge was constructed to accommodate the interstate and a boom in traffic. The Chamberlain Bridge was joined with another to make a one-lane pass on both sides, connecting I-90 business in Chamberlain to Oacoma.

That, I thought, was a much better tourist attraction than Wall Drug. Someone should build a restaurant and water park there. As I motored toward Sioux Falls, I wondered if Chamberlain's mayor would give me a consultancy fee for such a brilliant idea.

CHAPTER 14

Miles in the Midwest were mind-numbing. Merely moving thirty minutes felt like a month. The weather didn't help; hot and humid, not ideal conditions on a motorcycle. I tried to block it out, but even the best meditators would have had difficulty.

I wasn't expecting much when I began the ride on Interstate 29 going south toward Sioux City, Iowa. My choice of routes was another slog down the interstate. I wasn't thrilled by it, but I picked this way for expediency. I would grab breakfast there, then keep going south until I reached I-80, then head east.

There were only 285 miles to ride today, and since most of it was on the interstates, I would be done well before dinner. If all went to plan, I would end up in Des Moines. There was a sense of anxiety hovering over me, and I attributed it to the tedium of being in the middle of this country. My feeling was one of desolation, and I wanted to see a tree or a mountain, or I feared I would go mad.

When crossing coast to coast in United States, there is a dilemma that confronts motorists halfway through the journey. Unless going out of the way and traveling through South Dakota, drivers must pick one bland, colorless state to ride through, and believe me, it's not an easy decision.

For me, Nebraska, Kansas, Oklahoma, and Texas were the barren connectors that divide the expanse. Cornfields, wheat fields, dust fields, or oil fields were your choices, and not one of them was very appealing. I had been through them all, and I can say that I disliked them all equally.

In previous trips, I found that no matter which route I took, it was 400 to 500 miles of misery that can't be completed fast enough, unless you make the mistake of going through Texas like I once had. I took a southern route home and was on Interstate 10. I crossed into Texas at Beaumont and saw the sign that said 827 miles to El Paso. That doubled my pain, and I vowed never to take that route again.

Today's jaunt of fewer than 300 miles gave me hope that I could complete this mundane itinerary without too much psychological trauma. Trust me, Des Moines wasn't much better, but it made Sioux City look like New York City. Plus, I would be a day out from Illinois and civilization. All I had to do was keep it together mentally and move forward. There was no expectation of anything exciting happening, just riding and doing it in a blur of asphalt.

Sioux City came into view by late morning, and I pulled off to get some breakfast. I dawdled at the diner, reading the local newspaper and nursing my Diet Coke. I had knocked off eighty-seven miles and only had 198 remaining, and it wasn't even noon.

As I got on I-80, I noticed ominous dark clouds on the horizon. I was barreling toward them, and the minute the temperature dropped, I felt the first raindrop on my cheek. It was a typical summer thunderstorm, and I knew it wouldn't last long. They were brief but intense, and it was best to find shelter and wait them out. I found cover beneath an overpass, waited an hour for the skies to clear, and was able to proceed.

I let the storm continue to move east, then started Libertad back up and followed safely behind. Ensuring I would see no more rain, I donned my rainsuit and put the waterproof covering on my luggage. I don't care if there was a tidal monsoon or a Cat-5 hurricane, if I put on the protective gear, I won't see a drop of water. If I didn't wear it and there was one cloud in the sky, it would call its brethren, and they would stalk me like a cheetah pursuing prey.

I rode fifty more miles, and even though I had half a tank of gas, I decided it was time for a break. My mind was fighting me, as it often did. I had filled up when I pulled off for the thunderstorm, and it was already midafternoon. I had plenty of time to get to Des Moines before nightfall, but my ego kept trying to push me. I overruled Ego and its brother, Machismo, and pulled off in Atlantic, Iowa.

It was about eighty-one miles from my destination, and it would only take me an hour or so to get there, so this break didn't make me feel all that guilty. Atlantic had a gas station, so I could top off the tank and take a load off in the process.

As I exited I-80, I saw a man hitchhiking on the other side of the road. That he was bumming a ride was not unusual. That he was wearing a white dress shirt and tie was definitely different.

When I paid for my gas, I asked the woman behind the counter if she knew what was going on with the man. As I suspected, the small town was all abuzz about their well-dressed, carless visitor.

Seemed he appeared a few days before and had been at the local church. He got some people to donate a room to him for a couple of days, but then the charity ran out, and it was time for him to go. He had been there for two days trying to get a ride but had no luck. He was penniless, and those few facts were not enough to satiate the townsfolk's desperate need to know what this man was all about. Rampant speculation and rumors flew around like dragonflies.

The gas station employee heard he was a missionary. Another person had told her he was mentally ill. Running from the law was another theory. I was surprised that spy or terrorist weren't suspected.

Funny thing was that the mystery could have easily been solved if someone had just asked him, but while defaming a man isn't a faux pas in Atlantic, Iowa, talking to him about his background and travel was considered rude.

Though I possessed a strong imagination and would have

loved to contribute to this version of "Let me Guess Your Life," my curiosity overruled my desire to play this particular parlor game. I filled up the Harley and rode over to him for a soft interrogation disguised as a friendly chat, just in case he was a spy or terrorist, and knew fifty-two different ways to kill a man. Fortunately for my well-being, his life story wasn't nearly as dangerous.

Thomas Currier had been in town for the last three days and trying to catch a ride for the last two, but he had no luck. Part of the problem was that he wasn't traveling light, definitely a prerequisite in persuading someone to pull over. Encircling Currier were ten pieces of luggage. They held his life's possessions. Clothes, books, writing pads, mementos, and various sundries stuffed in suitcases and plastic bags resting by his side.

A child of God, Currier had been traveling the United States spreading the good word. He was a Pentecostal minister, and he would arrive at a town, go to the local church, and barter his grant-writing expertise in exchange for room and board and a chance to preach on Sunday.

It seemed like a good arrangement, but the church elders in Atlantic weren't interested in the deal. It wasn't the only town where Currier had struck out. He was finding it hard to peddle Jesus these days, even to those whose minds and ears were open.

Currier had been in the trenches as one of God's soldiers for most of his life. The fifty-five-year-old made it more formal six years prior when ordained as a Pentecostal minister. He thought he had a pretty good life, marriage, stepchildren, stable job, and a nice home in the San Francisco area. Then his wife asked for a divorce, and it seemed like his world had crumbled.

"It was a tough period," Currier recalled. "I wasn't sure what I was going to do."

The answer came in a vision Currier said was sent by the Lord.

"He told me what to do," Currier added. "So, I did it."

It wouldn't be the last time God spoke to him. This was his

calling, and he knew what he had to do. He packed up his belongings and started hitchhiking across the country. He usually stayed less than a week, and he worked exclusively for Christian churches, though he never knew where he was headed.

"The Lord directs me," Currier stated. "The churches have the need, but not the resources. I try to help them, and in turn, they help me."

He brought out a Bible but resisted the urge to preach. A Catholic currently studying Buddhism, I probably wasn't in his target demographic. I have never been a fan of those who foist their religion on another, and, to Currier's credit, he never did with me.

"I don't preach unless I am asked," he confessed. "I was at a truck stop once, and I started talking to a trucker. By the end of me talking, he was in tears, promising to get baptized in the next town."

He continued, "From day to day, to be able to witness people experience the gift of the Lord was pretty special," Currier contended. "That trucker was so grateful to have met me."

It was those moments Currier reflected on when he was standing in the cold or the rain, getting harassed by nonbelievers, or denied shelter by a church. The road was lonely, and there was ample opportunity for conversations and introspection, especially when depending on the kindness of strangers to give him a ride and waiting hours for that to happen. To pass the time, Currier worked on a book he was writing. It was about the end of the world, based on the "Book of Revelation," and he had filled numerous yellow legal pads with blue ink.

"The end of the world could come today, tomorrow, whenever," Currier predicted. "It will be fiery, not as moderate as people think."

I joked that it would be terrible if God ended the world before he finished the book and gave away the ending. Given Currier's current mindset, he failed to find the humor.

Today was one of the difficult days for Currier. God had told him to go to Atlantic, and he had obeyed, but with the local church not in need of his services, he needed to go to a town that could appreciate him. That wasn't going to happen until someone picked him up, and, so far, divine intervention was nowhere to be found. Homeless and hungry, Currier was rescued by the woman at the gas station, who took pity on him, giving him food and water. Someone else had paid for a night in the motel.

"He seems like a nice enough man," the woman observed. "But there was only so much you can do to help someone out."

The police had an opposing view of the town's benevolence and forcefully expressed it. They thought it was time for Currier to depart Atlantic, and one state trooper had made it his mission to ensure it happened sooner rather than later. He visited Currier on the side of the road and informed him he was loitering. Every hour or so, Currier had to move his belongings up the road thirty yards so as not to run afoul of the law.

Currier looked at the harassment optimistically, believing that moving around gave him a better chance to catch a ride, but it had been two days, and there was no luck. The wear of the road was showing both physically and mentally. Currier's attire was disheveled. His white short-sleeve shirt had a stain, and his dark blue tie was loose. His black pants were tight around his roly-poly belly and unable to be fully zipped. There was a touch of sunburn on his nose and forehead, and the warmer than usual August day had him sweating uncomfortably, conditions souring Currier's demeanor.

"I told the officer to pull out his gun and shoot me because I am about ready to step in front of a truck," Currier exclaimed. "I'm really frustrated."

To add to his plight, a semi had backed over one of Currier's suitcases earlier in the week. The other pieces of luggage looked like they had been accident victims as well.

Through all his trials, though, his faith remained strong.

"This was what keeps me going," Currier said, pointing to a passage in Proverbs. "It says, 'In all thy ways acknowledge Him, and

He shall direct thy paths.' The Lord has always come through for me. You have to live in Hell before the blessings come."

Before I left, I gave him twenty-five dollars and wished him well, telling him I hoped he got a ride.

"I can't see why I am having so much trouble," Currier said. "I look nice, and I'm not bothering anyone."

The words had barely left his lips when a yellow pickup truck pulled up and the driver offered him a lift. I helped him put his bags in the back of the truck and said goodbye. The smile returned to his cherubic face as he got in the truck.

"The day was getting better," Currier shouted, waving back at me as the truck pulled away. "God bless you."

CHAPTER 15

It was funny how my mood lifted after a good night's rest in Des Moines and my encounter with Thomas Currier. He made my life better. Adding to my optimism was that it was a mere 179 miles until I reached the Illinois border, and that was reason enough to change my disposition.

As I was humming along the interstate, the passing towns didn't seem to hold much interest, though I did stop in Iowa City for a break and some fuel. It wasn't because I thought I would find someone or something interesting there, it was because I was playing a dangerous game of how far I could go on the Harley before I ran out of gas. The distance between Des Moines and Iowa City was 119 miles, just about how much I could go on my 4.5-gallon tank. I had already switched over to reserve about a half-hour before, so I was pushing my luck, but I was bored, out among the cornfields. Fortunately, I made it to the city that boasts both the University of Iowa and the Herbert Hoover Presidential Library. Neither held much interest to me, so I gassed up and got back on Interstate 80.

Another forty-five miles east was a sign for Iowa 80, the world's largest truck stop. Right off I-80, at exit 284 in Walcott, Iowa, was the main artery for semi-trucks traveling east and west, and the truck stop provided a much-needed break for those who drove for a living.

Interstate 80 begins in San Francisco and runs approximately 2,900 miles until it merges with Interstate 95 near Ridgefield Park, New

Jersey. It was one of nearly 65,000 miles of interstate that were built in this country in the 1950s and 1960s after funding for the Interstate Highway System was encouraged by President Dwight D. Eisenhower.

The origins of the interstate routes went back to 1938 and President Franklin D. Roosevelt, who allegedly took a map and drew three lines north and south and three lines east and west to signify he wanted superhighways constructed. Part of the proposal called for the government to open gas stations along the road, but many in Congress vehemently opposed the idea of federally sponsored businesses, and Roosevelt abandoned that idea, instead letting others open businesses to serve both automobiles and trucks.

Eisenhower presented much of the funding for the roads sixteen years later and the major routes began construction. Even before the interstates were fully completed, they were hit with truckers who found the wide four and five lanes much easier to traverse than the two-lane nightmares they had been using, hopscotching from a state road to a rural route to try to move commerce across the country.

The oil companies owned many of the truck stops along the interstate, and, in 1964, Signal Oil constructed and opened the facility in Walcott, Iowa, running it under the Amoco fuel brand. Bill Moon was hired a year later to manage the truck stop, though there wasn't much to oversee in 1965. There was one lube bay, a restaurant run by another family, some gas pumps, and a small store. Moon added to the features through the years but expanded when he bought the property from Amoco in 1984. Showers were installed in a private driver's area, both of which were unheard of in the trucking industry, and soon were duplicated at similar facilities.

It was 1989 when the facility transformed into a state-of-the-art truck stop and tourist attraction. A new 58,000-square-foot store was added, and hanging from the ceiling was a 1918 Oldsmobile. There was also an extensive section of the store devoted to chrome products and other items of interest to truckers. Moon's dream was realized.

He didn't have much time to enjoy it, dying in 1992. His wife and family preserved his legacy and kept expanding. In 2006, they embarked on a four-million-dollar renovation that made Iowa 80 the largest of its kind in the world. What was a fuel stop on the Iowa-Illinois border was now approximately 240,000 square feet and featured a museum, gift store, restaurants, chiropractor, barbershop, movie theater, showers, stores, and served more than 5,000 people daily.

One unique business was upstairs, sandwiched between a barbershop and the facility's offices. There, a sign read, *Interstate Dental.* The proprietor was Thomas Roemer, DDS, the dentist who was a godsend to truckers. I saw the sign and went up the stairs to introduce myself.

Today in the dentist chair was trucker Deborah Bartlett, whose business trip was interrupted shortly after it began with a sharp pain in her mouth, adding inconvenience to near incapacitation. Bartlett intended on taking a load in her tractor-trailer truck west to California from near her home in Minnesota and would have made the trip in just under three days, if not for this unscheduled stop in Wolcott, Iowa.

As Dr. Roemer looked at the offending molar, Bartlett tried not to wince too much as air came in from her open mouth and increased the pain. The news was not good, but Bartlett's aching mouth had already primed her two states ago for the diagnosis. A crown would save the tooth, but a root canal was also necessary. She faced $1,500 for the work and at least two hours in the chair. A follow-up appointment would have to be made to take off the temporary crown and put the permanent one on her chiseled-down tooth.

Bartlett looked at her husband, who was the other half of this long-haul trucking team, and knew the answer before she even asked his opinion.

"Pull the tooth," she told Roemer.

It was the usual request at Interstate Dental, and while tooth extractions were routine, Dr. Roemer's office was not. He lived in nearby Davenport and had seen the truck stop hundreds of times, but never dreamed he would open an office there.

When Roemer graduated from dental school in 1988, his goal wasn't to have a clientele of long-haul truck drivers with rotting teeth and pus-filled gums. A small, suburban dental office in a strip mall, catering to soccer moms and their children, was the career path Roemer envisioned. He lived that life for years, and it left him empty.

"My practice was successful, but it wasn't very fulfilling," Roemer explained. "It got very routine. It seemed like it was the same old thing every day."

The patients came in and out and Roemer didn't feel any connection with them. Now and then, a break in the monotony brightened his day. The phone rang with some poor trucker in pain, who had pulled over at Iowa 80 and thumbed through the yellow pages looking for a dentist. Roemer's office was one of the closest, and he was exactly what they needed—a dentist who could always see them, treat them, and get them back on the road.

To get a trucker to pull off the road for anything other than gas, food, or mandatory sleep was like pulling teeth. Often, those three tasks could be done in one stop, with sleep the least important. One could always choke down some fast food while filling up and then buy a 128-ounce mug to hold coffee or caffeinated soda and be on the road with all the efficiency of an Indianapolis 500 pit stop. So, when truckers called Roemer, he knew they were in trouble, often squeezing them in amongst his regular patients. Since many had no insurance, extraction was the most logical choice.

"It's either going to cost them one-hundred dollars for me to pull it or five hundred to a thousand to do a root canal or put a crown on it. If I do a crown, they have to come back for the permanent crown. It's not that they don't want to save it, but they don't have the money or the time."

It certainly was a lot different than how he started out practicing dentistry.

"If you had told me back in 1988 that a majority of my work would be pulling teeth, I would have said no way," Roemer told me. "It's just one of those things. You don't think of dentistry as oral surgery, but I like it. It's not the same repetitive routine."

Roemer found these blue-collar workers infinitely more grateful than his usual clientele, and he soon got the idea to set up at the truck stop since it was so close to his house.

"I thought I could give it a try and see what happened," Roemer remembered. "I always figured I could start up a regular practice if it didn't work out."

The less than four hundred square-foot kiosk at the truck stop was perfect. Though the office was small, Roemer countered that the truckers have other options besides standing in his office.

"It looks like I have a closet-size waiting room, but really I have the entire truck stop," Roemer reasoned. "I have the biggest waiting room in the country, and it doesn't cost me a dime. They have a movie theater, place to eat, showers. If you are going to be bored here, you are going to be bored anywhere."

Roemer was anything but indifferent to his new location and customers. It was exactly the challenge he looked for in his career.

"I just enjoy the work I do out here," Roemer admitted. "I enjoy the clients that I have. Granted, it's not as busy, but it's less stress, less overhead, and a little more freedom."

The dentist gave up a lot of conventional luxuries when he made the move. He now was a one-man office, doing cleanings, dental surgery, paperwork, trash detail, and answering the phone, which rang frequently. Roemer provided his cell phone number on a sign outside his office so truckers can have it when they need it. Often, they will call from hundreds of miles away to give him warning for their arrival. He does not accept insurance, which was fine because most of these patients don't have it. Cash was the preferable form of payment for both doctor and patient.

Interstate Dental was one of three known truck-stop dentist

offices; the others were in Salt Lake City, Utah, and Memphis, Tennessee, though those dentists work primarily with people in the community. Roemer's business was almost exclusively for truckers. He didn't make the transition all at once, instead splitting his time between his suburban practice and the truck stop. It didn't take long, however, to realize the truck stop was a more satisfying use of his skills. Plus, there was another benefit.

"I work more hours now because it was a walk-in," Roemer explained. "I probably spend more time sitting here than when I had my regular practice. But there are days I pick up the golf clubs and leave. The freedom to do that is nice. If you think about it, I could put up a notice saying I am out to lunch for a week, and there is not really much people can say. If I am out of town, they are out of luck."

But Roemer would never desert his patients. In many ways, he relied on them more than they did on him. It was a relationship that showed Roemer why he chose dentistry.

"I have had guys call me from two states away telling me they want to stop by because they are in pain," Roemer said. "I am at home, but I tell them I'll be there when they get there."

Roemer's clientele literally come to him through word-of-mouth. Truckers squawk his praises on CB radios. Roemer doesn't need to advertise. His previous patients endorsed his work all along the highways, and it didn't take long before someone broadcasted his cell phone number as the preferred means of communication for truckers.

Most of the time the tooth was pulled without any complications, and the trucker could be on his way in about an hour. Some truckers, however, took a little more time.

"I have had up to thirteen extractions on a guy at one time," Roemer recalled. "I don't think there was any visible tooth structure above his gum line. They were all down to the gum line, and I took them all out. I had a guy once where I put my dental vacuum up to his tooth and it popped right out. How did I ever justify that fee?"

Though Roemer laughed about that incident, he knew his patients were in a less-than jovial mood when they came to see him. "You wouldn't wish a toothache on anybody," Roemer said. "Fortunately, I got them where I want them; they are in pain. Anybody who was going to take someone out of pain was going to be appreciated."

One patient was so thankful, he sent Roemer a gift.

"I had one guy send me six or seven sequenced two-dollar bills," Roemer gushed. "It wasn't even for the bill. It was just a thank you. That was neat. I would never see that at my other office."

Roemer's philosophy was more country doctor than the current mindset of many health professionals, which was "greet them, treat them, and street them." Roemer prefers to be as hands-on as possible.

"I tell them, 'Don't hesitate to call me,'" Roemer said.

Bartlett was certainly glad she had.

"Thank you very much," she mumbled through the gauze in her mouth. "I feel a lot better."

CHAPTER 16

Approaching Davenport, Iowa, there was an even bigger body of water before me, and I couldn't wait to get to it. I was going to spend much more time at the Mississippi River than I did at its rival, the Missouri.

Exiting I-80 to Route 61/North Brady Street, the business road for Davenport, I crossed the Arsenal Bridge, also known as the Government Bridge. It was built originally in the 1850s and had been redone in 1866; then the structure was replaced by an iron, twin-deck bridge in 1872 and refurbished in 1896.

I crossed it into Rock Island, Illinois, and then traversed the Mississippi again to Twenty-Fourth Street in Moline. I turned left on Fifth Avenue and began to look for a spot to watch the river, riding past the island to River Drive. I parked Libertad on the bank and sat there watching powerboats and the occasional barge travel up and down the tributary. I must have been there for two hours. It was so relaxing, I couldn't seem to pull myself away, even knowing I still had a little more than 300 miles remaining if I wanted to get to my intended stop of Milwaukee.

If I had seen the Mississippi as a kid on a family car trip back East, I don't remember it, though I doubt my father would have stopped anyway. He took these trips as a chore, and the itinerary had to be followed. There was no time for diversions, no matter how majestic.

While driving on one such vacation, we came upon the famous

Gateway Arch in St. Louis. My mother told me that was where Ronald McDonald lived, and my six-year-old brother and I begged my father to pull over. For an eight-year-old, Ronald McDonald was one of the biggest celebrities on the planet at the time, and stopping by to say hello seemed the polite thing to do. Maybe Mr. McDonald would have a famous cheeseburger and fries waiting for us. My father sternly looked at my mother, silently chastising her for getting us whipped into a frenzy. The howls of protest lasted until the structure disappeared from view.

So now, as an adult, I made a point to stop at famous landmarks and take my time to enjoy them. If I was late, I was late. The Mississippi was difficult to leave, but I tore myself away and reluctantly got back on the interstate.

Libertad needed gas, so I stopped in Knoxville, Illinois, and found a station. As I was filling up, I noticed two cars pull up over by the air hose pump. They came from opposite directions, but stopped short of each other, the front of each vehicle nose to nose.

In one car was a young man in his mid-twenties with two small girls. They couldn't have been more than three and five years old. In the other car, an old Station Wagon, was a woman about the same age as the man. She was sitting in the driver's seat and looked rather impatient.

It took me a minute to figure out what was going on with these people. The father opened the backdoor and unbuckled the girls from their car seats. The oldest jumped out and opened the woman's back door, securing herself into a similar car seat. The mom checked on her to make sure her daughter had done it correctly, then summoned the youngest. The child didn't want to leave the man's car. She began crying as he picked her up, and the wailing got exponentially louder as he put her down. The mom stood outside of her car, waiting for her younger daughter to walk to the vehicle, but instead, she collapsed on the asphalt and refused to move.

No amount of coaxing from either parent was going to get her to cooperate. They must have stood there for at least five minutes, trying different parental strategies to achieve the objective. First, it was cajoling, then it was threats, but nothing was going to move that little girl.

Finally, when it became painfully obvious to the parents that they weren't going to win, the mother said to the father, "Just pick her up." He complied, and the daughter started screaming. When he got close to the woman's car, she grabbed the girl from him and roughly put her in the car seat. The child's face was red from the outburst and the tears. Her older sister sat motionless, gazing out the window in the opposite direction.

The man waited for his ex-wife to leave, and she did, spitting gravel back at him as she pulled around his vehicle. His last image was his youngest screaming through a closed window. He waited a minute, started his car, and pulled out of the gas station in the opposite direction.

It was awful to see, and I got the feeling that this was a weekly occurrence. I couldn't imagine having to have to go through that every seven days, but these parents seemed to be immune to the outburst, acting like it was no big deal. They had the routine of the child exchange down, such as it was, and other than those four words the mom uttered, they didn't speak to each other the entire time in the parking lot.

I needed something to take my mind off what I had just witnessed. Fortunately, Peoria, Illinois, gave me such a distraction. I thought I was done with water for the day, but then Peoria Lake appeared. It wasn't as large as the other two rivers I had seen, but the Murray Baker Bridge more than made up for it.

Constructed in 1958, the cantilever bridge, which used steel trusses for support, was beautiful. It was two lanes in each direction, and once I got on it, I barely realized I was on an interstate. The design was traditional, with arches and encased in steel supports, but travelers could look out both sides with little obstruction. Had I been able to stop on the bridge, I would have, but there was no place to pull over. Instead, I went back and forth on it a couple of times, doing a loop so I was certain I wouldn't miss anything.

It was an unexpected highlight, and as I headed north on Route 89 to I-39 to Milwaukee, it made the miles go by a little quicker. I reached a stop I had been eagerly looking forward to since I left my house. It was a business called Growing Power, and I was there to see the founder, Will Allen.

He was near a pile of soil, and the first thing I noticed was his hands. They were large and thick with worn calloused palms that provided proof of a predestined profession, and they gently cradled an impressive mound of dirt as if it were a newborn baby. Will Allen was careful not to let any of it slip through his long, brown fingers as he showed its richness to a group of visitors at his urban farm and community food center.

Allen's philosophy was, "It all begins with the soil," and he worked the dirt like Mozart did a concerto. Allen believed in a somewhat revolutionary philosophy in regard to growing. He took dirt, mixed it with a compost of fruit peels, vegetable stalks, coffee grounds, leftover grain from a brewery, and other organic ingredients. Then he tossed in red worms, and nature usually provided him with soil fertile enough to grow just about anything.

"The worms are the real stars," Allen explained. "They do all the work."

The man may delegate the heavy lifting to the annelids, and, like any good farmer, he gives a majority of the credit to the earth, but he was the person responsible for growing fresh produce in an area that had been called a food desert. Before Allen set up shop in this largely African American neighborhood, the closest place to get fresh fruits and vegetables was seven miles away. There was no supermarket, and the main food source was nearly outdated boxes of macaroni and cheese at a place called Dino's Food Mart. Most residents ate at

McDonald's, Popeye's, and other fast-food restaurants.

But Allen didn't come here to save the citizens of Northwest Milwaukee. He just wanted a place to be a farmer again and grow his crops to sell. It was the second time in his life that Allen had become the accidental trailblazer, a role he never wanted but got when his dreams collided with reality.

He was built like a movie-star hero, at an imposing six-feet, seven-inches tall, but attractive, with piercing brown eyes and a warm smile, ready to employ, which he frequently did. Even at sixty-two, Allen still had an athlete's physique. Most days, he dressed in blue jeans and a hooded sweatshirt with the cut-off sleeves revealing massive biceps and forearms that looked like the basketball power forward he was in his younger days. When I visited him, he wore a green Miami University Hurricanes hat that hid his hairless head. On his left knee was a brace that was doing nothing but prolonging impending knee-replacement surgery the only hint of any physical vulnerability.

Limping, crawling, it didn't matter. If Allen had the chance to preach about the benefits of urban farming, nothing was going to stop him. He planted the seed in others and watched his vision grow.

"The stuff we do was wrapped around social justice, food justice to make sure everybody has access to the same kind of high quality, safe, culturally appropriate food that they want to eat," Allen described. "That's the kind of the theme of many of the people that come into this space."

It wasn't Allen's dream to work in a field. He was pushed into it by his father, who worked in construction but was a farmer first. His dad was a sharecropper in South Carolina, but moved his family to Rockville, Maryland, partly to get away from the racism of the South. Allen's father kept his love of farming and tried to pass that on to his children, who weren't quite as enthusiastic.

"I didn't want to work on the farm," Allen remembered. "I wanted to play with my friends, do anything but work after I got home from school."

Besides, he was getting plenty of attention as a standout basketball player at his high school and was attracting interest from major universities. Temple, Indiana, Penn State, and others were requesting Allen come to their programs, but he ultimately enrolled at the University of Miami.

Will Allen was the first African American athlete on the university's basketball team, a gutsy move that many of his contemporaries shied away from, but the teenager didn't choose the school for any pioneering reason. His choice was a little more selfish.

"I was into the girls then." Allen laughed and then quickly mentioned that he met his wife, Cynthia, there. "I really liked that school because of the weather and the fact that it was a Northern city in the South. At that point in time, it was a good choice."

It wasn't all good, however. Allen experienced racism while at Miami, and it didn't take him long to notice the inequities.

"When I went to college, those were the days when I would say one Black star athlete out of the whole state of Florida would go to a major White university," Allen recalled. "The school system there was so segregated. Schools were so poor, many of the students couldn't qualify, or even if they did qualify, they would not go through the process of getting selected by a college. Once you stepped out of the boundaries of South Florida, you were in a different world."

Allen received racial taunts when the team played away games, and hate mail would sometimes find its way into his dorm room mailbox, but he ignored the threats and excelled. On the court, he averaged 17.2 points and 12.2 rebounds per game, and he still ranks twelfth on Miami's career scoring chart with nearly 1,300 points in only three seasons, since back then freshmen were not allowed to play. He was second in career rebounds to NBA Hall of Famer Rick Barry.

One cause Allen did take up fervently was protesting the athletic department's decision to disband the men's basketball team. Even though he was a senior and done with his eligibility, he still led an unsuccessful protest against the decision.

Allen was selected in the fourth round of the 1971 NBA Draft by the Washington Bullets but never played a minute in the league. Instead, he caught on with the American Basketball Association's Floridians, where he played one season before the team disbanded.

Wanting still to play basketball, Will and Cynthia moved to Belgium where he played for five years. It was there that his love for farming was ignited. Allen traveled around the Belgium countryside and observed several farms, wanting to do the same at his house.

"It was funny. I swore I would never farm again when I left home," Allen laughed. "I found out I really enjoyed it."

So did his teammates, who were the main beneficiaries of Allen's labor. He and Cynthia would host team dinners and would feed the group with chickens they raised and vegetables they grew. It wasn't unusual for him to show up to practice with a basket of eggs to give to anyone who wanted them.

"It was just like when I was growing up," he recalled. "We always had food for everyone. It was great to be able to do the same there."

When Allen retired in 1977 at twenty-eight and moved back to the United States, he and his wife settled south of Milwaukee, where Cynthia's family lived on a farm and Allen could continue his newfound passion. The food he grew would sell at local farmer's markets but it was just a hobby; he was anchored in the corporate world. His first job was as an executive with Kentucky Fried Chicken, but he soon became a sales representative for Proctor and Gamble.

"I never planned on staying with Proctor and Gamble forever," Allen said. "It paid well, and I was able to put my kids through school. I had farmed on the side always. I had my real love and what I liked to do. I was able to manipulate that along with my job."

One afternoon in 1993, Allen was on a sales call, and he saw the piece of land that he knew would be the future home of Milwaukee's only working farm. It was on the site of an abandoned nursery, and there were far more weeds than viable plants on the property that was in foreclosure.

"I was driving down the street, and something made me stop when I saw the for-sale sign," Allen remembered. "I wrote down the number and called it and found out it was a city-owned property. I liked where it was, and by bringing in food from my farm, I could affect the community in a positive way."

At the time of my visit with Allen, Northwest Milwaukee comprised 16 percent of the city's population and was mostly a mix of Black and White residents. In 2010, the area accounted for 14 percent of the homicides and 15 percent of burglaries and thefts. It was not the worst part of Milwaukee, but the stretch on Silver Springs Drive that led to Allen's Growing Power was littered with liquor stores, fast-food joints, and check-cashing establishments.

Allen saw an opportunity for a plot of land that the city was eager to sell, and there wouldn't be a lot of interference from the neighborhood. He cashed out from Proctor and Gamble, got a loan from the bank, put together a proposal for the land, and waited to hear from city officials.

They were impressed by Allen's words and accepted his bid. He started building a community farm and then hired local kids to work there.

"It's completely not what I thought it would be," Allen noted. "I didn't think of any community project. I just wanted to sell my farm produce. About two years into the project, I helped a youth group that needed some land and wanted to grow an organic garden, and no one would help them. I got a call from a friend who asked me to talk to them, and I had this big piece of land in the back, and I let them use it."

His property became home not only to indoor growing areas but to hydroponic growing as well. The system produced farmed fish and simultaneously fertilized the plants with their waste. Allen said he had a proposal to renovate the farm and build more structures to grow more food. He had already transcended the neighborhood.

"The neighborhood hasn't changed that much. What has changed was that we built this infrastructure that has brought new people to the area," Allen said. "Many White people were afraid to come into this neighborhood when I first got here. But because of our programs and the way we operate, it pretty much changed all that in terms of people coming here and getting involved."

As I left, I purchased some radishes to snack on while I looked for a place to stay for the night. They were crisp and spicy, some of the best I had ever eaten. When I was getting gas, a middle-aged White man asked me what I was eating. I gave him a radish and a pamphlet I had taken. He promised me he was going to go over there.

CHAPTER 17

Leaving Milwaukee in the morning, I was only ninety-two miles from Chicago but had no interest in stopping there. Chicago was a city that had eluded my interest. It was a big city trying to pass itself off as a Midwestern town, and in my mind had achieved neither. It seemed gray and failed to have the same type of energy of its unmentioned rival, New York City. Other than stopping for some deep-dish pizza, blowing through the Windy City was my intention from the beginning of the day.

That mission was accomplished in less than two hours. I had ejected myself from the south side of the city and was on I-57, headed toward Champaign, Illinois. I made it there in fewer than four hours, before noon, and was pleased with my progress. I marked the occasion with lunch at a diner that had one of the best pastrami Reuben sandwiches I had ever eaten. It was the perfect celebratory meal.

Because I had made so much progress on the road, I had the opportunity to dawdle. As I was nursing the last of my French fries, I thought about how the trip had progressed. I hadn't shared my travels in a while with my friend Heather, so I gave her a call. It was just an excuse to see how she was doing. I had gotten updates from other friends about her battle with cancer. She had been fortunate enough to get in to see doctors at UCLA, and they were some of the best in the country at treating pancreatic cancer. Through her moxie, she had met a woman whose husband had battled the same disease and had donated a great deal of money to the university to open a wing in the medical center dedicated solely to this form of cancer. The woman also sponsored Heather to go to Switzerland for some experimental treatment that had shown progress.

There was part of me that had overwhelming guilt in regard to this trip. I felt like I wasn't being a true friend to Heather. We had been through a lot together, and she had picked me up more times than I could remember. But she always told me that the trip was something I was destined to do that I didn't have a choice. "Could you imagine how miserable you would be if you didn't go?" As usual, she was right.

When I called, she was in good spirits, and I hoped it wasn't an act to reassure me. She said they were seeing progress with the tumors, and her energy level had improved. She shifted to ask me how the trip was going. I told her about the highlights, and she seemed so genuinely happy. It was almost like she was deriving strength from it. When we hung up, I was confident she was doing well, and it put me at ease.

When I crossed the Illinois-Indiana border, I realized that this had been the farthest east I had traveled on my motorcycle. The old mark was Milwaukee for Harley-Davidson's 100th anniversary. It was a sponsored ride, something Harley does every five years, but the 2003 version was the centennial, and it was huge. I rode out there with my friend Ken, and he knew people in Milwaukee, so we had a place to stay. We partied with everyone from women to gay men to police officers to hardcore bikers. It was one of the best riding trips I had ever taken.

Now I was on an even better ride that was going to last longer and go farther. Though I should have had some sort of commemoration, there was none. I had barely thought about it until shortly after it happened. Plus, I was going to be much farther east in a couple of weeks, and that would be a mark that would be hard to beat.

It was another three hours before I reached Cincinnati, and I figured that, with about 500 miles under my belt for the day, I could stop here and start fresh in the morning. I found a little motel and sacked out for the night.

Leaving Cincinnati, I didn't see any options except Interstate 71. Grudgingly, I was forced to take it but got off as soon as possible. That much concrete had too many cars, and it reminded me too much of commuting. I wanted to desperately discover a back route or a two-lane highway. I found it about thirty minutes north of town, leading me to one of the best side roads I had been on so far.

Highway 22 paralleled the interstate for much of its path but treated users to pieces of Amish Country—green, rolling farmland and deep cornfields that stretched toward the Pennsylvania border. It was a path that required no map and created no stress. It meandered instead of rushed, glided instead of pulled, and flowed instead of pushed. The towns were genuine, not manufactured to accommodate a thoroughfare, with friendly people and history and character.

One of those was Sabina, Ohio. A town of approximately 3,000 people, it didn't even warrant mention on my map. The sign at the city limits read, *The Eden of Ohio.* It was a living Norman Rockwell painting. A policeman waved hello and smiled; people sat on their front porch and rocked the late afternoon away. Kids pedaled bicycles up and down the street, not having to worry about strangers abducting them.

The local paper was just four pages and had Bible school announcements on the front page. Ice cream socials were hosted for people who already knew about the event before the paper published it. Everyone was friends with everyone, and hard work plus a strong belief in God had kept this town thriving for 175 years.

The supermarket was down the road in the next town, and

there were no chain restaurants. One of the eateries in Sabina was a Frosties on Highway 22. I could think of no better place to get an ice cream cone than this epitome of Americana.

Inside, sitting in one of the plastic booths, was a young mother treating her three boys to ice cream. The oldest couldn't have been more than ten, and the youngest appeared to be around five. They were laughing in between bites of this simple pleasure.

Two booths down was Jim, a senior citizen able to leave his job at the post office after thirty-four years with a comfortable pension. He held court here daily with other retirees, discussing world events and offering solutions while drinking coffee.

Libby Hughes walked in and joined the young mother and her family. Hughes was in her early fifties; her two sons, thirty-four and thirty-five, were raised without their father. They grew up to be strong, responsible men and gifted her with three grandchildren. She enjoyed her latest role, after the turmoil of raising her two boys by herself. Hughes smiled at the young mother's challenges with her offspring, glad that her child-rearing days were behind her, laughing as the youngest struggled to keep his ice cream in the cup. She gave the younger matriarch a sympathetic glance that only someone who has had a similar experience can give.

Hughes's days of motherhood had been a constant struggle, filled with worry, made more difficult when her oldest son enlisted in the armed forces, fighting in the Persian Gulf War in 1990. It was not uncommon for young men in this town to sign up to fight, but it didn't make his decision any easier for Hughes.

"I never had a gray hair until he went over to fight," Hughes quipped. "It worried me so much."

She was lucky; her son came home and lived ten miles away, dutifully visiting his mother often as a good son should.

Other mothers in town were not so fortunate. Pam Saville's son, Brett Wightman, was killed in action in Iraq on August 3, 2005. There won't be any grandchildren for Saville, no surprise visits or phone calls asking about her day. The only memory she had of her son was an American flag and a letter of condolence from the government, telling her about her son's bravery in combat.

Mother's Day could be the longest and toughest holiday for Saville. While other sons brought flowers and gifts, her only memento was a bucket full of tears. Any parent who had lost a child will say holidays were the hardest days to get through.

Serving his country had been Wightman's calling, a most admirable path. It was all he had talked about. He proudly discussed his career choice as far back as high school. He was the all-American teenage boy, captain of the East Clinton High football team. In his senior year, he was voted homecoming king and was popular with just about everyone in Sabina.

Wightman's short military career was equally as inspiring. He achieved the rank of lance corporal when he was deployed with his unit in March of 2005. He died tragically six months later when the amphibious assault vehicle he was in hit an improvised explosive device while on maneuvers, the IED taking a young life that held so much promise.

The town mourned with shock and profound sadness. They buried the hometown hero on a summer Saturday afternoon. Before he was laid to rest, they had a public viewing in East Clinton High's capacity-filled gymnasium. The service was on the very football field he excelled on so many Friday nights years earlier. The procession featured approximately 180 cars.

As Hughes recounted the events, tears filled her eyes. She choked them back to finish the story, taking long pauses in a futile attempt to suppress the overwhelming emotion. Hughes and others realized that Wightman went to war for something he strongly believed in, though it was of little solace to those who loved him.

The war hero continued to be honored, even after his departure. Yellow ribbons adorned oak and elm trees, houses, and telephone poles. Local businesses prominently displayed signs of tribute in their windows. A foundation in his name was created at the high school. American flags were everywhere, all still at half-staff. A large billboard with Wightman's picture in uniform from the chest up was impossible to miss. To the right of his photo, it read, *In loving memory of Lance Cpl. Brett Wightman, January 11, 1983-August 5, 2005. You will be missed. Class of 2002.*

He will be rightly remembered as an American hero, but his legacy may have provided an additional effect. He and his fellow thirteen Marines, who died in the single deadliest roadside bombing up to that point, made people in this town question why their children were being sent to fight in a war, the purpose of which most couldn't figure out. The blind allegiance to combat was unwavering for years, but then, quietly, mothers and fathers who were losing their children began to wonder if it was worth it.

As of August 17, 2005, 1,857 members of the military had died in Iraq. Jim, the old guard, didn't want to debate the topic. He will go to his grave convinced the ultimate sacrifice was worth the objective, but when I asked him what the objective was, he could not produce an answer and ended the conversation. Saville was not hesitant or shy to ask why we were there. She told a local television station that she was not sure why her son, or anyone's child, was half a world away trying to kill strangers.

Hughes also couldn't fathom why.

"I think it's made a lot of people open their eyes," Hughes said. "Brett was a good kid. He didn't deserve this."

As Hughes considered this conundrum, the youngest of the young mother's sons, who had more ice cream on his shirt than in his mouth, walked toward the front door with the intention of reaching the street.

"Casey," Hughes said in an elevated voice of warning from one mother to another. 'Grab him before he goes out into the street and gets hurt.'

CHAPTER 18

The next two days would be spent visiting relatives. After nearly three weeks on the road, I was ready for it. My destination was Buffalo, New York, and I had 243 miles to cover from my starting point of Akron, Ohio.

As chance would have it, there was a professional golf tournament in Akron that week, and I stopped by to see some of the reporters I used to labor with when I covered the PGA Tour. It was strange walking into the media center and not having to work. It took me a minute to quash that anxiety I always got when I came to a sporting event.

Most of the people in this room loved what they did. Going to tournaments and writing about golfers was considered a dream job. They had found what gave them purpose, and I was happy for them.

The truth is, I had never considered it fun. There were enjoyable moments, but they were usually found away from the golf course. Discovering a new town or meeting interesting people was what I hoped for when I was on the road. I could not have cared less about who was leading some meaningless golf tournament that no one would remember a day or two after it concluded. It was work, often tedious labor. It wasn't digging ditches, and, sure, it was cool that Tiger Woods knew who I was and that I got a front row seat to watch most of his accomplishments. Having my picture in the newspaper once a week and getting recognized in the grocery store was also an ego boost. I realized, though, that was only temporarily satisfying.

When I would talk to some of the guys about how I felt, I could never succinctly explain my position. Besides, it would fall on deaf ears. They didn't want to hear that what they held so valuable was essentially worthless to me. I wasn't part of the club because of these views. Often, I ate dinner by myself and missed out on invites to play golf or go to parties. It was part of the consequences of my beliefs. Still, I enjoyed what limited camaraderie we shared. We would sit in the press room and joke about the day, complain about our editors, and argue over the most insignificant topics. That was the aspect of the job I missed. In some ways, however superficial, those were the deepest relationships I had.

Part of me was looking for that bond when I walked in the doors on that day. In an instant, I realized that whatever was once there was gone. I was even more of an outsider. They were cordial, and some even pretended they were happy to see me, but they let it be known through their body language that I was intruding. I would like to think there was some envy, that I was undertaking something they were too anchored in life to only dream of doing. There was no resentment on either of our parts. We were just in different places in our lives, and I finally came to that realization.

In a way, spending less than an hour there was a benefit. I wanted to get to Western New York and see family. Buffalo was where my mother and father grew up. They met in a bar, and the cake wasn't even cut at the wedding reception when my father was packing the car to take his new bride to California. He despised the cold and snow. Plus, I think he knew there was a better life for him out West.

As a result of their isolationism, I wasn't privy to their lives until well after my teenage years. This snippet of family history was theirs alone, and whenever I asked, I was given broad strokes. I knew my mom's mom died giving birth to her, and she was raised by an absent father and an abusive stepmother who left when my mom was in her teens. My mom raised herself.

My father's early years were much more serene. His father was a butcher, and his mom stayed at home. He suffered with rheumatic fever when he was a kid and had to spend about a year in bed. His best friend came over every day to play with him. They had been best friends for fifty years. When I was born, he was named my godfather. Dad tried to coax him out to California, but he was happy in Buffalo. Louis Steinkirchner, his wife Bernadette, and their kids, Carolyn and Paul, would visit a couple of summers when I was a teenager. They drove a beat-up orange Vega, and to this day, I have no idea how it made multiple cross-country trips.

Now it was my turn to go to their house. I hadn't seen Louie and Bernie in twenty years, and I was excited to be with them all again. I knew that a big plate of roast beef on a kummelweck roll, or *kimmelweck,* as some people spelled it, would be waiting for me. Beef on weck was a Kaiser roll with salt and caraway seeds, and the way Bernie made it, I swore I could have eaten ten of them. But I had to save room for the plate of Buffalo chicken wings that would be next to the sandwiches on the table.

I couldn't get enough of it in my belly. For those who had never tasted this territorial delicacy, it was worth getting on a plane and flying to Western New York. The roast beef was sliced razor thin and piled high on that specialty roll. Soak it in *au jus* and heap on fresh horseradish, and it was the perfect sandwich.

My mouth was already watering when I pulled into their driveway. I had been tasting this since Erie, Pennsylvania. Those hundred miles to Buffalo were torture, and had I not seen troopers in what seemed like every mile, hiding in turnouts, I would have sped faster along Interstate 90. Still, I shaved a few minutes off my journey, getting there just before five o'clock at night.

When they opened the door, it was like I saw them yesterday. Carolyn and Paul had driven ninety minutes from Rochester. The hugs from everyone were tight and genuine. I had a cold Labatt Blue beer in my hand before the door closed behind me. We went out to the backyard to enjoy the cool summer evening. While the winters were brutal, the summers more than made up for it. Cool, with a light breeze, the air was damp, meaning I was going to be treated to thunder and lightning later.

All four had questions about the trip. Louie wanted to know how the Harley was holding up. Paul inquired, when the women were in the other room, if I had met any girls along the way. Carolyn marveled at how I had the stamina and the resolve to ride as far as I had. Bernie was curious about how it was to be on that machine. I could tell by her questions that she wanted a ride on the back. It was the least I could do for the feast I was about to be served. I would have ridden her to Niagara Falls for this meal. A quick jaunt around the neighborhood was a bargain as far as I was concerned.

Three sandwiches and ten wings later, I was significantly stuffed. With thunder in the distance, we retired to the living room. We talked more about life, and I had a few more cocktails before I began my inquisition about my parents. Talking with their old friends was the only way I ever got any biographical information about them. I had learned about my mom's life from an earlier trip to Fort Collins, Colorado. High school sweethearts Jim and Hattie Haas had known my mom since they were kids, and they had given me some tidbits, including an anecdote about how my mother broke up with my dad and dated a New York state trooper. She had grown tired of my dad's stalling on a marriage proposal. He soon realized his mistake and won her back.

The tales on this night weren't as juicy but were still enjoyable. I found out how my father bought one of the only convertibles in Buffalo and insisted on driving with the top down nearly year-round. The evening went by faster than I hoped. It was nearing midnight, and I had to go. My motel was in Grand Island, about ten miles away, and the rain wasn't going to wait on my schedule. I wished that visit could have lasted a month. Reluctantly, I said goodbye and rode in a downpour that I didn't even notice. I sat on the balcony of the motel as sheets of water and bolts of lightning pummeled the area. When I went inside my room, I opened the window and let the storm lull me to sleep.

Before leaving the area the next morning, I wanted to ride by the house my father had grown up in, burned into my memory from a trip we made when I was eight. When I got to the residence on Grand Island, New York, I noticed that the meadow we had played in behind the backyard had given way to more houses. My dad's cousin, whom I had never met, bought the house from my grandmother, but I didn't want to impose, so I sat on the motorcycle and let memories flood over me. I remembered my grandfather gave us a ride in a wagon hitched to his riding lawnmower. The fort we had made from peat moss was long gone, but I saw where it once stood.

I stayed there close to an hour, and if anyone noticed me, they left me alone. I appreciated the reverence but didn't push it. I fired up Libertad and headed toward Vermont.

CHAPTER 19

My contempt for toll roads was formed early in my lifetime of driving, taking only a couple of trips on paid highways. While bumps on free highways and interstates were expected, on a paid road, I was paying for the privilege of getting my kidneys pushed up into my sternum. Silly me, I thought the concept of a toll road was to take the money collected and actually maintain or improve their conditions. Going east from Buffalo, I didn't have much of a choice, however, so I resigned myself to this asphalt abortion and got off as soon as I could. That was in Syracuse, 152 miles later. I grudgingly paid $5.60 and asked the toll booth attendant where Route 11 was located.

"It's the first exit off eighty-one, but why would you want to take that?" he asked. "Eighty-one goes the same place."

"Same destination," I replied, "but definitely not the same journey."

I don't think he understood. Traveling north, I passed through the small towns of Maple View, Pulaski, and Adams. They were all preceded by stunning scenery. Tall trees, cornfields, and ponds graced both sides as I rode up the two-lane road. With forests come deer, and my phobia of them instantly put me on alert. I kept expecting one to jump out in front of me, but fortunately, I made the sixty-seven miles to Watertown, New York, without incident.

My strategy was not to stop for the night in Watertown. I was going to go to Potsdam to be closer to the New York-Vermont border.

It was one of the crossroads one hits on a trip like this. I had seventy-five miles on a country road to reach Potsdam. It was six o'clock with about two hours of daylight remaining, and it was sprinkling. I sat off the side of the road and contemplated the decision. I wouldn't enjoy the next two hours, as I would be worried about getting there and paranoid that a deer was going to dart in front of me. If I kept going, I would be able to spend additional time in Vermont, a state I had never visited. The rain became more persistent. It made my choice for me. I turned the Harley around and looked for a motel.

After dinner, I stopped at a bar for a drink. There were five or six regulars at this watering hole in the old part of town that was built around 1803. There was a square with a fountain and a grassy area, and in the middle of it was a resident who practiced yoga. The evening was dark and drizzly, and he stretched and posed while working on finding his happy place. This amused the regulars in the bar. They went out and watched and laughed. Apparently, he did this all the time, and they used it as a source of entertainment as they washed down their beers. He also sang, played the guitar, and yelled in the square. He didn't harm anyone, so people mostly left him alone.

Still, the patrons at the bar couldn't understand why he did this. They thought him insane. I suggested he might be a little different from them. They looked at me like I had just insulted them, and in a way, I had. I finished my drink and left just as the man ended his yoga session. I waved, and he returned the greeting. I went to my motel and locked the door in fear of retribution by those I had inadvertently insulted at the bar.

Because it was a Sunday, I noticed the churches more as I ride through the small towns of northern New York on my way to Vermont. The parking lots, usually empty during the week, were filled with cars. My day had started at ten in the morning, and the people were already safely inside their places of worship.

Small communities, such as Carthage and Harrisville, were on Highway 3, and there were all types of denominations in those towns. I saw Protestant, Methodist, Episcopal, Baptist, Catholic, Nazarene, and a Calvary chapel as I passed through. It was then I realized how many churches there were in these small communities. One wouldn't think they would have enough people to fill them, but the packed parking lots proved this theory to be resoundingly incorrect.

Though I was born Catholic, I had been practicing Buddhism for a couple of years, which, in some ways, was more of a way of life than a religion. I still appreciated the Catholic Church, even if I didn't agree with everything it taught. Buddhism was more about peace than conformity; people were encouraged to find the answers not given to them instead of following a lifestyle blindly. It was my personal belief that there was room enough in this world for several types of religions, and if anyone had any type of faith, that was good.

My cathedral for this Sunday was the Adirondack Mountains. The pews of this church were before me, behind me, and to the sides of me. It was a beautiful day, with a scant number of loitering clouds to keep the sun off my neck for brief periods of the late morning. It couldn't have been more than seventy-five degrees. Even in August, there was a crispness in the air that felt more like fall than summer. I went northeast, chasing the trail of the Canadian border. I had originally wanted to go on Route 11, which was a little higher up and ran parallel to Route 3, but it would have skirted the mountain range, and I would have missed some incredible scenery. The trees were crowded together like a New York City subway platform at rush hour, rising a couple of hundred feet in the air. Closer to the two-lane road, the forest was not as dense, and through it, I spied the occasional pond. My knowledge of trees was minimal, but I did spot pines, maples, and beech. The Adirondacks were massive, six million acres, and I felt the enormity when I passed the sign to the entrance halfway up Route 3.

The first named lake I came across was Portaferry, just before Star Lake, and it was off to the left of the road. It was small compared to Star Lake and the others that followed. Star, Cranberry, and Saranac Lake were much larger, but I pulled over to look at this one. There were dead trees in front of it, sprouting up out of the water, spindly trunks with no branches. It was like they were guarding the lake, and it made me stay a respectful distance away. The other three bodies of water were more recreational, and people seemed to enjoy these lakes more than Portaferry.

After passing by those bodies of water, I stopped for breakfast in a little town outside of Tupper Lake, and, with the Sunday rush, had to sit at a table with a local couple who were already eating. They were gracious to let me sit at the opposite end of the table and extremely pleasant. The husband told me he had lived here his entire life. We talked about the town and motorcycling and each other's lives. It was a far better way to eat breakfast than reading the newspaper alone.

When I got on the Harley, I was invigorated, but Libertad was not. The altitude had messed with the carburetor, and she was being difficult. I worried about flooding the Harley with too much gas, feathering the throttle while enough air tried to enter the chamber to turn the engine over. It took a little finesse, but she finally coughed and spit to signal she was ready to go. We headed toward Lake Placid. The little resort town was the site of one of the greatest moments in sports history, and I had to play tourist for just a moment.

The 1980 United States Olympic Hockey Team's victory over the USSR was a thrill I was able to watch on television and have relived many times in documentaries. To see where it happened and touch the ice was pretty special. I had always loved hockey, and this was the sport's greatest hour. The size of the arena was what I noticed first. It was small, with a capacity of 7,800, and it didn't even look like it sat that many. That day, a lone figure skater was practicing her routines on the ice. Two teenagers and I walked around, and the ice skater didn't pay us any attention. Her coach, however, noticed me putting my boot on the ice and yelled at me from the top of the stairs to get off. His voice carried throughout the arena, and I reluctantly complied.

From Lake Placid, I continued northeast and came across an unusual body of water. It was outside the Adirondacks and was near the New York-Vermont border, the Au Sable Chasm, a box canyon carved out 10,000 years ago during the Ice Age. Natural waterfalls were formed from erosion. Its natural beauty stopped me in my tracks. I pulled Libertad off the road to gaze at the geological wonder.

Port Kent was four miles away, and it was there I caught the ferry to Vermont. The ferry ran hourly across Lake Champlain, and it was a nice way to get across the huge body of water that was named a Great Lake in 1998. That distinction didn't last long, however. Eighteen days after the designation, it was rescinded after the protests of residents.

While I was on the eighty-five-minute ride, I met three women from Montreal who spent the day down in the States. They were very nice and invited me to Canada, promising me they would be my tour guides if I went north. I had vowed before I left on the trip to stay in this country. They were enthusiastic about showing me their hometown and did make a tempting offer. They talked about the cathedrals and other attractions. I told them that I would visit one day.

I said goodbye to the ladies as the ferry docked in Burlington, Vermont. Libertad seemed anxious to get onto dry land, apparently not a fan of the water. She kicked over right away and was itching to get off the boat. I revved her a couple of times, then got onto the loading ramp and onto King Street. It took about two miles to find a motel, and that further irritated Libertad. I believe she was under the impression that we had more riding to do after we disembarked from the ferry. When I eased off the throttle to pull into the motel parking lot, there was a stutter from the Harley, almost like a cry of protest. I said out loud, "Don't worry, we'll ride again tomorrow." I'm not sure if that satisfied her, but it was the best I could offer.

No hands, taken by Ken Steinhardt

Crazy George Reiter

Ernest Lee

Harley packed outside Sunset Beach apartment

Charlotte King

Thomas Currier

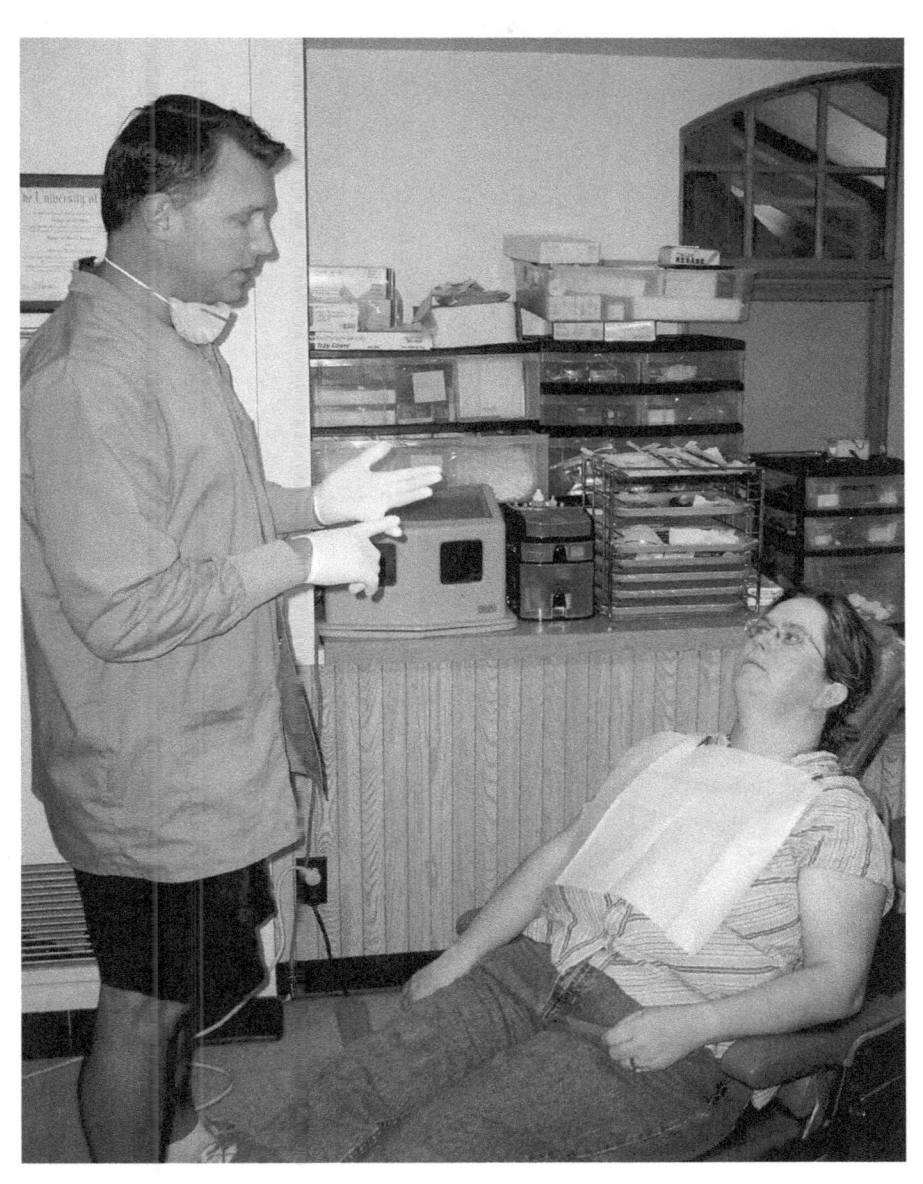

Dr. Thomas Roemer dentist

Me with Morgan Freeman

Brett Wightman

Puddin' Hatchett

Castle Otttis

Castle Otttis

John Evans

Michael Conyers

Minter village

Joe Minter

CHAPTER 20

This was a good day for highways. There were rain clouds, but they were a safe distance away, at least for the moment, and the cover they provided made the temperature enjoyable. These were optimum riding conditions, so I took advantage of them. The two-lane road of Highway 2 paralleled Interstate 89 but was lower than the main path chosen by many and offered better access to the scenery of the small towns like Jonesville and Waterbury.

This country tended to rebuild and renovate. The emphasis was on new, not tradition. Go to London, and one could eat at the same restaurant Charles Dickens lunched at. Here, if there was a dining establishment of character, local developers claimed eminent domain, razed it, and put up a strip mall with a Starbucks and an Olive Garden.

When I saw the signs for some of the towns that said they were chartered in 1763 or 1765, it made me smile. It felt like I was driving through a little piece of history—towns that existed before we were a country, founded most likely by people who came over on the Mayflower.

The apex of this experience came at Montpelier, the state capital of Vermont. I was rolling slowly through the main street of the town when, on my left, was the state building. The architecture was magnificent. I immediately stopped to take a picture and read the sign for the building.

It was the third time city officials had rebuilt the structure. The first was too small. The second, which was similar to this one, was destroyed by fire in 1857. This state house was erected in 1859. There were no signs of wear, which truly amazed me. I thought there would be some fading, chipping, cracking, any piece of evidence to show the building's age, but there was none.

From Montpelier, Route 302 stretched out toward the New Hampshire border and crossed underneath another freeway, Interstate 91. After passing that thoroughfare, I reached the border and got on a bridge that carried me over the Connecticut River. From there, I was able to wend my way toward the White Mountains.

Nestled in the White Mountains was Squam Lake, a beautiful body of water and where the majority of the filming for the movie *On Golden Pond* took place. Little Squam Lake was also in the movie.

It was at this lake that I met my first New Englander on this trip. His name was Michael, and he and his young son were up from Boston enjoying the private beach.

I was trespassing, as I was inclined to do, but he didn't seem to mind. Michael wore what seemed to be the requisite headgear for any male in the New England area—a worn, blue Boston Red Sox ball cap covered most of his late-thirties skull, but thinning, shaggy black locks of hair poked out from the sides of the hat. Though it was summer, Michael still had on a red and blue light flannel shirt, unbuttoned over a gray V-neck shirt. He did yield to the warmth by wearing khaki shorts and completed the outfit with topsiders and no socks.

Michael's eight-year-old son, Brendan, was busy exploring the lake's shoreline, picking up flat rocks and trying to skip them. He wasn't having much success. It was a bounce, maybe two across the water, then the stone would sink. Now and then, a rock would make three or four skips, and he shrieked with excitement at his accomplishment, then turn around to see if his dad had witnessed his feat. Before he could ask, Michael would say, "Nice throw, son."

In between tosses, Michael and I discussed everything from the Red Sox to the lake to the best route to Boston, but I wanted to go to Maine first.

"Oh, in that case, take Route 113 to 25," he said. "That will get you to Portland. Then take Route 1 and right about Saco, get on 9. That'll take you down the coast. You can get back on 1, and that'll go all the way into Boston. Lot better than the highway. You'll see more."

I knew I liked him for a reason. I thanked him for the help and continued down the road, following Michael's directions.

Getting across New Hampshire took no time at all, and I was in Maine before I realized it.

The road to Portland was short as well. I had nearly entered the southernmost part of the state and had about forty miles to Maine's largest city. I got there midafternoon, found a little diner, and enjoyed a lobster roll. As I ate one of the best sandwiches I had ever consumed, I wondered if I could get a dozen of them shipped home. I'm sure it was possible and costly, but in this case, it would have been money I was willing to part with to replicate one of the best lunches I had ever experienced.

From Portland, I took Michael's advice and headed south on Route 1 as soon as I got out of the city limits. I saw the sign for Saco, found Route 9, and took it east. I was surprised that I didn't see more of the Atlantic Ocean, but it didn't matter much. I was on my favorite type of asphalt—the two-lane road. There, among the trees of New England and rolling farmland, I was instantly at peace. It was a warmth that enveloped me and the exact reason I rode a motorcycle. There were just enough twists, and the scenery seemed to change colors, even though it was August and not October. I reached Kennebunkport, and I decided to take a detour to the Atlantic Ocean. I needed to put a foot in the body of water to add to my collection.

Some people measured travel by how many states or countries they've visited. I had friends who wanted to go to as many baseball fields as possible. I used water as my travel barometer. Rivers, lakes, oceans, gulfs, seas, I had put my feet in so many, but the Atlantic Ocean was a glaring absence from my resume. I parked the Harley, took off my boots, and stood in the chilly, shallow water of the world's second-largest ocean. I could now add it to my list of Pacific Ocean; Irish, North, Bering, and Caribbean seas; all five Great Lakes; Sea of Japan; Yellow Sea; and the Gulf of Mexico.

Or at least I thought it was going to make my list. When an old man was watching what I was doing, I thought I owed him an explanation. I told him about wanting to dip a toe or two into the Atlantic, and he said I hadn't accomplished that. Instead, my foot was in the Fore River. He said it separated Portland from South Portland, and farther east was the Atlantic. It dampened my celebration, somewhat, but I figured that I would be up and down the Atlantic Seaboard for the next three weeks and could correct the slight at some point.

Despite identifying the Atlantic Ocean incorrectly, this was still easily becoming one of the best days of riding. I got back on the state route and headed toward the New Hampshire-Maine border. From there, it wasn't long, though, before I reached Massachusetts. I marveled at Michael's directions and his advice. It was like we were kindred spirits, and his love of side roads equaled mine. I often wondered if people were put in my life for a reason, kind of like living angels, guiding me in some way or another. I believed guys like Michael were there to point me in the direction of beauty I could never find on my own.

My friend Heather was put in my life to teach me lessons I didn't know I needed. It was amazing how many times she saved me from myself and did it in a graceful, nonjudgmental way. I had lost count of how many occasions she had grabbed me by the hand and told me what I was doing was wrong. I was certain I wouldn't be on this earth now if it wasn't for what Heather did for me so many years ago.

As I got on the Harley, I began to cough and figured the tall pines of Vermont and New Hampshire had flared up my allergies. I was about to be proven wrong. By the time I reached Boston a hundred miles later, I switched my allergy diagnosis to a summer cold. My head was clogged, the fever was taking hold, and all I wanted was a soft bed to fall into. I found a motel, and the guy at the desk was another friendly sort. This caught me off guard. I had been to Boston twelve years before and found the people as cold as their winters. Even my mom's longtime friend, who lived in a small town thirty miles outside of Boston, had an emotional distance about her. She was joyless and somewhat bitter, and everyone I came in contact with there seemed unfriendly. Striking up conversations with strangers proved futile. I couldn't wait to leave.

This trip, though, was the exact opposite. The guy at the motel wanted to know my life story, and I was the one who ended the conversation prematurely. I felt bad, but I could barely keep my eyes open. I apologized, took my key, and surrendered to my illness.

The next day, the head cold took its toll on me, and the last thing I wanted to do was get on a motorcycle and ride. To me, there was nothing worse than a summer cold. They made no sense. Colds were for winters, when it was dreary and bleak, not when it was warm. I knew it was a virus that caused this affliction, but still, it seemed more logical to have a cold in December—not August.

With a foggy head and a body full of cold medicine, I headed south out of Boston. I realized this was as far east as I could go. From this day forward, I would be heading either south or west toward home. It took a minute to let that reality sink in. It was a prospect I knew would eventually come, but I had sort of put it out of my mind. If I didn't think about it, maybe it wouldn't happen.

There was nothing particularly thrilling that was waiting for me at home, and the adventures I had experienced in the short twenty-four days I had been on the road were already filling up a lifetime of memories. I hadn't thought about how long I would be away. I just figured I would know when the time was right to go home. Maybe I was waiting for a sign, but what if it never came? Would I be a vagabond for the rest of my life? It didn't seem like such a bad existence. I could easily see myself roaming the country, taking menial jobs to make enough money until I could get back on the road to the next adventure.

Of course, the reality was I had to return home at some point. Heather needed me. My mom probably did in some way, though she would never admit it. Then there was the career. I still had a steady job waiting for me, and the security of a regular paycheck was comforting in some small way.

I understood why people embraced that security. There were far fewer worries in life. One just showed up at a job, did the work, got paid, and if they were lucky, took a two-week vacation somewhere.

But that holiday was the highlight of the year. The rest of the time was this drudgery of working somewhere they didn't want to be. I knew a guy who had a two-hour commute to and from work every day. He got up at four in the morning, left his house in the dark at five, and was at work by seven. He was at the job until four in the afternoon, battled rush-hour traffic for two hours, and returned home at six. After a quick dinner and two hours of watching television and playing with his two children, he was in bed by nine. The weekends were spent going to youth soccer, baseball, or the occasional birthday party. If he was lucky and didn't get laid off or replaced by someone younger and cheaper when he turned forty years old, he might save enough to retire when he was sixty-five. But by then, the stress of this lifestyle would probably have affected his health to the point where he couldn't enjoy his life, but just wait out his golden years until he collapsed from a stroke or a heart attack.

It just didn't seem like much of a life to me. I liked the unknown. I relished being able to see places that people only dreamed of, and, if I had to sacrifice a career for it, I was all right with that. Of course, this could have been the cold medicine clouding my judgment, so I changed the subject in my mind and motored onward.

Traffic on the highway was light, and I moved south rather easily, coughing and sneezing most of the way. The summer air made me feel a little better, and I decided I was going to live from what seemed like my terminal illness the night before.

There was one stop I wanted to make, though, and when I crossed the border from Massachusetts into Connecticut, I saw the exit. Mystic, Connecticut, was a little seaport along the Atlantic Ocean, and when I was there twelve years ago, it was small and mostly filled with locals. Mystic had grown since then. The main street was packed with tourists walking up and down the block, looking in stores that were filled with souvenirs and crafts and other mementos of the town that were available to take home and put on a bookcase as a remembrance of their time there.

When I stopped for gas, I asked an attendant where the town's biggest attraction was. A man in his early twenties looked at me funny and said, "You don't want to go there. The food is terrible. They are just living off their reputation."

Mystic Pizza had been in the town since 1973, run by a couple named the Zelepos. It was a small, one-story family restaurant, and there was something magical, and, indeed, mystic about the pizza. It was in the sauce, and the family secret drew people from all around New England.

One person it attracted was screenwriter Amy Jones who wrote a movie about three young women working in the pizza parlor. One of the actresses in the movie was Julia Roberts, and when the movie premiered in 1988, it made her a star. It also gave the restaurant instant notoriety, though the Zelepos kept it the same.

On my initial visit in 1992, the wife cooked my pizza, and I couldn't believe how good it was. The slogan was *A Slice of Heaven*, and I couldn't disagree. When I went in the place this time, I looked forward to the same experience. I needed a little culinary comfort to get rid of this cold. The building was now twice the size it had been, and with the husband dying and the mom having since moved to Greece, the three sons had taken it over. They had focused on merchandising, and some people came in just for apparel.

Robert, the manager, was a personable guy who took a break from work to talk to me. We chatted for several minutes about the area, and he couldn't have made me feel more welcome. But the pizza had lost something. The magic was gone. There were nonfamily members in the kitchen pumping out pizza after pizza and, while it was still good, it wasn't magical. The sauce wasn't the same as I remembered it, and there seemed to be more spices in the pizza the first time I was there. I ate my two slices and paid the bill with a young waitress who could have easily been the inspiration for the movie. I walked out the door, passing a couple in their forties walking in. I thought they were out on a date, but they were looking for a poster of the movie to buy. Apparently, they had eaten down the street.

CHAPTER 21

The first time I ever saw New York City, I was twenty-eight and driving an old Honda Accord across the country. It had been packed with most of what was precious to me. The one missing item was Michelle. We had met three months before after I had already committed to take my first odyssey across the United States. By the time I reached her hometown, I was broke, homesick, and driving a car with a bad battery. I was about 200 miles into what was going to be a 1,100-mile, twenty-six-hour drive from Boston down to St. Simons Island, Georgia, where work as a food server awaited. There wasn't much time for sightseeing. I had to get enough money so I could drive the rest of the way back to Southern California.

Somehow, I had become woefully lost, and rather than stop and ask for directions or look at a map, I had placed myself in New Jersey. To get this off course was an extreme case of stupefying navigation. I still, to this day, have no idea how I managed it. I can only surmise that I crossed the Hudson River near Tarrytown, New York, and into South Nyack, New Jersey. In my feeble defense, I will say that it was about five in the morning, and I was running on copious amounts of caffeine, which clouded what little judgment I had. I headed toward Newark before I righted the ship and went east instead of south. I saw a sign on I-78 that said *New York City*, and knew my little detour was over. Just then, the Manhattan skyline came into view, and I was mesmerized. I got off at the last exit before the Holland

Tunnel, found a vacant lot, and had to keep the engine running, or I wouldn't have been able to start the car back up. I leaned on the hood and stared at the Twin Towers for at least an hour. It was the most awing cityscape I had ever witnessed. It was then I realized New York City was a place of infinite possibilities.

When I reached the George Washington Bridge thirteen years later, that same sense of euphoria returned. The towers were gone, but the city held the same allure. While others despised Manhattan, it held a dreamlike quality for me. My motel was in Queens, but this time, my diversion was intended. I took my fully packed Harley into the city and spent the next two hours roaring up and down city avenues, the sound from the pipes bouncing off tall buildings, setting off car alarms, much to my delight.

There would be about twenty-four hours before my girlfriend arrived. We hadn't talked as regularly as she would have liked, and this visit was her idea, not mine. If I'd had my way, she would have stayed home. I, however, wasn't getting a vote. At four o'clock in the afternoon, she was landing at John F. Kennedy International Airport, and I was going to take the subway to meet her. It was going to be a long weekend, probably longer for me than for her.

Libertad and I were at the Super 8 in Queens, a few miles from the airport. She wanted to stay in Manhattan, so I left my motorcycle at this motel the morning of her arrival, then went into the city to make sure the place we were staying was ready. I had a few hours to kill before I had to hop on the subway and go out to the airport to meet her. The two nights she was going to be here were not only going to be tedious but expensive.

In my mind, this would be my going-away present. We didn't have a future. I knew it, and I think deep down, so did she. Priya was twenty-five years old, fifteen years younger than me. We met on the internet. She liked motorcycles. I liked the idea of going out with someone who was in her twenties. The thrill faded almost instantly. I don't know why; it just did. It wasn't her fault. The age difference didn't matter. I had grown tired of women of all ages.

It was one of the reasons I was out here. Women came and went in my life, and I couldn't figure out why I didn't want to keep one. The pattern was all too familiar. I would go on the hunt, meet one, fall hard for her, then get bored and devise my escape soon after. Sometimes, they told me they loved me. Often, I lied and told them the same. It was an awful way to live, and unfair to them, and I knew it.

The romance was great in the beginning. I was excellent at courting. It was the chase I loved. Once I captured them, I looked for a way to release them.

Ever since Michelle, I had been like that. With her, it was different. We had a passion that I had never experienced before or since. Her, I loved. Her, I wanted to have children with. Her, I wanted to grow old with. But when I was young and didn't know how to love someone, it terrified me. It did her, as well. She took our breakup harder than I did at first. She was able to recover from the pain, while mine was just beginning.

Being back in New York, where Michelle had grown up and shown me so much of, the memories came rushing back as I floated around the city on the subway and buses. My transportation for the day would go by a place we had explored some fifteen years prior. I had gone there to meet her mom and visit her old neighborhood. It gave me a sense of comfort, and I was certain we'd be together forever.

Recounting that time made me smile. I was on the M11 bus going north up Tenth Avenue and soon wondered why it all went south with us. As I passed street after street on my way to Harlem, I couldn't come up with a reasonable answer. I thought about what life would have been like with her now. It made me happy, but ultimately sad that it didn't occur. I had thrown away this incredible opportunity, and I had no one to blame but myself.

One of the many gifts Michelle gave me was her knowledge of New York City. She showed me places I would have never found. She also advised me on how to deal with the citizens I came across. New

Yorkers were completely misunderstood. They had a reputation for being rude, but they were some of the warmest, most genuine people I had ever met once I got to know them. It was a city of eight million concierges. They were fiercely proud of where they lived. They wanted you to love their town as much as they did. It worked with me. I have spent time in cities all over the world—London, Marrakesh, Seoul, Toronto, Bangkok, and Dublin—and never felt the same way as I did about New York City.

It should be my test for any relationship. My ex-wife failed it. We spent a week in New York City, and all she could think about was how much it cost us. I showed her Greenwich Village, and she was worried about the twelve dollars she spent for a sandwich at Katz's Deli two hours earlier. Money was money, I told her. If we run out, I'll make more. She never quite felt comfortable with those words.

I looked at my watch and saw I had about two hours until I had to pick up Priya. I felt like I was on borrowed time. I tried to get my mind right or at least in a spot where I could make the best of this.

I took the subway and then the AirTrain to JFK. She was excited to see me, and I was more enthusiastic than I thought I would be. We stopped at my motel first to take a nap and then grabbed our bags and headed into the city. Before we left, I went to check the motorcycle in the Super 8 parking structure. It was locked up tight, but that meant nothing if someone wanted to steal it. I would worry about Libertad the entire weekend. I gave it a fifty-fifty chance she would be there when I returned.

Priya and I settled into the elegant midtown Manhattan hotel. My birthday was the following day, and we were going out for a nice meal. Little Italy was home to one of my favorite restaurants in the world called Taormina's on Mulberry Street. It was supposedly where famous mobster John Gotti used to get most of his meals when he was the Dapper Don. We started with a little prosciutto and melon, some linguini and clams, then lasagna. A bottle of wine would erase any lingering anxiety about the visit. After dinner, we went to a little café and had espresso and finger desserts. It was a great first night.

We hadn't been back in the hotel ten minutes when my cell phone rang. I didn't recognize the number, but the area code was from home, so I answered it. Ron, the president of the Assholes, the motorcycle group I belonged to, was on the other end. "John, Crazy was in an accident," he said. "It was bad. He's in a coma. He's not going to make it." I sat on the bed while Ron told me the details about my friend George Reiter, the man who introduced me to the club. George had been on his way to the hospital near his house to visit a friend. He was on his motorcycle. He got off the freeway and was waiting at a red light. When it turned green, he entered the intersection and was hit by a twenty-something guy in a work truck. Apparently, the kid was looking for his cell phone on the floor of his truck and blew through the light. George never saw it coming. At the request of his wife, Marti, he was in the hospital being kept alive by a life-support machine so the members of the club could come and say goodbye. I was the only one who didn't go to see him. Four days later, Marti had doctors pull the plug, and he was gone.

When I hung up with Ron, I sat motionless on the bed. Priya asked me what was wrong, but I couldn't talk. I don't know how long I was dazed, but it felt like forever. She kept asking, her voice rising with concern. I was finally able to spit out that George had been in an accident and was going to die. She had met him once and started to cry. I had known him for five years and could not produce a single tear.

CHAPTER 22

A day after the news about Crazy George, Priya was on her scheduled plane ride home, and I was alone back at the Super 8 in Queens. She had offered to stay longer, but I knew she had to return to her responsibilities. As I lay on the bed in the dingy motel room, I tried, but just I couldn't process what had happened. My one concern when I left on this trip was how Heather and my mother would be with me 3,000 miles from home. When they both reassured me that they would be fine, I relaxed. I had let my guard down, thinking that if they were fine, then everyone else in my life would be as well. With George's death, I had received the cruelest of sucker punches.

This wasn't supposed to happen. The guilt I felt not getting to South Dakota to see Crazy was overwhelming. It felt like I couldn't breathe, and being in a small hotel room in the basement of a cheap motel wasn't helping. The walls were closing in, and I did what came naturally—I fled.

Another bus ride through Manhattan was my choice of travel. When I reached the end of the line, I got on a different bus and headed in the opposite direction, staring out the window and gazing at businesses that were mostly closed because it was Sunday. People were sparse on the streets. They were all blurs anyway. I spent my time chastising myself for not seeing George one last time. Then I thought about all the adventures we had shared and ones that would never happen again. No more early evening chats in his driveway. No more motorcycle rides to Sturgis or Beatty or Yuma—or anywhere else.

Still, though, there were no tears. It wasn't for lack of trying. They just wouldn't come. Not by recollections or by force or internal pleading. That, more than anything, made me feel guilty. What kind of friend was I? I couldn't even show emotion for my friend over this tragedy. Jesus Christ, did I even have a soul? What kind of callous bastard was I? I loved this man like a father, and yet I couldn't find the empathy to cry for him. It haunted me even when I got back to the room. I lay awake for most of the night wondering why I couldn't grieve properly. Finally, the exhaustion of this conundrum surrendered to a few uneasy hours of sleep.

When I awoke, I didn't know where, or if, I wanted to go. With the memory of Crazy George dominating my thoughts, the last activity I wanted to partake in was the one that got him killed. While I mourned for my friend, I also had this natural thought, *Was I next?* Especially when I was riding 300 to 500 miles a day.

Trepidation was a biker's worst enemy, a cancer that spread rapidly if not quashed immediately. Problem was that my mind fought me and wouldn't let it go. These were the last thoughts I should be having, but they were the only ones, and I couldn't get rid of them. Some guys surrendered, gave up riding, and sold their iron horses. They lost their nerve and knew they would never get it back.

I was close. I must have been in bed for two hours staring at the ceiling with all types of wild thoughts running around my head. The first was the accident that took George's life. I put together what little information I had and visualized this horrific collision. I knew the freeway off-ramp where it happened. I had been on it a hundred times. I pictured George waiting for the signal to turn green, then thinking nothing of going through the intersection. I saw the truck running the red light and smashing into him and his motorcycle. George never saw it coming, but I kept replaying it over and over.

As I pushed away that thought, I toggled over to my accidents. I should be dead. I wasn't wearing a helmet for any of them. When you're young, you think you'll live forever. Now I wondered if I would make it to the next day.

The last scenario in my maudlin imagination was possible future accidents. This was an extremely destructive parlor game to play. In addition to my favorite and frequent thoughts of a head-on collision with a passing car on a lonely two-lane highway, or colliding with a deer, there were new editions I came up with to add to the repertoire. I could see myself being rear-ended by a semi-truck or getting knocked off the motorcycle by a bird hitting me or running over a large piece of debris on the interstate, like a tire or a rock. These catastrophes played in my mind like a loop. I had to get out of my head, or I was going to be stuck in Queens for the rest of my life.

It would be nice to say that I bravely decided to soldier on with the trip, that I reached deep down in my soul and collected the courage to push aside all my fears. The truth was that I had no choice. It wasn't like I could pull the Harley into the garage and call it a day. I had more than 3,000 miles left to get home, so I decided I might as well make the best of it. I packed up and left Queens before I could figure out some way to sell Libertad and take a Greyhound bus home.

CHAPTER

23

There were easy miles of riding, and there were hard miles. Today was going to be nothing but difficult ones. I began going through the Lincoln Tunnel back to Manhattan from Queens to delay traveling south as long as I could. I wasn't ready to ride, and I knew it. I stopped by Ray's Pizza on Sixth Avenue and Eleventh Street for a couple of therapeutic slices of pepperoni. As I ate them, I watched the world go by, procrastinating as long as possible.

Finally, I could wait no longer. I had chosen Atlantic City as my destination for the day. It was a short ride, only 125 miles from the city, so it wouldn't be too laborious. Plus, the bright lights of the casinos would distract me, keeping my mind off what I shouldn't be thinking about. When I reached the Holland Tunnel, it was one in the afternoon, and, taking my time on Route 9, I estimated my arrival at sunset.

As beautiful as New York City was, Jersey City, New Jersey, was equally as ugly. The smell hit me as I exited the tunnel on Route 139 heading to Route 9. It was what I imagined death smelled like. A rotting, vile, chemical-induced odor puked out of one of the industrial plants that I couldn't see. That odor took up residency in both my nostrils and wasn't leaving. The stink was like nothing I had ever experienced. I saw that there were businesses on both sides of the road that would indicate nearby houses. I saw a sign for a hospital, and there was a deli, as well as a gas station. I noticed a couple of auto-wrecking yards and thought it was something there. I couldn't put my finger on it, but I'll never forget that pungent, vile stench.

It made me wonder how people could live with this. I hoped it was a temporary situation, maybe a factory with some excess pollution belching out of its stacks. Just about the time I had accepted that I would never lose that smell from my memory, my eyes started to water. No matter how much I blinked, the tears wouldn't stop, and I could hardly see. That, coupled with the assault on my nose, made this ride much harder than it needed to be. I didn't want to stop because of the adversity and figured I would push through, hoping it would get better.

The dirt was next. It was on me instantly. Trucks kicked up pieces of gravel that pelted my face. When a semi-truck passed me on the other side, the usual blast of hot air was accompanied by a flying sheen of silt that got into my nose and the corners of my mouth. Even though I kept my mouth tightly shut, a speck would get in, and then I was spitting dirt as I rode down the highway. I looked into one of my mirrors and saw the accumulation of soil caked on my face.

The roads earned the dubious honor of being the worst I had ever encountered. Potholes, bumps, and grooves were all hazards I had to avoid. The lane shifted a couple of times, and if I hadn't been paying attention, it would have sent me into oncoming traffic. I couldn't escape the road conditions, but the smell finally left as I got on Highway 9 and headed south. Passing Newark Liberty International Airport, I welcomed the smell of jet fuel, compared to the battering my nostrils had endured the previous eighteen miles. From Jersey City to Toms River, it was seventy miles that felt like seven hundred.

Once I got to Toms River, however, the roads improved. They were smoother and less grimy, although the two-lane Route 9 was congested like it was rush hour. It was 2:30 p.m. on a weekday, so all these cars didn't make sense. There wasn't any construction or accidents. It bothered me to do so, but I reluctantly got on the Garden State Parkway and prepared to pay the tolls.

The highway was tree-lined for most of the fifty-four miles until the off-ramp for Atlantic City. It was a nondescript piece of thoroughfare, one of those stretches forgotten as soon as it was passed. I noticed myself trying to find anything memorable in the tall pine trees, but I came up empty.

Then I saw the deer. I had been warned by the signs a few miles back but found it hard to believe they would have so little taste as to pick this real estate as a place to call home. There they were, though, lying in the grass between the asphalt and the forest. They didn't seem to mind all the cars whizzing by. I was extremely irked by their presence. All I could think of was which one was going to run and jump in front of me. It caused me to slow down, much to the annoyance of the man in the car now honking behind me.

There was a curiosity for me regarding Atlantic City. Being on the West Coast my whole life, I had been to Las Vegas plenty of times but had never had the chance to go to the East Coast's answer to Sin City. My New York and Boston friends described Atlantic City as a seedy, slimy, depressing place, where degenerative gamblers went to slide even further into their addiction.

There were parts of Las Vegas where that depiction was accurate. Downtown Las Vegas thirty years ago was a place only the brave or naïve stumbled into. I went once, and I counted more drug addicts and hookers than gamblers. One didn't venture east of Las Vegas Boulevard on Fremont Street. It was sort of a demilitarized zone, and the mentally ill, as well as various sociopaths, regrouped before they made their way back to where the big-name casinos, such as the Golden Nugget and Binion's, were on the safer side of Fremont.

I didn't mind the seediness of downtown. It had a certain charm to it, much like Times Square in New York City, before they ran out all the peep shows and replaced them with family-friendly stores. Downtown Las Vegas got the same treatment years ago, and now the place had a covered roof and stages that blasted live music to the tourists who flocked there by the hundreds.

Atlantic City didn't seem to be much different than the Las Vegas Strip. It reminded me of a waterfront Las Vegas. It was not completely sanitized, but not grimy, either. I walked around and felt safe. Sure, there were some hookers who welcomed me to town, but they weren't overly pushy. Seemed business was just fine, and even though I didn't want to utilize their services, there were apparently plenty who did, so they just moved on to the next guy walking down the boardwalk.

The seven hotels were tall and glitzy, just like Vegas, and inside, they had all the amenities gamblers enjoyed. There were expensive shops and restaurants that provided a momentary obstacle before reaching the casino floor. The casino I went to seemed friendlier than the ones I had been to in Southern Nevada. The dealers talked to you, the people were happy, and the inside was bright but not blinding.

A relatively inexpensive way for me to gamble was playing poker. It's also a good distraction. I have sat at poker tables for hours in the past, and the most I have ever won or lost was a hundred bucks. I knew just enough about the game to think I knew something about the game.

Fortunately, the chump that night was not me. It was a college student named Dave. A nice enough guy, but clearly, he had come to Atlantic City to feed his addiction to gambling and alcohol, two items that definitely shouldn't be mixed. As we chatted, I found out that Dave lived in Long Island City, just outside of Manhattan in Queens, and had driven there earlier in the afternoon. He had been playing cards since five o'clock and was going to play until one in the morning. Then he was driving to Delaware to buy cheap cigarettes, then get a couple of hours of sleep before going to his job at a pet store. The cards were not kind to Dave, as they often aren't when booze made the decisions. He was down a couple hundred dollars and well on his way to blowing his whole paycheck.

Dave was probably the only one at the table who didn't know he raised his whole cards twice to look at them when he had a good hand, and if I picked up on it, I'm sure I wasn't the only one who noticed his tell. Part of me wanted to clue him in, but I figured that would upset the others I was playing with, so I just let him keep making the mistake.

When 1 a.m. hit, Dave was light $500, and the trip to Delaware was canceled since he had no money left to buy discounted cigarettes. He got up dejectedly, said a faint goodbye to me, and disappeared through the maze of gamblers on the casino floor. I played for a few more hours on the money I won from Dave and then called it a night.

CHAPTER 24

Hurricane Katrina was barreling north, and the weatherman was predicting that some of the remnants would spill over to the east. One of the biggest natural disasters in United States history had devastated New Orleans and parts of Mississippi but was now shooting blanks once it got past Tennessee. It was just spitting rain and had all the makings of a regular rainstorm. Still, I wanted to avoid it. Fortunately, I was spared the severity of the downpour.

My disdain for backtracking led me to an alternate route that would take me along the water and over some superb scenery. It was either that or get on the cold, scenery-deprived Garden State Parkway. I made the right choice.

I traveled south down Atlantic Avenue with the water on my left for about six miles until I crossed the JFK Memorial Bridge to avoid hitting a dead-end. Having the water surrounding me was of great comfort. This was a road with no pretense. It was just there for me, and I felt at ease as I made my way toward another bridge. The Ocean Drive Bridge was longer and higher than my previous overpass. From up high, I could see the Atlantic Ocean pushing into the Great Egg Harbor Bay. Fishing boats and a few sailboats dotted both sides of the water. I took it all in and was instantly at peace. I knew I was relaxed because the toll booth at the end of the bridge didn't even bother me.

Ocean City, New Jersey, was a typical touristy beach town. There were pizza shops and gift stores, as well as ice cream stands and bicycle rental places. The summer was winding down by late August, though there were still enough tourists milling around to keep the local economy flush for another month or so. I traveled from one end of this isthmus to the other, the ocean riding shotgun with me. I had to head inland for a stretch to get to the Cape May Ferry. As stunning as my ride had been so far, I needed a break, and I figured I would let a boat take me nineteen miles to Lewes, Delaware.

On the ferry, I had ninety minutes to reflect on what was coming next. I had heard last week that a memorial service had been planned for Crazy George, but the date was up in the air. I had asked one of the guys to tell me when it would be, and I would fly out to attend. I'm sure they would have understood if I didn't come, but there was no way I was missing this. I received a call that morning to tell me the date.

The ferry ride allowed me to hammer out logistics. I was angling toward Washington, DC, but needed to kill eight days before I flew back to California. I decided to depart from the nation's capital. I would drop my big bag at a friend's house, ride the Harley to the airport with a small duffel bag, and fly home. It was concerning abandoning the motorcycle at the airport. I had rolled the dice leaving her at the run-down Super 8 motel in Queens for a couple of days, so I felt fairly confident that Libertad would be safe in an underground parking garage.

I called my mom, who owned a travel agency, and booked a flight. At first, she didn't even know why I was coming home and didn't bother to ask. I finally had to tell her about my friend being killed on his motorcycle. There were no condolences and no empathy. She just gave me the flight information and said she had to get back to work.

When the ferry docked, I started up my machine and headed toward Highway 404. It was 117 miles from where I was in Delaware to Washington, and I needed two things. The first was a stiff drink. The second was to see my friend Chris, who lived near my destination. I sped west and made better time than I should have. I checked into a motel in nearby Manassas, Virginia, and called Chris. I soon met both of my objectives.

Chris was one of the funniest, smartest people I had ever met. We both shared a love of the writer Charles Bukowski, and we both dabbled at one point with Bukowski's lifestyle of hard drinking and even harder women. We met at the newspaper in Orange County, California. We were working for an intolerable sports editor, who was the poster child for the Peter Principle. The contempt we had for this stuffed shirt was hard to contain, and, as a result, we both knew we were never going to advance to staff writer as long as he was there.

We made the best of it. We did our menial tasks, covering high school sports and working desk shifts. A lot of nights were spent taking phone calls from outraged parents whose kids didn't get the coverage they thought they deserved. They were amusing as they screamed into the phone, telling us their Christ-child was the reason the team won the game. We had to be polite, but it was a challenge. Most of the conversations ended with the parent yelling, "I'm canceling my subscription!" or "I'll never buy your rag again!" Chris had the best retort. He would calmly say, "You'll be missed," and hang up the phone on them. In between phone calls, we would talk politics and philosophy, and Chris had a perspective that I respected and admired.

After work, we would get together and drink at a bar or play poker with other coworkers. Chris was much better at drinking than at cards, and as he got more and more inebriated, the fantasies he had about defiling a certain coworker became more colorful. It was talk that would get someone fired in today's politically correct climate. We just wrote it off as punch-drunk love, and that would be as far as it would go.

Chris left the newspaper before me. He had a calling to be a Catholic priest and was studying at a monastery in Central California. I went up and visited him and stayed in the rectory. The only trade-off was that I had to go to confession, then early morning mass. The priest demanded a cigar before my confession, which I was all too willing to part with as a condition of the deal to cleanse my soul. The next morning, I was up at six, sitting in a church pew like a good Catholic. As Chris and I returned to our seats after receiving the holy wafer and swig of sacramental wine, he looked at me and said, "Geez, John, we're drinking before noon again." That was why I liked him so much.

That was one of many stories we retold at the bar while we sipped vodka. Chris had long left the priesthood, wanting to teach, finding a more direct way to save souls. He was working for an old boss we had in Southern California, who had gotten an editor's job at the *Washington Post*. It was one of the few editors we both respected and admired. We sat for hours catching each other up on our lives and fondly recalling the past.

Though I didn't see him that often anymore, we had a lifetime of memories crammed into a few years. Chris was one of those friends that you talked to sparingly, but when you did, it was like you saw each other all the time. I'm sure I tired him with stories about Crazy George and all the mischief we got into in the five short years I knew him. I told him that I wished they had met. Even though the two were from vastly different worlds, they would have gotten along great.

Much like we had done in Southern California, we closed the bar. The bartender got tired of us, but we managed to get one more drink from him. That bought us forty-five minutes of holding off our demons. Finally, at two-thirty, the bartender threw us out. It wasn't the first time we got tossed from a bar. Spending time with a good friend talking and drinking was something I never seemed to experience enough in my life. It also ended way too soon.

CHAPTER 25

The memorial for Crazy George was set for Friday, September 9. I had a week before my flight. Chris was going to let me leave my stuff at his house. Then I would ride up to Dulles International Airport to catch an early-morning flight to Los Angeles. I had someone subletting my place in California, so I was going to stay at a motel while I was home. I would go to the memorial service the next day, then fly back to DC on Saturday and resume the trip.

Organizing that excursion had been simple. It was like a business trip, really, and I had been on many of those. The hard part was how I was going to kill the next eight days. I was truly a man without a home, and that hit me for the first time in the past month. It took me a minute to settle my anxiety. The best way to combat the feeling was just to have no itinerary and see what happened. Funny, but that uncertainty became strangely comforting.

I took a break from riding during my first full day in Washington and spent the day playing tourist. I took the subway into town from the little motel where I was staying in Manassas, Virginia. It was late morning and rush hour had passed. The subway car had a smattering of people but nothing like the mobs of commuters on it a couple of hours before. Like most public transportation in metro areas, no one wanted to talk. I was the only person in casual clothes. The men were in suits and the women in skirts with blouses and jackets. Even the people sitting together didn't converse. It was quite strange.

My stop was the last one on the Manassas route of the Virginia Railway Express, and when I emerged at Union Station from being underground, I was disoriented. I saw Columbus Circle and headed there. It was a pleasant stroll; the weather wasn't too hot or humid, despite being late summer and a couple of days shy of Labor Day weekend. The tree-lined streets provided shade as I made my way down Delaware Avenue. That was when the dome of the Capitol came into view. I headed toward it.

While the weather was tolerable, the crowds were not. Attractions were inundated as it was the last gasp of summer before families returned to the routine of school. The tourists were inescapable. I looked around the Capitol building and the nearby Library of Congress, but I couldn't enjoy them with all the people.

I reversed course, heading on Maryland Avenue toward the National Mall. The open space was still crowded, but that expanse of green parkland easily accommodated the masses. I made my way toward the Washington Monument, stopping to see the outside of many Smithsonian museums along the way. The first was the National Museum of the American Indian, then the National Air and Space Museum. I had to admire them from afar since the lines to get in prevented any other interaction. That was okay with me. I was perfectly content wandering outside.

My ultimate goal was to get to the Lincoln Memorial. Before that commemorative structure was the Washington Monument. I wanted to go inside, but again, I wasn't standing in line for two hours, so I kept walking. The Lincoln Memorial Reflecting Pool more than made up for my disappointment about the Washington Monument. It was stunning, and the reflection of the Washington Monument in the water was a sight that I lingered over. I sat on the edge of the water, fixating on that image.

Water called to me. It always has. I can spend hours gazing at pools, lakes, rivers, and oceans. It was ironic, in a way, since I have a healthy fear of drowning, even though I am a pretty good swimmer. I grew up around swimming pools and spent a lot of time at different Southern California beaches during the summer. The movie *Jaws* ruined the ocean for me forever. It's a rational fear for a teenager to have, but the panic of getting eaten by a great white shark has stayed with me to this day.

I reached the Lincoln Memorial at about noon. It was an interesting piece of architecture, and I marveled at its massiveness. I stood at the base of the steps and just stared at the large white columns of the Greek Temple-style building. It was impressive, and it caused me to stand and gawk for quite a while. I thought about Martin Luther King's "I Have a Dream" speech. He delivered it with the Lincoln Memorial as a backdrop on August 28, 1963, 363 days before I was born.

This field trip was proving to be exactly the distraction I needed, and I wasn't even halfway done. I was now going to walk to the back of the Lincoln Memorial, peek at the Potomac River, then head back to the subway station, utilizing the northeast side of the National Mall.

The Vietnam War Memorial was on that side, and it was something I was looking forward to seeing. It was the only war that I could identify with, even though I was a toddler when it was being fought. A lot of friends I knew had relatives who were there, and some of them openly carried the scars of what they had experienced. A couple of guys in the motorcycle club had served in that war, but they never talked about their time in Southeast Asia, and I never pressed them for details.

The memorial is a stunning yet understated structure. Simple in its design, the black granite had been imported from India. It was hard to fathom the more than 58,000 names that were on it. When I was there, a man and his wife were looking intently at the wall. I overheard him say he wanted to find fellow members of his platoon. When he discovered one of them, he broke down and cried. I realized I wasn't at a tourist attraction; I was at a sacred place. I paid my respects and left out of deference to those who had come to mourn.

I swung by the Korean War Memorial as I walked back to the subway station. It was more traditional in its design. With a *V* shape to the area, the most striking feature was the nineteen stainless steel statues of soldiers, most carrying guns and walking in what was supposed to represent rice paddies. There was a black granite wall as well, but instead of names of the deceased, there were photographs from the three-year conflict. There were no tears at this memorial, just people taking pictures and talking. The sense of solemnness was not as intense. I don't know if it was because this war wasn't talked about as much or because it was built after the Vietnam Memorial, as if an afterthought.

From there, I made my way up to Constitution Avenue. I wanted to see the White House. I knew there was no way I was getting in there. People have to sign up for passes months in advance through your congressman's office. I wasn't even sure who my congressman was. The federal government was just another authority figure I didn't want to bow to. I never had been a big believer in blind loyalty to the government. In many ways, I didn't even consider myself a citizen of this country. I fancied myself more of a passport holder to the world. It's an unpopular opinion, and one I don't share with a lot of people. I let those who have an unquestionable love of country wrap themselves in the flag and feel secure, while the very institutions they put so much faith in work as hard as they can to govern against those patriots' self-interests. The children of those running the institutions got deferments; your offspring died in wars that they profited from. Your health insurance wasn't sufficient, but members of Congress had the best medical coverage in the country. Most citizens had trouble affording a home. Congressmen had second and third homes they rarely saw.

No, I'll pass on not questioning authority, having learned years ago that the game was rigged, and nothing other than a full-scale revolution by the populace was going to change it. The gap between the haves and have-nots widens every year. Referring to the rich and powerful, the great comedian George Carlin once said, "It's a big club, and you ain't in it." My goal was to hope the government left me alone. They never did, but it was the only dream I thought I had any chance of fulfilling. The only problem was my vision didn't align with theirs. I didn't want to be the obedient worker that agreed with every law Congress or the president wanted to pass that would somehow negatively affect my way of life. Still, I was fascinated with historic places and determined to see as many of them as possible.

I made a left on Seventeenth Street and then a right three blocks later onto Pennsylvania Avenue. It was much different than the first time I saw this area. That was in 1992, the first time I went across the country. I was on an all-night drive from Boston to Georgia, where I had a job as a restaurant server at a resort waiting for me as soon as I got there. I wanted to see Washington, DC, even if it was midnight, and I was going to stay in the car. When I reached the White House, anyone could drive right past the front of the building. I was so excited, I must have driven by it ten times, just circling the block. I parked in front of the Treasury Building and called my girlfriend, Michelle, telling her how I was staring at the east end of the White House.

Now, Pennsylvania Avenue was closed to cars and had been since 1995. Big cylindrical metal bollards block off both ends of the street. The president's home seemed so far away, but that didn't seem to bother tourists rubbernecking through the black iron fence that was behind metal barriers. Those that wanted an unobstructed picture had to stand on the barrier and quickly snap a shot before a security guard told them to get down. I was not sure if anyone else noticed, but I could squint and see a couple of guys on the roof of the White House looking out at the crowd.

Sightseeing suddenly didn't seem so appealing. I left the hordes and headed back toward the subway station. It was time to move on.

CHAPTER 26

Relief washed over me as I left Washington, DC. I had felt trapped, almost claustrophobic. The coldness of the people in the nation's capital surrounded me wherever I went. It was absolutely the least friendly place I had encountered so far on the trip.

It didn't matter where I was, the reaction was the same. No one talked or even smiled. Walk down the street, and there were scowls or blank expressions. Sit in a restaurant, and I was ignored by people next to me, even if they were two feet away. One lunch spot I went to around the corner from the White House was as impersonal as a courtroom. I picked it because it was far from where the tourists would be, but in hindsight, I probably would have enjoyed dining with them more than the locals. In this place, there was no amiable chatter, like in most luncheonettes or diners, just hushed tones. All were dressed in either blue or black business attire. The ties on the men were all a bland color with their white shirts. They were career bureaucrats likely plotting their next political move. It was like the whole dining room was telling secrets.

Even the waitresses were stilted. They didn't ask how you were. They were all business and couldn't be bothered with such pleasantries. My server was a middle-aged woman with black hair and a touch of gray. She was plump, but not overly so. She had tight, thin pursed lips, and seemed ready to spit bile in lieu of conversation.

"What do you want to drink?" was how she greeted me.

"Diet Coke, please."

"You ready to order?"

"No, not yet."

She sighed heavily. I knew I had better have my meal selected before she returned with my drink or two guys in ill-fitting suits and dark sunglasses would be picking me up by each arm and escorting me to the sidewalk.

Fortunately, I had plenty of time to decide what I wanted. She was punishing me for my indecision. She had my drink in her hand and stopped to chat with one of the other waitresses. There was absolutely no sense of urgency. The place was half-empty, and I was one of two tables in her station. The other was two men in their thirties who were noshing on club sandwiches. After about five minutes, my time in restaurant purgatory was completed. She came over with my drink.

This special treatment wasn't reserved just for me. Everyone was dealt with in the same manner. There would be no triumphs of social interaction in Washington, DC, either on a subway, or walking down a street, or in an eatery. It wasn't for a lack of effort on my part. I seemed like an out-of-place optimist. My demeanor and body language were the opposite of the citizens who worked or lived here. I strolled. They walked briskly. I said hello. They looked away as I approached. I was being treated like a pariah, and once I realized I wasn't welcome here, I escaped.

Why it had to be that way was the topic I chose to dissect as I got on Route 50 to make my way toward West Virginia. There was a specific town I wanted to see in that state, and it was about a three-hour ride to get there. That would give me plenty of time to ponder why people got so obsessed with power and status.

My philosophy was more about caring than plundering. Living to grab control over someone, or something, was immoral to me. Status seeking, greed, and phoniness were of no use to me. They were prevalent in Southern California, and I had experienced the phenomenon countless times, mostly with women I had dated. It was usually about the time the entrée came at dinner on the first date when they were exposed. The questions were coy in nature, but obviously with an agenda. "What type of writer are you?" "Can you make any money doing that?" "Why not be a screenwriter? I hear they make a lot of money." "Why don't you own a home?" I probably should have brought a balance sheet and tax returns to the restaurant and saved us both some trouble. Of course, with their character, they still would have expected the free dinner.

In Orange County, California, the examples of obscene wealth were evident almost daily. The area even had a reality television show celebrating this narcissistic behavior. How big was my house? How many cars can I own? How much jewelry can I show off at dinner tonight? Honestly, it nauseated me.

I was at a park walking my rescue dog one time and got to talking with a woman who was the epitome of the Orange County housewife. Fake lips, fake breasts, fake hair, fake nails, fake eyelashes—she had it all. I'm not sure there was a real part on her. Unfortunately, her personality was as genuine as her numerous cosmetically enhanced parts.

We were talking, and two minutes into this conversation, I was looking for an excuse to end it. I had come this far, though, so I figured I would see how bad it would get. She did not disappoint. After we talked about her and all the possessions, she began to complain about her Christmas. She was holiday shopping and had to buy scores of expensive gifts for all her friends, who I assumed were doing the same for her. The biggest challenge was her twenty-something daughter. She required the latest and best of everything, and purchasing all these baubles was heaping added stress on her holiday season.

As she was prattling on and on, she caught her breath long enough to ask how my Christmas shopping was going. I informed her that I detested the commercialization of the season. Instead of participating in the mind-numbing process I found repulsive,

I spent my time doing charity work. I encouraged my friends and family not to buy me a gift. Spend the time with loved ones or undertake charity work. It was much more satisfying both, morally and financially. "It makes the holidays much more tolerable," I said.

For one fleeting moment, she had self-awareness about her vapid lifestyle, and I thought I saw her undergo an epiphany. I reached someone who I thought was unreachable. Maybe she would volunteer at a toy drive with me. I was so excited.

"I do a lot of charity work as well," she blurted. I asked her what type, and she, not surprisingly, was unable to elaborate. I wished her happy holidays and walked toward my car, defeated that I was unable to show her how meaningless her life was. It shouldn't have been shocking to me, though I held out the smallest hope. It's a battle I should have known I wasn't going to win. It was also the last time I ever had an interaction of deep meaning with a stranger. Now I just talk about the weather or some other benign topic with people I meet.

As I got back on the road, I wondered if I could keep that pledge.

CHAPTER 27

The farther I got from the nation's capital, the better I felt. By the time I hit the border going into Virginia, my mood was considerably brighter. The same could not be said for Libertad. She was not happy and was taking it out on me. She was running hot and, as a result, was unresponsive. I knew the answer rested with the oil. It had been about 5,000 miles since the last oil change, and even though I was running synthetic, it was time for some attention in that area.

Winchester, Virginia, had a Harley-Davidson dealership, so I aimed for the small town in the Shenandoah Valley. When I arrived, they had time to do the oil change and check out a couple of other concerns.

My biggest worry was the front brakes. They were soft, and I figured they needed new pads. My brake caliper was from a Honda Goldwing that an old mechanic had put in and didn't tell me about. I found that out when the Virginia H-D mechanic spent an entire day trying to figure out what kind of brake pads I needed.

Fortunately, I had a set of my brake pads with me. The Harley mechanic next noticed that my rotor was grooved. We decided to replace that also.

He had the Harley all torn apart but couldn't get the brake pads to fit in the caliper. I was lucky my new mechanic back home was around when I called. He told me the solution was to grind the brake pads down. The service guys at Harley wouldn't do that, so the guy just tightened the brakes up and put everything back together as it had been.

With all the work and delays, it was closing in on sunset, and I only had about two hours of daylight remaining. I could have easily made it to Martinsburg, West Virginia, since it was only about a half-hour away, but I wasn't motivated to ride, so I decided to stay the night in Winchester.

I was a big believer in fate, events happening for a reason, but I couldn't figure out why this day had been such a waste and why I was stuck in this little town.

The answer rested at 608 South Kent Street. That was the current home of Richard and Melissa Lozeau. They had been living there since April, and when they first rented the three-bedroom home, they didn't realize they were residing where a musical legend had grown up.

| | |

A lot of people who lived in Winchester at the same time as Patsy Cline never much liked her, and the feeling was mutual. One of the most influential and beloved country singers of all time couldn't find that same adoration in this small country hamlet.

It was a hard life for Cline from the moment she was born on September 8, 1932. Cline's mother was fifteen years old, her father forty-two. They married a week after Cline, whose real name was Virginia Patterson Hensley, was born. The family, which added two more children, moved nineteen times by Cline's sixteen birthday. Her father deserted the family shortly afterward. Cline's mother moved her three children into the modest two-story house on the east side of Winchester. That was where the working-class poor lived. Cline was a high school student in name only. She never went, instead working jobs ranging from slitting chicken throats in a slaughterhouse to cleaning busses at the local Greyhound station to working as a soda jerk at Gaunt's Drug Store. It was a life right out of a country-Western song. It was also the destiny of someone from the east side of Winchester.

It was the wrong side of the tracks, as far as those who lived on the other side of town were concerned. The west side was more affluent, with doctors, lawyers, and other professionals in that area. The only time they wanted to see east-side residents in their neighborhood was when they came to clean their houses or mow their lawns.

They shopped in different stores and prayed at similar but separate churches. Their children were educated at better schools. At home, the rich kids were taught that those White-trash kids had dirty faces and minds. You didn't talk to one of them, much less date one. The arrangement had worked for years, at least for those on the right side of town.

Cline might have been poor, but she wasn't downtrodden, and she absolutely wasn't demur. She got her unapologetic sass from her grandmother, who told Patsy to stand up for herself. Her grandmother taught her more lessons than any school could have.

The singing voice came from God. Cline would perform every chance she got. Her mother was a seamstress and sewed most of her stage costumes, glimmering cowgirl outfits. Cline honed her gift at bars and honky-tonks all around Virginia and other neighboring states, her mom driving her daughter to gigs. Often, they were the only women in the place, and Cline was the only female on the stage. She wowed those who saw her, and they couldn't believe a teenager had such a sultry and powerful voice.

At twenty, Cline began to perform with bandleader Bill Peer, who convinced her to change her first name from Virginia to Patsy. The next year, she married Gerald Cline. A year after that, in 1954, she got her first record deal. It took three years after her first record, but she got her initial taste of fame when she appeared on Arthur Godfrey's *Talent Scouts* television show. She performed "Walkin' After Midnight" and won the competition.

While her professional life blossomed, her personal life had all the makings of one of her sad ballads. She divorced Cline in 1957 and married Charlie Dick the same year. The two had a complicated union. They loved each other but fought constantly, most of their rage fueled by alcohol. Cline confided in close friends about their battles but stayed with him until her death.

That fateful day came way too soon. On March 5, 1963, Cline was returning home from a benefit show when the small plane she was on crashed near Camden, Tennessee. She was thirty years old. Though she had moved to Nashville years earlier, she was buried in her hometown of Winchester. For decades, the simple gravestone at Shenandoah Memorial Park was the only evidence of her ties to Winchester. A street with her name was proposed, but it never happened. The townsfolk remembered only a young, brash Cline, and they weren't ready to forget, or forgive, her past.

Now, forty-two years after her death, the residents may be ready to look beyond what many perceived as her immoral behavior. The town sponsored a festival earlier this year and, on September 3, 2005, was going to dedicate a sign in front of her home designating it a historical landmark.

The town of approximately 24,000 people now has a Patsy Cline Festival that runs during Labor Day weekend. The Patsy Cline fan club also wanted to turn her home into a museum, which thrilled a lot of people, except the Lozeau family.

They were paying about $200 less for the home than they would a comparable place and Richard would have liked to sign a longer lease to ensure that he and his family could stay there. He stood outside the house and visited with me, showing me around.

"This was a great place," said Richard, who moved there from Providence, Rhode Island, about three years ago. "The school system was good, and it's a nice place to live."

Richard had even started fixing up the house. A painter, he had replaced the lime-green paint with white, and black for the shutters.

"The people who come here don't bother us much," Richard said. "They take a picture and look and then leave. No one comes knocking on the door."

The family did get to meet country music star Lynn Anderson. She was in town and wanted to see the house. She was the only person they have let in to see it, and they were rewarded with autographs and pictures.

Saturday was going to be a big day at the house. Politicians had finally approved a plaque to be erected in front. The city was expected hundreds of people, but the Lozeau family wasn't too worried.

"It should be pretty exciting," Melissa said. "We will have a front-row seat for it so that will be good."

CHAPTER

28

It was the first wrong turn I made on this trip, and I was surprised it hadn't come sooner. I had logged about 3,700 miles in forty days with no mistakes. When I was home, I couldn't drive two days without going down the wrong street.

My wayward direction on this day mattered little. I was still just killing time before I had to get on a plane in Washington, so staying on the road I was on was just going to be a slight detour. After leaving Winchester, Virginia, I headed west on Route 50 toward Capon Bridge, West Virginia. Somehow, though, I managed to turn north, and, instead of staying on Route 50, I ventured onto Route 600. That led me to the town of Gainesboro, Virginia. I should have known something was amiss about twenty minutes after I made the wrong turn. I didn't see any signs for my destination but figured I was close. Part of my certainty that I was going in the right direction was unavoidable. As a carrier of the male DNA, there comes an entrenched stubbornness in all matters of navigation, especially in my lineage.

This affliction dates back several generations in my family. My father had it, as did his father, as did his father. The Reger clan had a ridiculous history of driving aimlessly for hours on end. To stop the vehicle and ask for directions would be to acknowledge weakness. If my great-great-grandfather had been the captain of the ship that brought him and his wife to America from Germany, they would have ended up in Greenland rather than Ellis Island, and we would have become a proud family of seal furriers and ice fishermen.

It was a miracle the divorce rate in the family was nonexistent, considering the stress it caused when a Reger couple got into an automobile. It was the only occasion I witnessed my parents fight. Ninety percent of the time, my mother and father were the most loving couple I ever saw. Put them in a car on a road trip, and they fought like they were mired in a ten-year bad marriage.

When I was a young teenager, my parents were in a rented Volkswagen Beetle in Mexico City, en route to the hotel from the pyramids we had visited, my brother and me in the back seat. They got into a traffic circle and couldn't figure out how to get to the hotel, which was visible from the road. My father drove around and around, yelling at my mother about where to go. She was as obstinate as my father and informed him she had no goddamn idea where to exit. I thought for a moment my father was going to stop the car in the middle of his fifth go-around in the traffic circle, take custody of my brother, give me to my mother, and send my mom the divorce papers once he got back to the States.

My parents have the dubious distinction of being the only couple to get lost on the way from Los Angeles to Las Vegas. If one had never driven from Southern California to Las Vegas, understand that there was literally one way to get there. Any one of four west to east freeways in metropolitan LA runs into Interstate 15. Go north on I-15, and four hours later, the lights of Sin City greet you. It was impossible to get lost. Well, apparently not for Don and Peg. They found themselves inexplicably on the way to Arizona. To this day, I have no idea how they got lost, especially when big signs directed those who were directionally challenged toward Las Vegas. No explanation was ever given.

Given this genetic flaw, the best I could hope for was to turn around before I drove to Canada. Berkeley Springs, West Virginia, was where I finally surrendered, and it was only because I needed gas.

My new path put me on Cacapon Road. Now I was riding

parallel to the Maryland-West Virginia border and the Potomac River. As detours go, I could have undergone worse. After hitting the town of Forks of Cacapon, I was on Route 29, where I soon got back on Highway 50, going from forest to more bucolic scenery. Then, outside of Romney, West Virginia, doublewide mobile homes began to dot the side of the turnpike. There was one on a small hill that seemed to represent the area. The paint had long since eroded, a casualty of the elements. It had cardboard where two windows once were. Three nonworking cars sat in the high grass to the right of the front door, where a fourth car was but looked like it would soon join the other three. The poverty was palpable. I found myself juicing the throttle, embarrassed that I was staring at the dilapidated dwellings, and wondering how people in the richest country in the world lived in such deplorable conditions.

Eighty miles later, I was in Elkins, West Virginia. I had a self-indulgent reason for seeking out this part of the country. Reger, West Virginia, was listed on the internet as a town, but it was not on any map that I had. I narrowed it down to somewhere between Elkins and Buckhannon, but there were twenty-five miles between the two towns. After driving twice from east to west and back again on US 48 with no luck, I sought assistance. I pulled into a gas station in Buckhannon and asked if they knew where Reger was located.

Of the three people working at the station, no one had even heard of the town. They were as helpful as possible; one guy even called a friend who worked for the post office. They told me there was a Reger Street, as well as a Reger Cemetery, and Reger Chapel, but those were all in Buckhannon. I thanked them and went on down the street.

A West Virginia State Police substation was on my right, so I pulled in figuring someone there could help. Two troopers and a dispatcher later, the town was found, but getting me there took some work. The one trooper, who had lived in the area his entire life, found the vicinity on the map after two attempts and gave me directions.

Off I went, with correct directions, but with no sign for the town of Reger, I was never positively certain where it was. I had a pretty good guess and knew I was in the neighborhood, but I couldn't definitively stop and proclaim this was it. I don't blame the officers; it was not exactly a bustling town, but it did point to a disturbing trend I have seen as I go across the country.

No one seems to know anything outside of the immediate area where they live. This wasn't the first time I had asked for directions, and getting people to tell me even basic information had proven difficult.

When I was in Vermont, I had asked a guy at a gas station where a local motorcycle parts store was, and he shrugged. I went two blocks down the street from the station, and there was a big, bright sign illuminating the name of the business.

It isn't just directions, but basic travel questions. If someone asked me how far it was to San Diego from my house, I would be able to give them a reasonable estimate of two hours. When I queried about distances between towns, the reply was usually one of uncertainty. I don't want exact mileage and had said as much, but even giving me rough estimates proved to be a challenge.

It puzzled me and made me wonder why I got so many blank stares when I asked these questions. If I was getting erroneous information, I wouldn't mind, but it was the ignorance that was frustrating. Did people not care about the area they lived in? Were they not able to travel around where they lived? Had their world not expanded beyond their town? Was I asking the wrong people?

I went three miles down Old Elkins Road from Buckhannon to the area that was supposedly Reger. I saw a man sitting on the porch of a modest one-story house. It was obvious to me that he was put on this earth to amuse me, so I decided I would have a little harmless fun with him. I liked teasing people, always had. Every now and then, when I saw an opportunity, the devilish side of my persona took over.

I parked the motorcycle just off the street and waved as I took my helmet off. I said hello well before I reached the porch, as to put him at ease. He was happy to see me; I was probably the first nonlocal he had encountered in months. There was no reason someone who didn't live here would go down this road, much less stop. There was nothing of note here, just a smattering of houses.

For my impending street theater, the man on the porch was a goldmine. He told me his name was Claude and that he had lived there his entire life. Claude was eighty-six-years old, very spry, and extremely alert, but he did talk with a measured drawl, seeming to select his words carefully. I envied his being as healthy as he was and hoped I had a similar disposition if I made it to my eighties. There was a twinge of guilt as I started my ruse, but I justified it as innocent fun and pressed on.

"So, Claude, how do you like my town?" I asked.

Appropriately puzzled, he paused to process my question. When he could not wrap his brain around my inquiry, he replied, "Say again?"

"My town, how do you like living here?"

I pulled out my wallet and showed him the name on my license. He did a double-take and wouldn't release my identification right away. He studied it, looking at the name, and I could almost hear the gears grinding inside his head.

"Your last name is Reger?" he finally asked.

"Yes. My family has owned this town for five generations."

"They have?" Claude exclaimed. He suddenly got more animated. It was like he had just met a celebrity.

"My great-great-great-grandfather settled this land. He discovered it on the Lewis and Clark Expedition. They kept exploring, but he liked it so much, he stayed and put in a claim for it. Built a log cabin somewhere around here."

Claude listened intently. My oral history of his hometown was like uncovering the Dead Sea Scrolls. I had him hooked, and it was time to reel him in.

"My great-great-great-grandfather fought off Indians from the front of the log cabin. He turned them away with nothing more than a musket. He never pulled out the arrows stuck in the front door."

"You don't say," Claude said, impressed. "He sounds like quite a man."

"He loved it here," I continued. "He made all his clothes from bear and rabbit pelts. Even had a coonskin cap."

At this point, Claude leaned forward in his rocking chair to ensure he didn't miss any details.

"He found a wife in Buckhannon, and they started a family. Had my great-great grandfather and a daughter. He took over the town when his dad died. They had six kids. The oldest, my great-grandfather, took control of the town. He wanted to put in a general store, but the folks in Buckhannon didn't want the competition and ran him off. None of us has been back since, except to visit."

"That's a shame," Claude lamented, genuinely disappointed at the fate of the Reger clan.

"We retained the name and still get a piece of the tax revenue," I said. "Whenever we are in the area, we stop in and make sure people here are happy."

"I think I met your grandfather one time," Claude volunteered. "Nice man, looked a lot like you."

"That's what everyone says. Spitting image, my mom used to say."

Just when I thought I had exhausted this prank, Claude requested I sit for a minute while he excused himself and walked inside. I figured he was taking a bathroom break, but he came back out holding a single piece of blank paper and a pen.

"I'd be honored if you would sign this," Claude exclaimed. "My neighbors won't believe I met you."

"I'd be happy to," I replied.

I scribbled the following: "To Claude, I'm glad that you live in my town. All the best, John Reger."

I bid Claude a fond farewell, shook his hand, and got back on the Harley. I gunned the engine and waved as I took off down the street, the smile glued to my face as I headed the two hours to Charleston, West Virginia.

CHAPTER 29

It was hard to ride a motorcycle while giggling, but the more I thought about my stunt, the more I chuckled. It soon turned to nearly uncontrollable laughter, and I'm certain the passing drivers were pondering my mental state. People don't often see a big, burly, bearded biker laughing like a loon riding down Highway 48. That thought only made my hysterics more animated. It was like getting a second payoff on my practical joke.

It kept me smiling as I headed toward Charleston. I reached the small town of Weston, an area that straddled Interstate 79. I stopped for gas and asked the clerk how far it was to Charleston. He told me he thought it was about an hour down the road. It was getting close to dark, but if I only had sixty miles to cover, especially on an interstate, I could make it with some daylight remaining.

I could have gone north to Clarksburg, West Virginia. I knew it was only about thirty minutes away and that I would have had no problem getting there before sunset. But I wanted to head south so that was the direction I pointed Libertad. The first mileage sign I came across was five miles down the highway, and I knew I was in trouble. I was ninety-two miles from Charleston. Retreating would have been prudent, but my stubbornness and the Reger family genetic defect overruled logic, so I pressed on southward.

The light was disappearing, even though I was speeding to try to keep it in the sky as long as possible. The sunglasses were starting to become a problem, but taking them off meant no eye protection, and the wind at eighty miles per hour made riding without them impossible.

I rode for another twenty miles in semi-darkness, and I pulled into a rest stop to switch into amber-colored eyeglasses for night riding. It was the first time I needed them in more than a month of travel.

I don't like riding in the dark. There were way too many variables I can't control. I must look out for objects on the road, or potholes, or drivers who can't see me. Then there was the deer. For the remaining fifty-three miles, I drove with my head on a swivel, gripping the handlebars with clenched fists. The woods were on both sides, and the possibility of deer was there.

I had a sliver of light, and I wanted to take advantage of it as long as I could. There wasn't much traffic, and I straddled the centerline, giving me a better chance of avoiding animals and potholes. The road was relatively smooth, and speeding wasn't as dangerous as it could have been. I knew that if I could get twenty miles from the city, the woods would disappear, and my anxiety with it. Nothing jumped out at me, and I saw the exit for Charleston. I found the first motel and pulled in for the night, vowing not to get caught in the dark again.

The next morning, I ate breakfast and saw that Kentucky was hosting Louisville in a football game in Lexington in two days. I hadn't seen a sporting event in a while and thought it would be fun to watch an in-state rivalry.

The Kanawha River paralleled the road at the beginning of my day, and I watched boats push barges down the large body of water while small pleasure boats weaved around them. The view didn't last long, as Route 119 started to run away from the river, and soon

I was in the hills that stretched toward the Kentucky border.

The highway was one of the better ones I had been on. It was not a popular road and was free of traffic, even though it was a holiday weekend. Libertad and I had it pretty much to ourselves, and I opened up the throttle, letting her wind through the gently twisting path. She seemed to respond to routes like that, especially when there was no one else around. Because it was not heavily traveled, it was in good condition and easy on my back.

My forty-two-year-old body had been a concern on this trip. It was showing signs of betraying me. My back was bad before I left, but I got a massage, and that seemed to help. I had been careful not to overextend it and had been doing a series of stretches in the morning to loosen it up. I have my duffel bag on the passenger seat, and that acted as a support so that my posture was good when I rode.

The biggest problem was the beds I slept on at various hotels and motels. Mattresses that were soft or thin or warped were usually in the places I stayed, and they did more damage to my back than the Harley. Libertad had done her share of harm to other parts of my body. Gripping the handlebars six to seven hours a day had caused my hands to go numb. My feet were the bigger concern. My machine's foot pegs were fashionable and got lots of compliments from admirers, but they had little function. I changed out the pegs in South Dakota, switching to a larger one with more room for my feet, and that helped tremendously. The ride was much more comfortable now, but traveling an average of 200 miles a day for more than a month would make anyone sore, and I certainly was.

It bothered me a great deal that I was getting older, although, obviously, it was inevitable. I was almost certain I won't be the first person to live forever, but for many years, I thought there was an outside chance. Now I was resigned to my mortality, and it had become evident in how I live my life.

No longer do I take those unnecessary chances to cheat death; of course, some would argue that riding a motorcycle across the country would fall into that category. Not really, however. The open road was always safer than a city full of cars with distracted drivers. Nothing was guaranteed, but I liked the odds of a two-lane, sparsely populated country road versus a Los Angeles freeway at rush hour.

Life was about playing the odds. I had always taken a shine to the longshot, but as I advanced in years, even money looked safer and better. I feared that my edge was deserting me, and that would be tragic. I think everyone should have a little drama to beat back the mundane, which had killed many a person.

My life was about to be rather dull for the next four days. I stayed in Lexington for two of them, with the highlight being the football game.

On Monday, I headed back to the Washington area, where I was to catch a plane back to California for George's funeral. The next two days were not going to be enjoyable at all. They were merely days of transit, not discovery, and it meant moving at a fast pace and not seeing much. When I was on the interstate, the time went faster, eliminating any deep thought. Gone was my wandering nature. I was in the machine, pulled along the great freeway with everyone else, jockeying for position, tailgating those who didn't get over to the right soon enough, and barely looking to the left or right of me. There was no scenery, just road, and miles that had to be conquered, not enjoyed. My mind calculated how soon I could get to the next place. How long could I ride until I had to stop for gas? The only advantage was that the gas stations on the interstate made it easier to get right back on the freeway.

On Tuesday before sunset, I pulled into the same Manassas, Virginia, motel I had stayed at the week before. I checked in and marked the thirty-six hours until I would get on an airplane. It was the longest day and a half of my life.

CHAPTER 30

The sun wasn't awake yet when I saddled up and headed the eighteen miles to Dulles International Airport from Manassas, Virginia. My flight was at six in the morning, and I wanted to get there at least an hour before it departed. I didn't even notice the dark, and with a smattering of cars on Route 28, I was able to think about topics other than traffic.

It felt strange going home. I certainly didn't believe I would be headed back to Southern California on an airplane. There was a part of me that didn't want to go. Actually, there was more than a part. Just about all of me resisted getting on that flight. The more desirable way would have been to keep riding—my first instinct.

Running from unpleasantness was always the first instinct. It was my nature. I put off doctor's appointments. I left relationships when they got to be too much work. I quit my job when I felt boxed in. The reason for this trip had a lot of those elements; at some point, though, I had to confront those fears. I could only run for so long before my body and mind tired. I learned that fear never left, no matter how much distance I put between myself and it.

Flying back home represented a small victory. In the past, I would have found an excuse not to go. It was a selfish way to live, and as self-absorbed as I was, the pain I inflicted on friends and family wasn't even noticeable to me.

Belonging to the motorcycle club helped teach me about

relationships. The sense of family with the guys was something missing growing up. It made me care more about people than before. Between them and my friend Heather, I was turning into an actual feeling human being—quite an adjustment.

By the time I landed at LAX, most of the uneasiness had left, and I was even a little excited to be back home. My friend Warren picked me up at the airport and took me to my motel. We stopped for lunch and caught up about the trip. It was nice to be with Warren. We didn't get to see each other as much as we used to. Life just seemed to get in the way.

In the morning, a member of the club picked me up at the motel, and we headed toward the local bar, where all the other guys in the club were meeting. I knew today was going to be difficult and had been in a state of numbness since going back to the dingy motel the previous night.

The Huddle had been the local spot for the Orange County Assholes for years. The story I was told was that Crazy George and some of the guys used to congregate there for happy hour after work. There were about five of them, and they had talked about starting a club but couldn't come up with an appropriate name. One day, they were whooping and hollering in the bar, and a guy came in and asked the bartender, "Who's that group of assholes over there in the corner?" It was the perfect name, and the club was born.

I hadn't told them I was coming. Some had been following my travels, and, as far as they knew, I was on the East Coast. When I walked in, people were stunned to see me. Someone yelled, "John! What are you doing here?"

Instantly, I was mobbed by members and their wives. Hug after hug followed in a procession that must have taken five minutes. Wives kissed me on the cheek, and the men gave me big bear hugs. Some were able to lift me off the ground. They were truly glad to see me, as I was them. They were family.

Biker Bob was one of my favorites. He was a Vietnam War

veteran and had shown the most interest in my trip. He gave me advice like a big brother before I left. We talked while I was on the road, and I filled him in on my travels. He pulled me aside and asked me why I interrupted my trip to come back.

"We would have understood if you hadn't come," he said.

"Crazy would have done the same for me," I replied.

"I'm glad you came," he said. "Love you, brother."

"I wouldn't have missed it," I said. "Love you too, brother."

We all had a toast of Crazy's favorite drink, a shot of Jack Daniels. To this day, I have no idea how he drank that crap. I choked down my shot in his honor, and we all headed to the parking lot.

There were few spectacles as grandiose as a group of Harley-Davidsons riding in procession. Everyone had their motorcycles but me. Club members I had never seen ride had their steel machines ready to go. There were about forty of them, two abreast going up the freeway to the memorial site. I was beside in a car staring at the guys riding up the highway, and though I was jealous I wasn't among them, I proudly smiled.

When we reached the Shriner's Lodge, where the memorial service was being held, there were about a hundred more Harleys in the parking lot, as well as countless automobiles. Crazy had a lot of friends, and it seemed like they had all shown up. Recreational bikers sat next to hardcore ones. Most of the outlaw clubs were represented. Members of the Hells Angels, Vagos, Hessians, and Booze Fighters were all in the audience.

Crazy George's purple Harley was at the front of the auditorium. The officiant began talking about his life, and the tears started to flow, just not mine. There were some of the toughest guys I had ever seen sobbing like babies, and I sat there like a statue.

Friends and family came up and gave testimonials. The service lasted a little more than an hour, but it ended too soon. After the conclusion, I approached Crazy George's wife, Marti, and offered my condolences. We talked briefly, and she told me how much her husband liked me. It showed me what a strong woman she was, offering soothing words to me instead of the other way around.

We all spilled into the parking lot. It was strange; we didn't know what to do next. It took a minute, but someone suggested going back to the Huddle. I said my goodbyes. I wanted to be alone. Biker Bob dropped me off at my motel and asked if I wanted him to stay. I reassured him that I was fine. I spent the rest of the day thinking of nothing as I lay on the bed and stared at the ceiling with the lights off. I fell asleep in my clothes around midnight, not having moved an inch.

The next morning, I was back on an airplane flying toward our nation's capital. I was reading a book of Charles Bukowski short stories to kill some of the five hours, using one of the memorial cards as a bookmark. I pulled it out to look at it again. On the front was a picture of Crazy George riding this little go-cart he had made. I remembered it had a 50CC engine, four wheels, and a metal chair bolted to the frame. He had designed a crude steering wheel and often cruised up and down the block. The smile was quintessential George, part joy, part mischief. I thought about all the times I saw him ride it, honking the bicycle horn as he traversed the neighborhood.

As the memory got clearer, the tears started to trickle, and then with each recollection, they started to stream. The mourning of my friend had finally begun.

CHAPTER 31

Much to my surprise, Libertad was in the Dulles International Airport parking lot, right where I had left her. She was a little dusty, but otherwise fine. I tied my duffel bag on the back seat and fired her up. It seemed that the rest had agreed with her. I, on the other hand, needed a little time to acclimate myself to once again riding on two wheels. Pulling out of the parking structure became an adventure. I was on the second story, and the first two turns to get to the ground level of the garage felt like I was in driver's education. I took the initial corner too sharp, nearly dumping the Harley on its side. I recovered from that miscalculation just in time to approach the next right turn. That maneuver was less eventful, but there were more style points lost.

Getting out of the airport without causing harm to either my machine or myself was a minor miracle. It was a small measure of comfort when I reached Highway 28 and was able to drive in a straight line toward Manassas and my motel.

I had to make a stop at Chris's house to get the rest of my belongings. He had been gracious enough to hold onto them while I went to California. I offered to buy him lunch, but he was getting ready to go to work. It was small compensation for his kindness, and I was disappointed we couldn't have a meal together before I moved on to the next destination.

Next stop? Undecided. I had put any thought of traveling on

hold while I was back home. I even debated whether I wanted to ride back or ship the motorcycle back. George's death had affected me more than I wanted to admit. He was the first biker friend who had been killed, and, naturally, it made me reflect on whether living this lifestyle was worth it. The whole point of this journey was to ride without negative thoughts. I was supposed to be free, both in my ride and my life.

I figured I only got so many lives, and I was starting to get close to my quota. I had had three guns pointed at me, one discharged. I was supposed to be on a small airplane that crashed. Throw in the three motorcycle accidents, and going by myself across the country on two wheels probably was pushing my luck. I was well past the age of believing I was invincible. Of course, giving up now would be to admit failure, and there was more than enough history of my not finishing what I started.

As I was contemplating my future, I decided to buzz around Washington DC. I wasn't ready to go back to the motel and stare at four walls. Besides, I thought a little wind therapy would help me come to the right decision. As I was making a loop around the Capitol, I went down a street where the Washington Monument was to my right, and on the corner was a lone man holding three signs. I pulled over to meet this unassuming demonstrator. Quietly, almost unnoticeably, John Evans stood there, a protest of one, trying to get his message across to anyone who would slow the car down long enough to read his three homemade signs.

The fifty-seven-year-old, stout African American told me he traveled from Indiana to the nation's capital last year because he felt he had to object to an injustice he had suffered. The decision wasn't too difficult to make. Evans had lost his home, his car, and his savings, paying for the medical care he said the government owed him.

Sergeant Evans had fought in Vietnam and was proud of defending his country. But he came back with post-traumatic stress disorder, long before people knew its devastating impact on soldiers. The government didn't want to pay for his treatment, he said. Evans suffered from the disorder for decades, paying for health ailments, including a heart attack, out of his own pocket. He filed for bankruptcy because he owed the hospital money and had nothing left to sell.

Last September, right after the Labor Day holiday, he decided President George W. Bush and others needed to hear his grievances. The government had repaid Evans some of the money he felt he was owed, but his possessions had long been sold.

"What am I going to do?" Evans asked. "My house was gone. My car was gone. It's too late for me."

Evans's chance at retirement or even a normal life was over. He didn't want to sue his government for the money, nor did he seek any media attention. It was not his style. He just wanted future servicemen and women not to have to endure what he did.

For several hours every day for the past year, Evans took his three homemade signs and stood on this street corner adjacent to the Washington Monument and kitty-corner to the World War II Memorial.

"This war we are in is bad," Evans said of the Iraq conflict. "They are coming home with stress. Nobody treated us for stress; they just gave us more stress."

Evans was as modest as his signs. There was nothing provocative on them. Nothing titillating, looking to shock those who read them.

One sign was yellow and said in black lettering, "Without our veterans or troops, we would not have a country." It also directed people to a website, www.forgottenvets.com. The sign in his left hand asked a simple question. "Should we clean up our own home before we start with somebody else?"

The white sign that rested on his chest and stomach, held by a white string around his neck stated, "No donation," and asked, "Will our troops be treated for stress with stress like I am now?" and at the bottom said, "Lord help us."

There were other writings on the back of his signs, but no one got to see them since he faced oncoming traffic, and it was difficult enough to read the front. The hope, Evans believed, was that people would see his signs, remember the website, and then learn more about his cause there.

Evans was a God-fearing man, only looking to help his fellow veterans and soldiers. He had no press agent, did not set up across from the president's vacation spot, and was not planning on a media-filled bus caravan across the country.

The only traveling Evans did was from his small studio apartment near downtown to this site. Occasionally he went to the Capitol or the front of the White House to protest but found it much more peaceful where he was.

"There are too many tourists there," Evans explained. "They don't want to read my signs."

The people in passing cars did try to read them, and some even honked their horns in approval or waved to Evans. He returned the wave, almost embarrassed, but ultimately glad that someone recognized what he was doing.

"It's not right how they treat our veterans and our troops," Evans exclaimed. "We need to treat them right when they come home."

The vigil would continue, Evans deduced.

"I am out here every day I can be," Evans said. "I'll be out here until I die, or it changes. I think it will change, at least I hope it does."

"I hope so too, John," I replied. "I really hope it does."

As I headed back to the motel, I saw the Capitol Building in the background, and it instantly made me feel dejected. That was where the people who could help John Evans worked, and they didn't even know he was out there. Even if they did, I doubted they would care.

CHAPTER 32

My decision for the next stop was made around one in the morning. I wanted to be in St. Simons Island in a couple of days, and there were two ways to get there from Manassas. The first was to hop on the interstate and head directly south. That route was 655 miles, and making it in two days would have been easy. The second choice was to head east, first to the coast, then zigzag about. That added about 150 more miles but was going to be much more pleasant for my eyes. If I got up early enough, though, it wouldn't be as difficult to make it in two days. I opted for that route and fell fast asleep, at peace with my decision.

Interstate 95 provided a quick conduit to Route 17. Forty-five minutes later, I saw the Rappahannock River as I drove through Fredericksburg, Virginia. I liked the alternate name for Route 17, "Tidewater Trail," and hoped the water would accompany me for a while. Tall pines blocked my view of it for most of the next hour, but it was comforting to know it was alongside me. When I reached the town of Tappahannock, the river shot back into view and was larger than when I had seen it in Fredericksburg. From there, although the river went back into hiding, I would glimpse occasional pieces of its existence when it ran underneath a small bridge or was feeding into a creek.

The next chance at seeing water was the York River, and when I approached the city of Gloucester Point, Virginia, it confirmed my decision to take this out-of-the-way direction. Mature pine and elm trees were on both sides of the highway as I entered the town. When I reached Gloucester Point Beach Park, I could see an incline was imminent. Then the York River poked through the trees until the large tributary was visible on both sides of the bridge. At the end was Yorktown, Virginia, and I took the opportunity to pull off to the side at the bottom of the bridge and admire the water to my right.

I was also fortunate to stumble upon a site that was so steeped in history. Colonial National Historical Park was the site of the Battle of Yorktown where General George Washington led troops to a victory over the British in the American Revolutionary War. Walking around and seeing the Yorktown Victory Monument, authentic cannons used in the Yorktown battle, and how the people lived at that time was better than anything I had read in a history book in high school. The break was unexpected and put me behind schedule, but it was worth the diversion from the itinerary. It did force me to alter my plans slightly. Instead of trying to get to Columbia, South Carolina, I was going to have to spend the night somewhere in North Carolina. Entering that state was something I was not looking forward to. I tried to push it out of my mind and enjoy what I had left of Virginia.

My angst was momentarily forgotten as I went through Newport News, Virginia, and reached the James River Bridge. That four-and-a-half-mile bridge was the longest one I had ever been on. I found out from a local at a gas station where I stopped to fill up that it was once the longest one built over water when it opened in 1928.

That would be the last highlight of the day. In forty-six miles, I would be entering North Carolina. The first sight of the Virginia-North Carolina border, a knot in my stomach formed. I looked for the first town with a motel. I needed a strategy for tomorrow for the best path to traverse through the gauntlet. I found a motel in Murfreesboro, North Carolina, and checked in.

| | |

My cavalier attitude toward speeding came to a screeching halt when I crossed into North Carolina. As far as those in power in the Tar Heel state were concerned, I was a fugitive. My troubles dated back to 1999 when I was covering the US Open golf tournament in Pinehurst. On the way to the tournament, after landing at the Charlotte airport, I got pulled over by a state trooper, my lead foot finally catching up with me. He clocked me at eighty-five mph when I should have been going fifty-five. He gave me a stern lecture about recklessness, and I resisted telling him that if I wanted a sermon, I would go to church. Wisely, I kept my mouth shut and humbly took my speeding ticket. Of course, it didn't stop me from hitting the accelerator the moment he was out of sight.

When I returned home from the tournament a week later, the summons was in my mailbox. The total for my sin was $215. *No problem,* I thought. I wrote the check and then noticed on the paperwork that they didn't accept checks. I called the traffic court and inquired about my payment options. The clerk informed me that my choices were a money order or cash. I told her I lived in California and couldn't run down there with cash, and I wasn't paying for a money order. I could give them a credit card, but she told me they didn't take those, either. Well, my smart-aleck gene kicked in, and I said, "What, you don't have banks in that cousin-humping state of yours?" Probably not the *A* answer. I sent the check. They returned it, and my stubborn nature decided this was the hill I was going to take my stand on. I never paid the fine.

At the time, I figured I would never return to the welcoming state of North Carolina, but I was wrong. This was my second appearance in a year. I had been there two months earlier, covering another US Open at Pinehurst. I drove as carefully as an octogenarian on his way to church bingo for the week I was there. I obeyed every law they had on the books, and some I thought they might have forgotten about. Fortunately, I escaped without incident.

On this late summer day, I practiced the same prudence for

the 300 miles to the South Carolina border. The night before in my motel room in Murfreesboro, I mapped out my battle plans with the same military precision Dwight D. Eisenhower had used for the D-Day Invasion. The best strategy I surmised was to take back roads, assuming they wouldn't be as littered with law enforcement. Opting for Route 11, rather than I-95, would, I hoped, keep me away from Johnny Law Hillbilly. Ten miles into my ride, a state trooper came up next to me. I started sweating more than Richard Nixon in the 1960 televised presidential debate with JFK. I threw him a wave, and he returned the greeting, speeding on past me after his visual inspection.

The sigh of relief almost knocked the wind out of me. I pulled off to the side of the road to collect both my breath and my nerves. After a few minutes, I calmed down enough to resume traveling. Fortunately, I didn't see any other cops, though North Carolina also uses unmarked police cars, so I made certain I was adhering to all the speed-limit signs I saw. It was an unnerving way to ride. I didn't see much scenery since I was so focused on looking for any car I thought had a lurking cop. It took me over two hours to go eighty miles. One site I did see was a sign for the Craven Correctional Institution. I wondered if that would become my new home.

After passing the prison, I had had enough of two-lane back roads and shot west across Route 70 to reach Interstate 95, figuring I could blend in better on a major thoroughfare. Also, on an interstate, I would only be dealing with troopers instead of local police when I passed through small towns.

While on I-95, I saw a multitude of multicolored billboards for someplace called "Pedro's South of the Border." The signs were relentless and visually unavoidable. They had sayings like, *Chili Today, Hot Tamale!* and *You Never Sausage a Place.* There was no end to the puns. It did make the long, boring stretch of interstate a little more appealing.

The lesson I had learned in Wall, South Dakota, with the bombardment of billboards telling me how close I was to Wall Drug

Store, was this: the more signage, the bigger the tourist trap. That, of course, wasn't going to stop me from pulling off the highway. Pedro's was right over the North Carolina-South Carolina border, and I was fairly confident they didn't have an extradition treaty with their neighbor, so freedom would once again be mine.

When I exited the interstate, the road curved until a giant concrete statue of a Mexican caricature, which would be offensive today but not in 1950 when the place opened, greeted me with a sign that said *South of the Border*. The bandito's legs were split so as to provide an entrance. In its heyday, this was a must stop. It was the halfway point between New York and Florida, and many a weary father was browbeaten by his screaming children to pull over.

Now, however, Pedro's was like an aging movie actress trying way too hard to hold onto fame that left years ago. The rest stop was fifty-five years old, and time had caught up with Pedro's. The attractions that had lured in so many when they first opened now look dilapidated. The go-kart track was closed, and the main appeal was fireworks, illegal in North Carolina, but easily accessible here.

My fascination with Pedro's had caused yet another delay to my schedule, and getting to Columbia, South Carolina, by late afternoon was going to be a challenge. Fortunately, I didn't have the speed limit restrictions I had had in the previous state, so I was able to make up time.

It was around four in the afternoon when I arrived in Columbia, and I hoped the reason I came to this city was still there. He was, sitting at his familiar spot on the corner of Harden and Lady streets.

I had talked to Ernest Lee before I left for my trip, so I felt like I already knew him. I threw him a welcoming wave as I hopped off Libertad, parking next to his mobile trailer. Lee had occupied this vacant lot for years, practicing his craft, visiting with those that stopped by, and selling his artwork. Lee was nicknamed "The Chicken Man" because chickens were the primary subjects of his art. He used thin pieces of plywood as a canvas for a lot of his paintings. The more colorful the poultry, the better it sold.

An artist since the age of twelve, Lee attended Gertrude Herbert Institute of Art in Alexandria, Virginia, and Rose Hill Art Center in Aiken, South Carolina. He came to Columbia in 2000 and set up shop outdoors. Ironically, Lee resisted painting chickens at first. A friend had suggested it, but Lee wasn't swayed.

"I told him ain't nobody going to buy a painting of a chicken," Lee recounted. "I really didn't want to paint a chicken. Who would?"

His friend convinced him, and soon Lee found that there were, indeed, a significant clientele awaiting.

"I had to find my calling," Lee explained. "I wanted to do all types of painting, but someone told me to do my own stuff. I had to find me. You don't know what you are going to do before you do it. I had no idea I was going to be The Chicken Man."

Lee was similar to a group of artists known as "The Highwaymen," African American men who painted landscapes in the mid-1950s in the South Florida area. Art galleries in Florida would not display their work because of the color of their skin, so they went door to door, selling their art out of the trunks of their cars to people or local businesses.

"I heard about them, but I never met any of them," Lee said. "I wish I had. What I'm doing someone did before me."

While the medium and business model were similar, Lee's style was distinct. His depictions of the fowl had a human-like quality. They were animated and vibrant. Many wore hats, and they were always talking and singing. Because the images were unique, people recognized his talent and started snatching them up. Lee figured he had sold 5,000 of them.

"At first, I couldn't paint a straight line," Lee said. "I prayed about it, and the Lord gave me this talent. Then I was painting all the time. It was a lot of hard work. I knew I had painting in me. I just had to let it come out."

Even then, he wasn't convinced that people would want to buy what he was painting. He gave a lot of his early work away for free. Now, though, Lee was a local celebrity. His artwork was in many local businesses and homes. Though he painted other subjects, such as palmetto trees and celebrity portraits, he was comfortable with being known as The Chicken Man.

"Be what you are," he said. "Don't be what you ain't. Because if you be what you ain't, then you ain't what you are."

CHAPTER 33

It seemed whenever my soul needed recharging, St. Simons Island, Georgia was where I ended up, and the person most responsible for ensuring that my despair was erased was Michael Conyers.

I don't even remember when we met. He just showed up one day at a mutual friend's house in Long Beach, California. The three-bedroom rental was the perfect hangout, and guys in their mid-to-late twenties were floating in and out of the place all the time. I lived down the street in an apartment with my childhood friend Jeff, following him to Long Beach to go to college. Two of the house's residents were also students at Cal State Long Beach. The other occupant had just graduated. Michael was bored with St. Simons Island and had come out to Southern California for a change of scenery. I always admired him for just picking up and moving to someplace he had never been. It didn't take him long to make friends no matter where he was, and Long Beach was another example of that.

The house hosted a poker game every Friday and Saturday night. We would play cards all night and then go to breakfast at a little diner around the corner. Michael was always there, even when we weren't playing cards. Though he got along with everyone, he and I seemed to click immediately. We were kindred spirits, the same vagabond minds in search of our next adventure. We roamed the city and the surrounding areas on our motorcycles. One summer day, we watched the movie *Easy Rider* and spent the rest of the day pretending we were Peter Fonda and Dennis Hopper riding down Pacific Coast Highway. The Pacific Ocean was on our right and nothing but dreams and adventures in front of us. We rode forty miles on PCH, eventually stopping in San Clemente. There, at a bar, we talked about taking the motorcycles to Mexico one day. There was also a trip in place to ride our motorcycles across the United States. Michael told me he had friends scattered all around the country, and we could sleep on their couches or floors.

That dream died when I totaled my motorcycle in a crash. I had been rear-ended by a car as I was stopped to let a guy cross the street. I bounced twenty feet down the asphalt, and the police estimated the driver hit me at thirty miles per hour. I was at the hospital and called the house because I knew everyone would be there. They told me they had just started playing poker, and I was instructed to take the bus home. Fortunately, my friend Jeff picked me up, but he didn't take me home; he took me to the house because they needed another player for the card game.

My motorcycle was replaced with an old Honda Accord I got from someone relieved I would be in a car instead of on two wheels. My motorcycle went to the scrap heap along with my dreams of discovering America with Michael. He had lost his riding buddy, but never his friend. I vowed to him that someday I would get another motorcycle, and we would take that trip.

Other exploits didn't involve motorcycles. We would hang out until the wee hours of the morning at a local coffee house, talking and playing chess. It seemed like we both got the biggest pleasures in the simplest moments. He was always able to read my mind and tell me exactly what I needed to hear, even if I didn't want to hear it. It was a gift that few people have; it's one of the reasons we got along so well.

Michael had journeys I couldn't be a part of. He went to Mexico with some friends, spending a weekend south of the border. When he returned and told me about it, I instantly regretted not going. I figured we would get down there someday.

One day, Michael announced out of the blue that he was moving back to St. Simons Island. He had seen enough of California. Even wanderers return to where they were most comfortable. I tried to convince him to stay, but I knew he had to leave.

He had talked so much about St. Simons Island, I felt like I knew every inch of it, but it was still tough to see him go. On the day of his departure, I awoke with a hole in my heart. I drove around aimlessly for hours; the loss of my friend was a pain I had never experienced before. I told myself I would see him again, but it didn't make his absence any easier.

Today was going to be the third time I would see him since he had moved back home, and, like the previous visits, I was showing up a beaten man.

My first arrival was in 1992. I had been on my inaugural car trip across the country and ran out of money in Boston. Michael was working at a restaurant on nearby Jekyll Island, and I called him out of desperation. He told me he'd find me a waiter's job at his work, and after a twenty-six-hour drive from Massachusetts to Georgia, I was working two days later. The job earned me enough money to get home.

The second time was a few years later. I was on a newspaper assignment and was in the midst of a nasty breakup with a woman I thought I was marrying. When I flew into Jacksonville, Florida, I drove the eighty-five miles to St. Simons Island, not knowing what I wanted in life. Nothing seemed to matter. The despair was crushing my spirit. After three days with Michael, all was well again in my world.

The healing energy he possessed was what I needed most now. The grip of George's death didn't seem to be letting up. In thinking about George's death, I couldn't overcome the fear of possibly dying on this trip. I knew Michael would understand since he owned a motorcycle for years and had experienced the same thoughts. Everyone who rides will tell you the thought of crashing was in the back of their mind, but the idea of crashing gets more vivid when it happens to someone you know.

When I left Columbia, I had fewer than 250 miles until I would reach Michael's house. It was a straight shot down I-26, which connected to I-95. About twelve miles away, I emerged from the Georgia Pines to see a bridge. When I reached its apex, the Atlantic Ocean came into view. The Torres Causeway was where my sight of water met with its smell. Warmed by the late afternoon sun reflecting off the bay, I smiled.

When I pulled up to his house, Michael and his two dogs greeted me. I gave each of them a big hug. I unpacked the Harley, threw on some shorts, and the four of us took a little walk down to the beach. Not far into the walk, Michael asked how I was doing. He had been reading my dispatches about the trip I was posting online, so he knew that George had been killed. As we walked downtown, Michael said hello to anyone we encountered, and they all seemed to know him. We passed a lot of the stores and bars I remembered seeing on my last visit here five years before. Little changed with this coastal town the locals dubbed "Mayberry by the Sea." The biggest news concerning local businesses was that Frannies had closed. The owners, Fran Kelly and Lisa Cook, struggled to keep the restaurant afloat, ultimately losing the battle, and their famous Brunswick stew went along with them. That meal had been part of my healing prescription.

As we reached the pier, the shrimp boats were returning, seagulls following behind, picking any remnants of the crustaceans off the nets. It was close to sunset, and the sun's reflection was bouncing off the water. The scenery made it easier to talk about George's death. We must have spent an hour on the pier, side by side, leaning on the wooden railing, looking out on the Atlantic Ocean. It couldn't have been a better conversation. Michael talked me through the grief, as well as my anxiety about being on the motorcycle.

"This was something you were meant to do," he told me. "You

can't quit now. Think of everything you'll miss if you do."

I hemmed and hawed, making excuse after excuse as to why I shouldn't continue. He softly kept me on point, not allowing any of my reasons for quitting to become valid. As he refuted each point, he showed all the skills of a defense attorney in a court trial. I knew there was no way I was going to sway him. He had convinced me to keep going. I thought about it later that night before falling asleep and realized I had lapsed back into a familiar pattern of not seeing something through to completion. There I was on that pier, trying every trick I could think of not to finish this trip.

I don't know if Michael realized it, but he had another reason for me to keep going. I would like to believe that he was on the ride with me. Not physically, obviously, but in spirit. It appealed to his wandering soul. To see a fellow adventurer give that up was unacceptable. He had ties to the island that prevented him from going. His dad lived there, and he had a steady job that allowed him to live comfortably. Although in some ways he had surrendered to normalcy, there was no chance he was going to allow me to accept defeat. I believed he needed this journey as much as I did. He wasn't ready for this trip to end, and therefore neither was I. My sleep that night was some of the most peaceful rest I had ever experienced.

The following two days, Michael and I spent traipsing around the island like teenagers. There were no cares, and the biggest responsibility was walking the dogs twice a day on the beach, finally dipping my feet in the Atlantic, but that seemed more like fun than work. In between walks, we got into spirited matches of Putt-Putt golf and then ate lunch at local places in town. At night, Michael knew of a poker game. At around two or three in the morning, we would call it a night, and just like we had in Long Beach twenty years ago, we ended up at an all-night diner, having breakfast before we went to bed.

The time went far too fast. On the afternoon of my departure, we had lunch, and Michael slyly asked about where I was headed next. He wanted to make certain I wasn't backing out. I assured him that I had no intention to ship the motorcycle home and hop on an airplane. He was convinced that I was excited to proceed. Noticeable relief crossed his face.

Michael should have been a psychologist, and informally, he was just that. He had talked me through several tough situations. My fear was always that I got more out of this friendship than he did. I don't think I'll ever be able to fully even the ledger, but as I drove toward Orlando, Florida, I made a promise to try to do so for the rest of my life.

CHAPTER 34

The only remaining relatives who were alive besides my parents and brother lived just outside of Orlando. My father's only sibling and older sister, Carol, had been in central Florida since I was a teenager. My aunt and uncle and their son had moved to Poinciana nearly three decades ago. When they arrived back then, there was no one there. It was twenty-five miles from Disney World, but it might as well have been a thousand. Getting there was a labyrinth of side streets. Their house was the only one on a cul-de-sac called "Snapper Way," and the only neighbors behind them were my uncle's sister and her husband, who had moved with them. It was perfect for both couples. They all cherished privacy and solitude, and this community provided those qualities in abundance. Going to the store took twenty minutes, and downtown Orlando seemed much farther than the thirty miles.

I joked one time that they had better not need an ambulance because it would take the medics four days to figure out where they lived. That was frighteningly prophetic when my uncle was hit by a car on his bicycle while riding around the neighborhood. The driver left the scene, and it took my aunt and the emergency personnel two hours of searching before they finally found him lying in a ditch. He was banged up but had survived. I visited them often, but the only one I ever connected with was my aunt. I could count on one hand how many times I had seen my cousin, and I wasn't going to see him on this occasion, either. My aunt and her sister-in-law were now widows. They were in their sixties, and the two faced an uncertain world. Change was often unsettling, but especially so when one got older.

The rest of the world discovered Poinciana, and houses sprang up in the development like weeds. Now the town was spread over two counties. The commute to Orlando was tolerable and people were willing to sacrifice a little time in the car for affordable housing. I noticed all the changes from the last time I had visited, and when I pulled into my aunt's driveway, I saw that four other houses had joined hers.

"The honeymoon is definitely over," my aunt lamented as we sat in her kitchen. She saw the daily construction on her block as well as other streets. "I wish we would have bought some of the lots back then and kept it empty here."

In addition to the four homes on her small street, hundreds of other dwellings were being built around her. The main street had a stoplight, the Walmart had opened two years prior, and golf courses constructed around housing developments replaced wetlands. The very congestion of people and traffic my aunt sought to avoid found her and invaded her life. Going to the small post office had become a two-hour ordeal because of the boom in population. Driving anywhere had to be carefully considered. If an evacuation was needed because of a hurricane, it would be disastrous since there was still only one road out of town.

Her car had been broken into, and locking the doors to the house became a necessity long ago. An alarm system was installed and firearms were purchased. Her two dogs could no longer roam the neighborhood because of the increased traffic. They were as disturbed by the commotion as my aunt.

Her options were slim. She didn't want to move yet feared the crowds would win. Where to go? It seemed like finding a slice of paradise was difficult both then and now, and, as soon as it happened, others discovered it as well.

As I sat in her kitchen, she doted on me. Her refrigerator was stocked with an abundance of food that I couldn't eat in a month, much less the day and a half I was going to be there. I felt guilty having her wait on me, but it was what she had spent her life doing with my uncle and cousin. They were not the most motivated people in the world, and the father had taught his son that women were to serve men. It was different than how my mother had raised my brother and me. On one visit, we were eating dinner, and, when my uncle and cousin were finished, they got up from the table and went to the couch to watch television while the rest of us completed our meal. I thought my mother was going to have a seizure. My aunt saw nothing wrong with their rudeness.

I remembered that dinner and let her make me an extravagant lunch because she truly loved to take care of the boys in her family. She laid out four different types of cold cuts for just as many types of bread, and I had my choice of mayonnaise, mustard, ketchup, relish, and even Thousand Island dressing. My sandwich came with two styles of potato chips, carrot sticks, a green salad, sweet pickles, as well as dill. We topped off the meal with chocolate chip cookies and a slice of apple pie with vanilla ice cream.

I feared what was in store for dinner. I offered to take her out to the restaurant of her choice, but she had no desire to leave the house. She hadn't waited on anyone in a while, and this was like a vacation for her, in a way. Her smile made me feel delighted inside, or maybe it was the pie talking.

With not a lot of information about my parents, this visit with my aunt provided an opportunity to get some Reger family history. The last time I was there, I found out that my mother's father was a dreamer who never followed through on any of his visions. He also had the unenviable task of raising my mom by himself, since my mom's mother died while giving birth to her. It had explained a lot about how I was raised—the emotional distance and having to figure a lot of stuff out for myself. My mother didn't know how to be a parent; there was no one to teach her. That flaw was inadvertently passed on to her children and was probably a big reason why my brother and I didn't have kids.

On this visit, we talked about my father, and I began with some details Aunt Carol already knew. He was stern and believed he showed that he cared about me by putting food on the table and clothes on my back. When he came home from work, he had a drink and gave out signals that he didn't want to be bothered. When I was in Boy Scouts, my friend Jeff's dad was the one who took us to campouts and overnight trips. My father wasn't inclined toward such ventures.

My aunt was surprised by my father's hands-off approach to parenting. Their father had been involved in their lives. He taught my dad how to build objects, like a tree fort in the backyard. My grandfather also showed my father how to fix broken items around the house. It was how he got so handy. We rarely had to call someone to repair a broken toilet or install a garbage disposal. I was deemed to be inept at such projects and was largely shunned from helping with household repairs. My brother showed more aptitude in that area, and thus was the household's apprentice handyman.

One revelation about my father was that since he was the baby of the family, my aunt, along with my grandmother, contributed to his upbringing. It was almost like having two mothers, and it was something my father got quite used to. He never had to do much domestically because my aunt and grandmother did his laundry, cooked, cleaned, sewed any buttons that fell off his clothes, and darned any holes in his socks. It made me wonder how he existed so well with my mother, who showed little interest in being a servant to him, my brother, and me. I was fine with this arrangement, but the other two males in the family, I believe, had a harder time coping.

Aunt Carol and I talked until midnight, then I had to break the bad news to her that I was leaving in the late morning. She would have let me stay a week if I wanted, but I knew I had to press on toward

California, and there were other states I wanted to visit. I could tell that she was crushed, and I felt terrible. I did stay the following day until noon, getting two more meals. It was of some comfort to my aunt, but I could see the tears welling as I rode off down the street.

CHAPTER 35

The ride from Orlando to Ponte Vedra Beach, Florida, wasn't going to take long, but I had gotten a late start on the day and needed to make up time to ensure I made my lunch with friends. The trip was mostly on the interstates, and the 142 miles seemed to fly by. If time permitted, I would have shot across central Florida and gone to Cape Canaveral before heading north. It was an additional sixty miles, and I knew from experience that once I got on a two-lane beach road, all kinds of delays could occur. Traffic, construction, an accident, all could plug up a road in an instant, and if any one of those happened, I would have been lucky to get to Ponte Vedra Beach by Christmas.

The interstate was the smart play from an efficiency standpoint. It was almost all four lanes from door to door. I caught I-4 in Orlando, and that sent me north and east until it ended at I-95. From there, it was sixty-five miles until Highway 98. It soon joined I-295, and nine miles later, I was on Route 202. In twenty minutes, I was eating lunch with my friends Dave and Dave.

Like most of my friends whom I encountered on the road, they asked me how the trip was progressing, and I was more than happy to fill them in on my exploits. As lunch was winding down, I told them I was looking for unusual people and places, and they immediately told me to head south on A1A toward St. Augustine, where I would see something of interest. When I asked them what it was, they both chuckled, and one Dave said, "You can't miss it. It's on the right side of the highway before you get to St. Augustine."

The mystery intrigued me, and even though I would be headed south instead of east, I accepted the backtracking. From Ponte Vedra Beach, it was thirty-two miles, so that much regression I could handle. Besides, it would get me back on the coast, and I could ride with the scenic Atlantic Ocean to my left and the Guana River on my right.

Just as I entered the Vilano Beach area of St. Augustine, Dave's cryptic roadside riddle was revealed. Sticking out from a cluster of palm trees was a castle that looked like it had been plucked from Ireland and set to rest in the most unlikely of locations. It was stunning, and I was immediately drawn to it. I turned down Third Street to a gate that provided a better view of the majestic structure.

Though I knew I shouldn't have, I climbed over the gate and went up to the front door of the castle. My trespassing went unnoticed until I ran into a few teenagers who lived in the house in front of the castle. I inquired about the structure I had been gawking at, and one of the kids ran and fetched her dad. Rusty Ickes was extremely guarded when I met him, which was completely understandable, since I had trespassed. He was a peaceful man, however, and despite his initial mistrust, he warmed up after I profusely apologized for coming on the grounds without his approval.

I blamed the captivating beauty of the castle for my transgression. It was like I couldn't help it. I was lured by its beauty and foolishly walked up to it in a sense of hypnotic awe. After about my fourth apology, Ickes looked at me and said, "You want to see the inside?"

The instant I met him, I sensed Ickes was an extremely serene man. His movements were very deliberate. No step or word was wasted, and he spoke in measured tones. His personality carried over to the castle, with Ickes having meticulously thought out every part of the structure. A deeply spiritual man, Rusty told me he wanted the castle to be a remembrance of Jesus Christ, and there were signs hinting at his deep spirituality. The front of the castle had a large cross above the entrance. There was another smaller cross on the east end that faced Jerusalem, and the blocks of concrete atop the towers were made to look like the crown of thorns placed on Christ's head at the crucifixion.

The design had a lot to do with Rusty's Roman Catholic upbringing, his religious education received while growing up in Bermuda. He still had a lot of the Caribbean in him. Tall, bearded, with long hair in a ponytail, he wore cargo shorts, a T-shirt, and sandals.

As Ickes opened the large wooden door, he gave me an oral history of his art that had turned into a building. The idea to erect a castle came to him in a series of dreams that told him to build it in his backyard, and the visions kept coming. The work had three focuses—let the elements flow through freely, create a cavernous area for a humbling effect, and construct a structurally sound building.

Rusty had owned this two-acre property across from the beach since 1976 and decided he would follow the apparition. He, along with his friend Ottis Sadler, started the exterior on May 1, 1984. They set out to design this as a landscape sculpture resembling an Irish castle, though neither had been to Ireland and both knew little of that type of architecture.

"The building was simply allowed to exert its own insistent will," Rusty explained. "I knew nothing of what I was building. The visions were what guided me."

All the material used to build the castle was gathered at construction or demolition sites. The workers had either leftover material they didn't want or were tearing something down. Ickes, who had a construction background, knew exactly what was needed.

"It was the proverbial rejected stone." Rusty chuckled. "In some cases, we were doing them a favor by taking it away."

Rusty and Ottis used split-face concrete blocks, steel-reinforced rods, and poured concrete. Ickes and Sadler worked side by side, laying every block themselves. After four years, the castle was fifty-one feet high, featured four towers, and weighed more than seven million pounds. There were eighty-eight windows, but no glass; the openings allowed wind and light to flow freely throughout the castle.

"When we reached that point, there was a sense of completeness," Ickes recalled. "It was its own being. We just made sure it was an honor to Jesus Christ. We wanted to stay true to that vision."

The castle needed a name, and again, it came to Ickes in a dream. He wanted to title it in honor of his friend, Sadler. Ickes initially wrote it down as *Castle Otttis*, the third *t* a typographical error. He liked the exotic nature of the name, however, and kept it. I pointed out that the three Ts together looked like the crucifixion of Christ, with the "good thief," Saint Dismas to Christ's right, and the "unrepentant thief," Gestas, to his left. Ickes smiled knowingly and didn't say a word.

Explaining this architecture to the city bureaucrats was another matter. They weren't thrilled with the project, and about halfway through the construction, a code enforcement officer visited Ickes and informed him that he needed a permit. Through a little divine intervention, the city made the mistake of designating the castle as a garage, and work was allowed to continue.

When the exterior was finished, Ickes was unsure of what to do with the inside. A woodworker named Lee Carpenter appeared at his door one day, inquiring about the castle. He told Ickes he would handle the entire interior. Carpenter erected eight cypress wood staircases that spiraled in different directions and forms. The second story had an altar, pews, pulpit, and bishop chair made from southern heart pine pulled from an old general store built in the early 1900s. It took Carpenter three years to finish the interior, completing work in 1991.

While Ickes was a Christian man, Carpenter put touches of other religions in the castle. He carved a Star of David in the wood on the second story, and a yin-yang symbol adorned the floor on the third level.

When it was completed, Ickes began hosting a church service on the last Sunday of the month. Although it was intended for all faiths, Ickes didn't call it a nondenominational service but an interdenominational service.

"There was too much negativity in the world," Rusty stated. "I wanted a place of love. That was what this is."

MTV producers were scouting locations for a proposed show called *Fear*, and they thought the castle would be a perfect set. One of them called Rusty. When he didn't respond, two people from the music network showed up soon after, knocking on his door. They tried to convince him that this would be a great scary place. He said little, walked them to the castle, and showed them the inside. After experiencing the beauty and peace of the castle, the two left, apologizing for wasting his time.

"This was not about fear," Ickes declared. "This was about love."

That powerful emotion was what Ickes wanted Castle Otttis to portray, and he had enthusiastically shared his vision via free tours for school children, senior organizations, and other groups. People from all over the country came and visited, and many from Great Britain marveled at how it mirrored what they had at home.

"They always say this should be in their backyard, not mine," Ickes said. "I always have to laugh at that."

Photographing the castle was permitted, but Rusty was quick to get out of any frame taken.

"This was about the art, not me," Ickes exclaimed. "I don't own it. In some ways, it owns me. I am just a part of it."

The one attribute Rusty didn't count on was the most powerful. It was the overriding sense of peace people felt when they entered the castle. For me, it was an almost celestial sensation being inside Castle Otttis. Even though I had trudged up two flights of stairs, my breathing was relaxed, my body felt lighter, and my mind was never clearer. I stood at one of the windows that faced the ocean and listened to the calmness of the outside. A light breeze made a slight whistle as it passed through the cinder blocks.

Ickes smiled; he knew what I was experiencing. It was an

emotion that he had seen in others countless times. He interrupted the silence and told me he would be back at his house and to come there when I was ready, but to take my time.

I followed his advice. In a state of meditation, I stared at the altar, thinking of nothing but seeing everything. Then I pivoted back to a window and gazed out at the ocean with a sense of rapture. My body was relaxed, and any stress I had carried vanished. The clarity I felt was gripping—and terrifying. I had my own vision in Castle Otttis. The rest of the trip seemed to splay out in front of me. There was no itinerary, per se, but I could see where I was going and what I might be experiencing in the next couple of weeks.

After about an hour, I made my way back to Rusty's house. He appeared before I could knock on the door, inviting me for dinner and to stay the night. I thanked him for the offer but informed him I should be on my way. I felt like I had imposed enough. I also didn't want to distract from my still-present tingling euphoria. I said my goodbyes, got on the motorcycle, and headed northwest. I was in Valdosta, Georgia, before sunset, the feeling still pleasantly trapped inside my soul.

CHAPTER 36

The phone rang at five minutes after eleven in the morning in the shabby motel where I was staying in Valdosta, Georgia. The front desk clerk rudely asked me if I was leaving today. The time to depart had been five minutes earlier, but I had told another employee that I was running a little late, and she didn't seem to have a problem with it. This woman, however, wasn't willing to give me any extra time.

I had learned early on in this trip that, at an establishment like this, it was far wiser to pay in cash. I had been charged an extra night at a motel in Fort Bragg, California, and trying to get the sixty dollars taken off my credit card was impossible. Mastercard said the charge was legit, and when I called the proprietor of the offending motel, he suddenly forgot how to speak English. I chalked it up to what I called *road lessons* and felt fortunate I was only out sixty dollars.

This clerk was hinting at trying to get me to pay for an extra night, but we both knew that wasn't happening. She decided the best way to handle this situation was to berate me on the phone until I bent to her demand to leave immediately. I told her I would be out in about ten minutes. She didn't seem to care much for that response, so I told her it would probably be more like twenty.

"Keep up the attitude," I informed her, "and I won't leave until noon."

She hung up the phone and began a passive-aggressive contest, which resulted in a test of wills. First, she sent the cleaning woman down to pound on the door. I anticipated this move and put out the do-not-disturb sign. She countered by having the gardener rev up the leaf blower outside my window. I turned the television up louder. She thought she had me when she cut off my telephone. I used my cell phone instead. I knew she was going to cancel out my hotel key, so I left the door ajar when I went across the street to grab something to eat.

I delayed my shower and took my time packing. When I finally arrived at the front desk, smoke spewed from her ears. She told me to have a nice day through gritted teeth. Who won the war? Neither of us. She heaped more aggravation on her already stressed-out day, and I spent the next forty miles chastising myself for engaging in something so ridiculous. It was a supreme waste of energy as I could have been pondering more cerebral issues.

Usually, these types of confrontations don't bother me. I had spent the past two years trying to rid myself of senseless interactions and focused on more positive uses of my time. Now and then, however, my competitive nature sprung up, and I would rise to one of these pointless challenges.

As I rode away, replaying the morning in my mind, trying to purge it before I beat myself up any further, I stumbled across a beautiful cotton field in bloom, white puffs bursting out of the knee-high plants. I turned Libertad around and parked on the other side of Route 84 and walked toward the field, excited to see this raw material for the first time. The lea was large, and it made me wonder who picked all that cotton. I doubted there was a machine to do it, but I saw no activity at all in the field, even though the crop looked ready to be harvested.

Pieces of cotton had fallen from plants now soiled on the ground. I pulled a fresh handful from a boll and noticed how easily it separated from the branch. It was extremely soft and felt comforting in the palm of my hand as I made a fist. I stood in the sun and slowly pumped the cotton, consciously monitoring my breathing as I squeezed. Though it was hot and sweat poured off my face, I stood there for ten minutes repeating the motion, tightly pressing the cotton through my fingers, watching it, trying in vain to escape my grasp.

By the time I got back on the Harley, my frame of mind was once again right. I continued down the road, thinking purer thoughts as the cotton fields followed me on both sides. By the time I reached Blakely, Georgia, on Route 27, I was roasting. The 92 degree air temperature had combined with 86 percent humidity. The sun had won this round, and I sought shelter. I found a gas station and pulled in for some relief. I went into the bathroom and soaked my black T-shirt. After my feeble attempt to cool off, I basked in the store's air-conditioning. To stall further from getting on the Harley, I bought some lottery tickets, a purchase made out of sheer boredom.

After my second bottle of water, I could no longer procrastinate my departure. The clerk was sympathetic to my plight and allowed me to put some ice cubes in my do-rag, which would help keep my head from overheating while under the half-shell helmet I wore. My shirt got another soaking, but I knew this was pointless. It would be bone-dry four exits up the freeway.

By the time I reached Montgomery, Alabama, it was three hours past noon, and the heat seriously affected me. I found it hard to breathe in the stifling humidity, and I was trying to shake off the dizziness that had affected me for the last thirty miles. I wanted to get to Birmingham, which was a mere ninety miles away, but thought it was better to stay where I was. My body was telling me something was wrong, and I listened. I found a local hospital emergency room and went inside. After an hour of sitting, my name got called. The nurse asked me a bunch of questions, took my temperature and my blood pressure, and left the room. The doctor came in shortly thereafter and told me my blood pressure was through the roof. I wasn't surprised since, added to the intense heat, I had existed on a diet of fried, high-fat food for the last three months. He gave me a prescription for blood pressure medicine and told me I was also dehydrated. He had an IV put in my arm, and I drank water while I waited for it to empty. That night at dinner, I added more water to my diet and had a salad, feeling like I had made a major life change.

| | | |

Saturday morning in the fall in Alabama meant only one thing—University of Alabama football. The Crimson Tide was playing Arkansas in a few hours, and the sense of anticipation was already building four hours before kickoff. I went into a diner for breakfast, and I was the only one in the restaurant who wasn't dressed in red. Most of the people had some sort of shirt with the Alabama insignia. It went well with all the cars out in the parking lot that were adorned with Crimson Tide stickers. At one point, an overenthusiastic fan yelled, "Roll Tide Roll!" in the middle of the dining room. The rest of the patrons started yelling and hollering, and I found myself in the middle of a pep rally.

It was interesting to witness the fervent crowd so dedicated to a college football team. I never experienced such allegiance. In Los Angeles, sports fans were known for arriving late to games and leaving early. The team was secondary. It was all about being seen. Courtside at Laker games was, at one point, the most coveted ticket in town, not because of the success of the NBA basketball team but because of all the face time a person would get on the national television broadcasts.

I would not see Alabama defeat Arkansas, twenty-four to thirteen. My day was going to be spent with another celebrity. He was not as well-known as a star Alabama coach or football player, but he probably contributed something far more valuable to the state.

Joe Minter was an artist who lived in a modest home in southwest Birmingham, just around the corner from Martin Luther

King Jr. Drive. I pulled up to the blue single-story house surrounded by an assortment of what many would describe as junk. I looked at potted plants on the left side of the driveway and heaps of scrap metal on the right, all leading up to the porch. That was where I found Minter's wife, Hilda. Even though it was oppressively hot and humid, she was resting in a chair, looking out onto the street.

She greeted me like she knew I was coming. I told her I wanted to see her husband. He wasn't home, she informed me, but said I was more than welcome to walk around the property and view his work.

"He's at an anti-war rally," Hilda told me. "But he should be back in a bit."

Before I toured the yard museum, I sat with Hilda and asked her how her husband discovered his talent.

"He didn't know he had this gift at first," Hilda explained. "He just got touched by God Himself."

Minter never took art classes. He was a craftsman who made school furniture. When his employer went out of business, Minter worked in construction, then road crews and other blue-collar jobs.

In 1989, he told his wife he got what he called a vision from God and began a project in his backyard to illustrate the struggle of African Americans in this country. One piece led to another, and soon Minter's backyard was filled up with different exhibits.

One scene was of the Birmingham church bombing that killed four little girls. Each of their names was on a separate folding chair. Another piece depicted a jail cell, statues of dogs around it with a police officer. One of the most moving pieces to me was a sink with a sign over it that said, *WHITES ONLY*. It was a simple piece, but very moving.

His art was a mixture of sculpture and scripture, with a religious and political message in most of his work. As Minter gathered material from the side of roads, thrift stores, and flea markets, Mrs. Minter wasn't quite sure what to make of her husband's mission.

"I just couldn't understand it," Hilda recalled. "I said, 'My God, what are you doing?" He knew what he was doing."

Minter had always been talented with his hands. Hilda recalled when he was a child, he built a seesaw for him and the children to play on, and also crafted his own bicycle out of discarded parts.

"He was always handy," Hilda gushed. "He could fix anything and build anything as well."

The gift was now shared with others. The village was open for anyone to see, and if Hilda and Joe were home, chances were they would come out and act as docents, answering any questions someone had.

"I don't get many visitors," Hilda said. "It was nice to have the company."

About that time, Joe returned from the anti-war rally, claiming it a huge success. It even gave him some ideas for future works of art. Peace was a central theme in his work. In the far corner was a parcel of land they were able to buy when the home on that property burned. On it was a display questioning the Iraq war.

Minter's father fought in World War I and was a mechanic. When he returned home from combat, however, the only job he could get was a caretaker at a Whites-only cemetery. His plot was at Grace Hill Cemetery, bordering Minter's house.

The village was a continuous process, as was Minter's artwork. In a house across the street, aptly named The Art House, current works were being stored, ending up in museums or out in the yard.

"It's so full, you can hardly walk in there," Hilda said.

"I know everything that's in there," Minter countered. "I will use all of it at some point."

Every piece that Minter built had a meaning and was close to his heart. The message was there and available for anyone to hear. We just had to go and listen.

CHAPTER 37

The day was already dark, but I didn't realize how black it was going to get. My goal was to leave Birmingham in the morning and make my way toward Clarksdale, Mississippi. The nasty remnants of Hurricane Rita, however, put a stop to any travel I wanted to do on this fall Sunday in the deep South. The rain began in the late morning, the thick, heavy clouds eliminating most of the light. The downpour only intensified, and my decision, although frustrating, was the right one. I wasn't going anywhere today; instead, I was going to be a hostage in my motel room.

There was no cover for Libertad, and she was getting drenched. I felt terrible because I could do nothing to help her. I had my own battle to wage, though. The boredom of being confined to a dingy motel room with a television that had twelve channels, and none of them particularly interesting, was my own little personal hell.

By the afternoon, I was somewhat saved by professional football. That would help stave off the tedium. The only problem was that the games were constantly interrupted by thunderstorm updates from television weather women with either bleached blonde hair and enhanced breasts or men with bad combovers, fake tans, and whitened teeth. So, while the former beauty queen and failed character actor parading as meteorologists told me that it was raining and that the whole state was on tornado watch, I wondered if this motel would stand up to even a modest breeze.

This establishment was one of those one-story dumps on the side of the highway that was fronted by a gravel driveway. With faded paint and a checkered past, such motels were often the last refuge of the desperate road traveler. There were three types of guests. The first was the most obvious—the drug addict, hooker, or parolee on the run, who paid in cash and, as long as they don't burn the place down, had a hideout.

The second classification was the hapless guy who was falling asleep on the road. He had underestimated the time it would take him to get to a decent part of town and needed to get into a room. He doesn't know the area and is afraid he would pass out and cross over into oncoming traffic, killing a family of seven who were returning from a church function.

The third scenario involved the guy who was too cheap to pay for a safe motel, and too scared to sleep on the side of the road. That would be me. These motels were fairly secure and the interaction with the other occupants limited. As long as there was a deadbolt on the door, there was a flimsy feeling of security.

Unfortunately, this was not the case at the Fleabag Inn. I was in what appeared to be the five-year reunion of cell block C. They had decided that I had crashed their little get-together and weren't at all happy about it.

I stayed in the room and prayed they didn't realize the door was as thick as a communion wafer, then I turned the television up to drown out the cries of those poor lambs who happened across their path.

By four o'clock, I was famished and had no food in the room. The rain was taking a short break, so I decided to make a run for it. I opened the door, looked out, saw no one, and walked briskly to the bike. I hopped on, fired it up, and took off before my felonious neighbors realized I was a vulnerable target. I went across the intersection to a mini mall, featuring the one type of restaurant that can be found in most cities across the United States. No matter how small a town was, one could be assured there was a Super Asian Buffet, and I figured it would be an appropriate last meal.

The mystery, besides the meat, was how Asian immigrants find these towns and how they know another countryman hasn't squatted there first. Do they all sit in an outdoor square in Outer Mongolia, divvying up which family was going to open one of these buffet-style restaurants, like a mobster family carves up territories? I imagine the conversation goes something like this:

"Ok, I get Minot, North Dakota."

"That's fine, my family will take Plum Springs, Tennessee."

These restaurants had become small-town America's answer to fine dining. The proprietors had a rock-solid business model that rarely failed. Give the customers a myriad of unhealthy culinary choices that were mostly high in fat, sodium, calories, and carbohydrates, and they will beat down the doors to get in and gorge. Some of the typical menu items were sweet and sour pork, chow mein noodles, fried shrimp, egg rolls, fried rice, and gas station-quality sushi. The central theme was Asian, but there was other artery-clogging cuisine available. Pizza, spaghetti, and hot dogs were in the trough, and those with fingers that looked like Vienna sausages pawed at the food like they were starving, but with the rolls of fat poking through the bottoms of polyester shirts and the tops of matching pants, proved otherwise.

I looked like a male model compared to most of the customers there, and it made me feel good about myself as I went back for thirds. I actually found chicken and green beans. Vegetables were as welcome here as Dr. Atkins, and seeing one almost sent me into shock.

I was tidying up my ice-cream bowl when I looked outside and saw that the rain had returned. I had eaten enough for a Mormon family.

The distance between the restaurant and my motel was about one mile, which didn't seem like a lot, but when getting pelted with stinging water, it quadruples the mileage. I waddled outside with a full belly and, from afar, there she was, my vision of loveliness.

Her name—who cares? I sure didn't. I just knew that, for the next twelve hours, she was going to make my life a little less lonely.

She wanted a ride over to the Kmart; of course, she did. *There must be a sale on jug wine,* I thought. It was a little out of the way, but I was feeling like I needed some Karma after the self-assault on my digestive tract, so I agreed to shuttle her over there.

She was in her late forties but looked older. Years of drinking and abusive men will pack the pounds and years on a woman. She was short and having trouble slinging her leg over the seat to get on the bike. She was not very flexible, either, and I was guessing physical education was an elective course when she was in high school.

I took her over to the store and dropped her off. She said she would be over to my hotel room in an hour. Usually, I would take that as a brush-off, a line uttered instead of saying thanks for the ride. With her, I knew she would be there. Her options were limited.

Like an unwelcome relative visiting on a holiday, she was right on time. She knocked on the motel room door, and I opened it, pretending I was glad to see her. She was carrying a bottle of vodka, two liters of Sprite, and a six-pack of beer. I would have to fight her for a taste of any of it.

"Make me a drink," she exclaimed as she came in the door. Her speech suggested she had had a few pops on the walk over. She was wearing black stretch pants, a blouse, and tennis shoes. She sat on the other bed and drank, telling me her sad tale. They all have a sad tale. This one was pretty pedestrian as they go. Her boyfriend of fourteen years cheated on her with a younger woman and hit her when she confronted him. She had a hint of swelling around her right eye that she had tried to camouflage with as much cheap makeup as Kmart would sell her.

The trick was to pretend I was interested in her woes. Nodding helps; an occasional "That's awful" worked as well. During the conversation, she gave me clues that she was looking for company.

"He kicked me out of the hotel we were staying at," she said. "I am not sure where I am going to stay tonight."

She was making herself comfortable on the second bed, but if she was going to stay in this room, she would be sleeping in the same bed as me. I told her that. She put up a small fight about how she hadn't slept with another man in thirteen years and talked about how she didn't want to cheat on her boyfriend. But would she leave him? Doubtful. You didn't think she was going to leave him, did you? He'll get sick of the other chick, or she'll sober up and leave. He will go to the nearest bar and find this one and she'll go back. It had probably happened on several occasions before.

"If I sleep with you, you are going to break my heart," she said. "I can't have you break my heart."

Listen, I don't want your heart, I don't want your soul, I don't even particularly want you, but it's raining out, and I'm bored, and you are here, and that's the way it is.

Of course, I didn't tell her this. I convinced her I wouldn't break her heart, and, after four more drinks, she believed me.

We rolled around on the bed for a while, and I tried a little foreplay with her to show her I cared. Three minutes tops, then it was time. It didn't take long. She wailed, and I grunted, and in a matter of minutes, I was done and started to fall asleep. She, on the other hand, was all aglow. That was bad for me since now she wanted to talk and talk about topics that included me—or us.

One encounter and they started picking out china patterns. She asked me how long I was staying, and I told her for another day, so she didn't completely flip out. In the back of her vodka-soaked brain, she plotted on how to keep me there for another month or how she could move out to California and set up a house with me.

Finally, the liquor provided the knockout punch, and she fell into a light snore. I stayed awake for another hour, wondering how much further this was going to drive her to the bottom of the bottle.

In the morning, she surprised me with another go-round. I

looked at it as a going-away present. She viewed it as the beginning of the rest of our lives.

She dressed and left for work, which was at a dry cleaner. She manned the counter, but it was the Mexican woman who worked in the back who had the keys. The owner, a Pakistani, was a good judge of character and trusted an undocumented worker more than he did her.

I told her I'd pick her up from work, and then we could go have lunch. She didn't believe me, and I was impressed she figured it out. I said goodbye and went back to the motel. I showered, dressed, packed, and loaded the Harley in less than an hour. I left Birmingham and headed toward Mississippi.

As I rode, a twinge of guilt creeped into my thoughts. I tried to block it out, but it was starting to get to me. Two miles out of town, I saw a billboard for a religious radio station. The ad was pretty radical: *Repent, or Burn in Hell!* I had soiled the South with my sinning seed, and I wondered as I rode, *Can even God forgive me?*

CHAPTER

38

There were still clouds in the sky and in my mind as I aimed Libertad toward Mississippi, the ones overhead providing me with protection from the ninety-degree heat and high humidity. The same could not be said for the ones swirling around in my head. They offered no refuge from my dubious evening in Alabama. Still, I pressed on, hoping the Magnolia State would provide a sunnier day.

My first destination in Mississippi, however, would be the sight of one of this country's bleakest historical events. Two hours after I left Birmingham, I stopped for gas at a little Mississippi town called Scooba. I continued west on Highway 16 for about an hour until I reached Philadelphia. I wanted to go down the same road that was the site where three civil rights workers were killed in 1964.

James Chaney, Andrew Goodman, and Michael Schwerner had been working for an organization that was trying to register African Americans to vote. The leader of the Mississippi Ku Klux Klan ordered Schwerner assassinated. Members of the Klan showed up at the Mt. Zion Baptist Church in Philadelphia, looking for the twenty-four-year-old. When he wasn't there, they beat some of the congregation and burned the church to the ground.

Schwerner, along with Chaney and Goodman, went to see the site of the arson. On their way back to Meridian, they were stopped by Neshoba County Deputy Sheriff Cecil Price. Price, who was a member of the KKK, arrested them for the burning of the church.

They were held in jail for several hours and then released on bail. As they were driving late in the night on County Road 492, they were stopped again by Price, who put them in the back of his car and took them up a country road, where they were met by other Klan members. The group went down an unmarked road and executed the young men, then buried them side by side in a dam. It took two months for the FBI to find the bodies, tipped off by a Meridian Highway Patrol officer. The case, dubbed "Mississippi Burning" by the FBI, sparked national outrage and was the catalyst for Congress passing the Voter Rights Act later in 1964.

It was daylight when I traversed the same path Schwerner, Chaney, and Goodman took that fateful night. County Road 492, County Road 515, and Highway 19 all had an eerie feel. It had been more than forty years, but I still felt the desolation of those two-lane roads, only trees and weeds on both sides. I thought about the horror they must have faced and envisioned the three of them being shot by members of the Klan, who probably celebrated the dubious achievement. I wondered if they were killed instantly or if they suffered. Were they still alive when they were dumped in the dam? How could those who knew live with themselves? What about those who weren't an accessory but were told later? I tried not to imagine what those murdered men faced that night, but it was hard to put it out of my mind. I sped off once I reached Highway 19, the chills reaching up and down my spine on a hot summer day.

I stopped in town for lunch at a local restaurant. Coincidentally, one of the men who had been involved in the killings had been sentenced two months earlier, after a trial that came four decades later. The local news was illustrating Edgar Ray Killen and his part in the murders. He was the only one in the group who saw serious jail time. In a way, it was payback for what happened in the '60s. He was now eighty years old and confined to a wheelchair. The state declared victory with the sixty-year sentence. The television reports declared justice had been served. What struck me while I watched news reports at the trial was a local preacher who repeated several times how the town was not like that anymore. It was almost like he was trying to convince himself, in addition to the reporters he was talking to.

Understandably, there were no plaques in the city marking the event. It was a piece of history they would rather forget, and I didn't blame them. The town had other issues. Downtown was barren. Main Street had several closed businesses. The area didn't have much to choose from as far as restaurants. I settled for a Kentucky Fried Chicken. Inside was a mixture of Blacks and Whites eating and talking, but at a distance from each other, a sort of implied segregation.

It reminded me of my time in Georgia, working as a waiter at the Jekyll Island Radisson, a job that my friend Michael had gotten me on my first trip across the country in the early nineties. One of the coworkers I gravitated to was an African American busboy named Johnny. He was in his mid-fifties, short, with a slight frame and a balding dome. At first glance, he appeared broken down but was much stronger than initial appearances would indicate. His hands were bigger than they should have been, considering his height, and they were weathered from his fingertips to the base of his palms with scars, callouses, and wrinkles. They accessorized well with his worn face. Years of hard work and an even harder life showed in the lines running on his cheeks from his nose to his ears, like rings chronicling the age of a sequoia tree. Those coffee-colored eyes, though, told a sad tale of a life beaten down by others.

Despite five decades of hardship, his demeanor was outgoing and friendly. Any resentment he held toward others, any justifiable mistrust of strangers, was never revealed. I found him to be one of the most pleasant, amiable people I had ever worked with. Johnny and I would talk about almost everything, but he was apprehensive to divulge too much about his life. His wife had died, but I never learned how. He was living alone in a single apartment and didn't have other family close by. He worked and he slept, and that was about it. Once a week, Johnny and his friends might go to the local bar and drink a beer or two. Isolation seemed to be an amicable relationship. Johnny bummed rides from other employees or took the bus to work. If the bus stopped running and he couldn't get a ride home, he walked back from the island to the landlocked town of Brunswick, where he lived, nearly fifteen miles away.

He seemed to enjoy slowly opening up to me, and I got the feeling I knew more about him in ninety days than anyone he worked with or his small circle of friends. It might have been because he knew I wasn't staying. It was far easier to confide in someone who was departing and can't hurt you than to spill secrets that could become public.

One day, as my time there was coming to an end, he and I were sitting alone eating lunch. Michael had the day off, and Johnny and I had just finished a trying gathering of about a hundred women from a local ladies' club. I found Southern women with self-perceived, high-ranking social status to be contemptible when they weren't being completely loathsome. Their behavior was condescending and phony, and they have no redeemable qualities. They would run wait staff like dogs and then leave two dollars for a $100 check. They called me "sir" in a way that accented their insincerity. Some of the women called Johnny "Boy." It made my blood boil and, while he took it as normal, it made me want to spit in their coffee. Not that I ever did that. No, that would be wrong.

After a four-hour shift that seemed like two weeks, we were in our break room enjoying our meal and usual conversation. I had four days remaining and was eager to get home. I was also just as enthusiastic to get Johnny to take my job.

"You know I'm leaving next week, right?" I asked him.

"Yes, I remember."

"You should take my job when I go. You would be a better waiter than I am."

"Naw, not for me."

"Why not? It's more money, and I could put a word in for you."

"No," he said, his voice rising.

"I think you would—" I began to say, but Johnny cut me off.

"No," he said, his voice growing even louder. "It ain't nothing I want to do."

He got up and took his plate into the kitchen, almost snarling at me as he passed. I couldn't figure out why he had gotten so upset. I thought I was trying to help him. I must have sat there alone for a good ten minutes, rerunning the conversation. Just as I was about to give up, it finally dawned on me. Johnny was never going to be a waiter because of the color of his skin. The clientele wouldn't allow it. He was just good enough in their minds to take the dirty plates away but not deemed worthy to serve them their food. It sickened me for the rest of the day.

I found Johnny with the dishwashers and approached him. He wanted nothing to do with me or an apology that he would never have accepted. I should have known better than to suggest such a proposition. If I didn't know how it worked down here, I should have. Dangling hope to a man who would never be allowed to reach for it was a social crime worse than any that those appalling women could have committed.

While I was eating my fried chicken on this day, I wondered what happened to Johnny. He had left not long after I did, and Michael didn't have any idea where he went. As I hoped he found a better life, I saw an elderly Black woman approach the counter to order her lunch. The young, White girl serving her was courteous and respectful.

I had seen the same at other places in the town. I saw a White man open a door for a Black woman and a Black and a White teenager walking down the street talking and laughing. My time there was brief, and I know it can't be concrete proof, but I didn't see any signs of the old South. It made me hopeful.

Down the road from Philadelphia, on the other side of town from where the three civil rights workers were murdered, were two casinos. They were monstrous structures; one was called Silver Star and the other, Golden Moon. Both had hotels attached to them and were part of the Pearl River Resort. They looked out of place, but it might keep alive a dying town. More importantly, it may replace the reputation Philadelphia had tried to shed for forty years.

The following two hours were spent in anticipation of my next destination. I was headed toward the Mississippi Delta and the birthplace of the blues. Blues music was one of my favorites, and I was going to be immersed in the area that saw the blossoming careers of legends such as John Lee Hooker, Muddy Waters, Willie Dixon, and B.B. King.

King's hometown was on the way, off Route 82 in Indianola, Mississippi. It was a small town, and, other than the sign greeting me when I entered, nothing else had been done to mark the legend's contribution.

"They were talking about building a museum," said Charlie, a barber in town who was attending to my shockingly long curls. "They haven't gotten it started though, don't know if they ever will."

The town was struggling; there wasn't much keeping it going, and it could probably have used a tourist attraction. It was too bad there wasn't a museum honoring King. Charlie could have been a docent if they ever did erect a place honoring the blues icon. He told me the story about how King's famous guitar, "Lucille," got its name. King was playing an old juke joint in Arkansas early in his career. It was a classic shack, lit by Christmas lights strung around the walls, no tables or chairs, the cold night warmed by a fire in an old oil drum. While King played, two men got into a fight and knocked the drum over, setting the place on fire. King, as well as the patrons, fled out the doors. In the confusion and panic, King forgot his guitar. He ran back into the burning building to retrieve it, nearly getting trapped in the inferno. He barely escaped, managing to save his musical instrument. When he inquired about why the two men were brawling in the club, someone told him it was over a woman named Lucille. He named his guitar after her as a reminder never to take another risk like that.

I thanked Charlie for the haircut and the story, tipping him more than the cost of the cut. I got back on the motorcycle and headed up Highway 49 toward another area rich in blues history.

Clarksdale, Mississippi, was about an hour north of Indianola. At the intersection of Route 49 and Highway 61 was a sign marking the famous spot where legendary blues guitarist Robert Johnson was said to have sold his soul to the devil in exchange for musical immortality.

Around the corner was a barbecue place named Abe's, a tremendous little restaurant with some of the best barbecue I had ever eaten. It had been in the same location since 1924 and was simple, cheap, and delicious. It was the perfect early dinner before I checked into the Shack Up Inn. My lodging was on a former plantation, just outside of town, and there were old sharecropper shacks to sleep in. They had air-conditioning, but little else had been done to them. Wood floors, tin siding in the shower, and a big front porch to sit on in the evening. It was pretty cool.

Bill, one of the owners, was a great guy, and he and some of the locals sat out in the early evening to drink and talk.

"We are out here most nights, solving the world's problems," Bill said.

I sat with them a spell and enjoyed the company. They were all nice people and gave me a lot of insight into the area. When it got dark, I got on the Harley and rode into town to see if I could find anything to do. Since I hit Clarksdale on a Tuesday night, it was going to be a challenge to quell my boredom. The live music didn't get going until Thursday night, and the area was desolate. I found an open beer joint called Messengers on Dr. Martin Luther King Road. An old woman was playing slots, and no one else was in the place. The bartender, George, was sleeping in a chaise lounge he had set up behind the bar. When I approached the bar, he shot up, somewhat startled he had another customer.

I drank a beer, and we talked about why the town was so quiet, even by Tuesday night standards. George thought it had a lot to do with the casinos that had been built up Highway 61 about forty miles from Clarksdale. I asked him if anyone had music I could catch, and he thought there was one place down old Route 61 that might.

When I showed up, the place looked pretty scary. There were crack whores walking up and down the block and a club called Red's with smoked windows so you couldn't see inside.

Red's was an original juke joint, a small, dingy box of a room with homemade decorations, bottled beer, and great music.

The only ones in the place that night were two rather large Black men and Red himself, a middle-aged African American with a quick smile. They were watching baseball on television, which, along with a small lamp behind the bar, provided the only light in the place. When I walked inside, there was an uneasy feeling on both of our parts. They probably thought I, in my biker outfit, was going to toss the place, and I thought they could take about four seconds to beat the ever-living crap out of me.

It was those kinds of preconceived notions that led to a sort of détente between us, and, after a couple of beers, we all let down our guards and had a good time. They even felt bad that I wasn't hearing any blues music and turned down the television and put on a compact disc featuring blues artists I had never heard of before. Red talked to me above the music, telling me all the acts he had had in his place. I asked him how long he had been open, and Red just smiled.

"I've been doing this too damn long to remember," Red replied.

I was bummed I wasn't going to be around Saturday because he was having a little jam at his place with three bands, and it sounded fantastic. I left a little after eleven, thanking them all and shaking their hands. I didn't see any blues bands, but I did meet some great people. It was a surprisingly excellent first night in Clarksdale, but it would get a whole lot better on Wednesday.

A blues musician was going to be playing at the Ground Zero Blues Club, an establishment that actor Morgan Freeman, who grew up in Clarksdale, co-owned.

Freeman also owned a restaurant called "Madidi." I figured I would eat there and then head over to the club. Freeman was one of the few actors I truly admired, and he was in one of my favorite movies, *The Shawshank Redemption*.

There is a line in that film that had become my mantra: "Get busy living, or get busy dying." I caught myself saying it frequently. I figured I would patronize the restaurant as a small thank you for Freeman's work that had not only entertained me but had changed my life.

I had no clue he was in town, and when I heard his voice a few tables over, I couldn't believe it. I asked the waiter, "When Mr. Freeman has a moment, can you send him over to my table?" Much to my amazement, he got up and headed toward me. I thought, "Holy hell, now what do I do?"

Freeman couldn't have been more gracious. He had seen my Harley outside with the California license plates and remarked that I was a long way from home. I told him I was discovering America. He told me that I should meet Puddin' Hatchett.

"He comes into my blues club every day at noon," Freeman said. "Go talk to him. He's a real character."

When Morgan Freeman tells you to do something, you don't debate it. I would be at Ground Zero Blues Club the following day at noon, waiting for a man named Puddin' Hatchett.

CHAPTER 39

The best con Puddin' Hatchett ever pulled off was one he probably never knew he had accomplished.

It was a two-part scheme concocted effortlessly by the lifelong confidence man. The first segment was a basic card trick that the seventy-six-year-old resident of Clarksdale, Mississippi, had performed countless times on unsuspecting rubes whom he convinced through words and actions that they could beat him out of five dollars by picking the correct card. On this day, the mark for this simple card trick was me. The second part would come after I begged him to show me how he pulled off the first part.

After talking to Morgan Freeman the previous night about Puddin', the famous actor had left me full of intrigue. Freeman purposely wouldn't tell me much about Hatchett, wanting me to discover the trickster's unique life on my own. I looked forward to meeting Hatchett and didn't have to wait long for him to arrive at Freeman's Ground Zero Blues Club. Precisely at noon, a shiny red Cadillac pulled into the parking lot, and a tall, resplendent, Black man emerged from the automobile. He came from the house he lived in his entire life, ready to ply his trade on this sunny fall afternoon.

When he exited his car, he carefully but purposely put on a black Panama hat with a white band to protect his head from the blistering afternoon sun. The rest of his sartorial ensemble included a unique black tropical-print shirt with a variety of colorful logos (including playing cards), pressed brown slacks, and shined tan wingtip Oxford shoes.

The hostess smiled when he came through the doors, and he returned the greeting, adding, "Hello, sweetheart." The bartender called out his name from the other side of the room. The cocktail waitress gave him a loving hug.

Hatchett made his way to a table in the middle of the club, where he would be for the next five hours or so. He pulled out a tall chair and gingerly sat. He took out the tools of his trade from a small black bag he carried, pulling out a deck of cards from a torn box first. Then he fished out a pair of what he called magic dice.

Nothing was left to chance. His position at the table was exactly halfway between the bar and the entrance, giving him sight lines to both. He had acted as the self-appointed greeter of Ground Zero Blues Club for years, but that was just a ruse to unarm any suspicious customers, doubtful of what his true motives were. The warm, welcoming charm Hatchett oozed was also meant to put his victims at ease as he drew them into his lair.

Today, it was a couple visiting from England, both in their early fifties, traveling around the South. New Orleans was the next stop on their itinerary. They came over to Hatchett, attracted to him like bears to honey.

Hatchett asked them where they were from, how they liked the town, and if they had been to Freeman's restaurant or eaten lunch at Abe's. It was then that he produced the cards and, with as much precision as a septuagenarian with arthritis can muster, shuffled them. He then brought out the magic dice, holding them in his large brown hands. He shook them, and two fives appeared. Another shake and snake eyes popped up. His final shake brought up two sixes.

The couple was impressed and, thus, ready for the next phase. Hatchett performed some simple card tricks. He fanned the cards out facedown and had the wife pull one. She revealed it to me and her husband but kept it hidden from Hatchett. She stuck it back in the deck. He shuffled the cards and then pulled her card out, showing it to her.

After a few minutes of entertainment, Hatchett innocently asked if they had ever heard of three-card Monte. It was a variation on the pea-in-the-shell game. He produced two fives of clubs and a five of hearts.

"It's simple," Hatchett said to the Brits. "You just have to pick out the five of hearts after I move them around."

He showed the cards and then put them facedown, three in a row. Next, Hatchett moved the cards around, and, when he stopped, the husband had to pick where the five of hearts was among the three cards. If he did, they won double what they had bet. If he didn't, Hatchett kept the money.

Hatchett flipped over the card, the husband picked, and, of course, it was a five of clubs—not hearts. Professor Puddin' had just given them their first lesson in the education of the streets. The cost was twenty dollars. Funny thing was—the couple wasn't the least bit upset over being hustled. The man smiled and took their picture with Puddin', thanking him as they left.

They might have known the game was rigged, and if there was any doubt, one just had to look out onto the parking lot and see Hatchett's bright-red Cadillac. It represented only a miniscule sum of the money he had made performing three-card Monte over his lifetime.

Hatchett told me some days were better than others. He came in the afternoon, worked a little, then went to a local casino to play blackjack. He returned in the evening when the music started, greeting and hustling anyone brave enough to come over to his table.

"A man bet me three thousand two years ago," Puddin' recalled. "That's the most money I've ever won."

Hatchett averaged between $800 to $1,000 a week, and he estimated he had made a couple of million dollars at this over the last fifty-eight years.

"When I was eighteen, I didn't want to work a regular job,"

Puddin' recalled. "I didn't want to steal, didn't want to deal drugs, and I didn't want to beg. But I knew I wanted money."

One day, he encountered a younger teenager who was dealing three-card Monte, and Puddin' asked the boy to teach him. Two months later, the two were in Fort Hood, Texas, taking money off anyone foolish enough to play with them.

"I knew I was going to do this the minute I saw him do it," Puddin' explained. "I loved it, and I got real good at it."

In those days, travel was necessary because there weren't tourists coming into Clarksdale, like in recent years, so Hatchett would take business trips just like a traveling salesman, making some money and returning home to his wife and their nine children.

"When I first met my wife in 1961, I told her what I was doing," Puddin' recounted. "She asked if I could make a living doing this. The next week, I bought her a car. I told her, 'I ain't got no job, but I'll take care of you.'"

Hatchett also doesn't have a formal education and was unable to read and write, but he had gotten along just fine.

"There was always enough people to make a living off of," Pudding explained. "There was always enough people coming by I could knock off."

Unlike other hustlers who run the con with speed, Puddin' went slow; he always had. It was his style. He also didn't use a queen of hearts, which a lot of throwers employ, opting for the five of hearts.

Another trademark trick, and the one he saved for me, was to take the five of hearts, put it in my hand, turn my hand over, and then never touch my hand again. When he did it to me, I watched intently, making sure there was no switch of cards when he turned my hand over. He took the fives of clubs, one in each hand, turned them over, and moved his hands side to side with the cards. Then, after about thirty seconds, he stopped.

"Where's the five of hearts?" he asked.

I turned over my hand, and there was a five of clubs.

"Now I know how you are a millionaire," I exclaimed, handing him a crisp twenty-dollar bill.

Puddin' laughed a deep, wry chuckle that only a successful con man emits. It reminded me of that scene in Damon Runyon's *Guys and Dolls* where the lead character, Skye Masterson, talked about hustlers.

"One of these days in your travels, a guy is going to show you a brand-new deck of cards on which the seal was not yet broken. Then this guy is going to offer to bet you that he can make the jack of spades jump out of this brand-new deck of cards and squirt cider in your ear. But, son, do not accept this bet, because as sure as you stand there, you're going to wind up with an ear full of cider."

Puddin' continued to wet the ears of people who came in, despite many of his victims knowing they would be hustled.

"It's like a casino" Puddin' said. "They know they can't win, but they keep going up there. I'm a little slower than I used to be, but I can still throw cards I ain't retiring. I only work a few hours a day. The rest of the time, I am at the casino."

I innocently inquired, "Okay, you have to tell me how you did that."

Hatchett just smiled, but this time, I was the one who wasn't going to let him off the hook. I begged, pleaded, cajoled, and tried every manipulative trick I could think of to get him to divulge his secret. Finally, after twenty minutes of my prattling on and on, he relented.

"You come back through here again, and I'll tell you," he relented, confident that the odds of my returning to Clarksdale were slim.

As I departed Clarksdale a few hours later, I decided that I was going to save myself a trip back to Mississippi and figure out how he pulled this trick. It occupied my mind for the 485 miles to Norman, Oklahoma. Fortunately, I was on Interstate 40, so I could get lost in my thoughts on the thoroughfare, not having to worry about wildlife wandering onto the road or people turning left in front of me.

My concentration was fully centered on how Hatchett got a five of clubs into my hand after showing me a five of hearts. I was certain it was when he turned my hand over, but there wasn't enough space or time to make a switch. Or was there? No, impossible; maybe it was a magic card, like the dice he owned. Maybe the card had a sheath and changed when turned over. That was the only plausible scenario I could come up with.

Of course, I could never be certain how the trick was played. As I pulled into a motel in Norman to settle in for the night, I knew Puddin' had gotten me again. As I checked into the motel, I could swear I had cider leaking out of my ear.

CHAPTER 40

When I woke up in Norman, I realized I was one time zone closer to the one in my hometown. I had gone from Eastern to the Central time zone the previous day, and by the end of this day, I was going to knock off another hour and be in Mountain time.

The reality that I was headed home had fully gripped me as I packed up the Harley, but it wasn't met with the usual dread. Any previous milestone, like when I drove as far east as I could and then knew I was going to be pointed west, made me melancholy. It was a small indication that I was on the backside of my journey. Sadness followed the epiphany, and it typically took at least half a day to shake off my funk.

This time, however, a slight relief had replaced the usual trepidation. I had been away from Southern California for more than two months, and there were aspects of home I truly yearned for. Sleeping in my own bed was the primary one. It was a comfort that I had taken for granted. There wasn't one mattress I slept on so far in my journey that was as comfortable as mine. Now, I will admit that I'm rather finicky about my sleeping surface. I prefer an extra-firm mattress. The harder, the better, and being in a motel room that charged thirty dollars a night, chances were the proprietor had not gone the deluxe route in appointing his guest rooms. In some of the places I stayed, I was stunned there was a bed at all.

Thus was the life when traveling on the cheap. Frills were for rich people. I was content with my lumpy mattress, paper-thin sheets, a small bar of soap, and threadbare towel. One amenity I did have trouble sacrificing was the water pressure in the shower. When riding all day, my face and arms attracted what seemed like pounds of dirt and bugs, and I didn't think it was a lot to ask that the showerhead produced a stream of water rather than a trickle. Hell, in some of the places, a trickle would have been an upgrade. I started looking for places with swimming pools, and, if the shower was inadequate, the pool functioned as my place to get clean. Not very hygienic, I admit, but it was efficient.

One feature of the road I would miss was the food I discovered. Either by local recommendations or dumb luck, I was able to eat very well during my travels. There always seemed to be a food or restaurant a town was known for, and the residents took overwhelming pride in it. Some of the cuisine I would remember for the rest of my life.

There was an order of apple pancakes at The Original Pancake House in Salem, Oregon. The German dish had Granny Smith apples in the batter that was oven-baked with hints of cinnamon and brown sugar. In Montana, I had a steak that was so succulent, I swore they slaughtered the cow in the kitchen right before they cooked it. The Buffalo wings and roast beef on kummelweck rolls I had at my godfather's house in Buffalo, New York, I could still taste two states later.

Of course, there were food rivalries where I felt I had a duty to inject myself into the debate as an unbiased judge after consuming the competing cuisine. People who live in a town where a particular dish was similar to one in another location will defend their specialty as passionately as they do their town's sports team. There were two of the more famous regional food discussions I decided to weigh in on after visiting those towns. The first was Chicago deep-dish pizza versus a New York City thin slice. This was a matter of dough density preference. I much favored the thin crust of a New York pizza over the deep-dish variety in Chicago.

I also delivered a strong opinion on Carolina barbecue versus Southern style. The Carolina version strictly used pork and was drier than its counterpart. A spice rub and vinegar were usually put on during the cooking process, but there was no tomato-based sauce. The sauce was why I preferred the Southern style. The assortment of meats, including sausage, beef ribs, pork ribs, and lamb, was another advantage Southern style had over Carolina barbecue.

I managed to also get involved in the Great Philly Cheesesteak Conflict. The two principals involved were Pat's King of Steaks and Geno's Steaks. The two dueled daily on opposite sides of the corner of Ninth Street and Passyunk Avenue in South Philadelphia. Pat's had the advantage of being credited with inventing the iconic sandwich, but Geno's claimed to have perfected the delicacy. The food feud had the intensity of the Hatfields and McCoys, and there was no one in the city who didn't have an opinion on which restaurant's cheesesteak was better. Both were made on hoagie rolls with steak, gobs of melted American cheese, and grilled onions. The difference was how the meat was served. Pat's steak was chopped while Geno's was served in strips. I consumed both on a summer afternoon and, after careful consideration, chose Pat's. I liked the tradition of the chopped steak and found it easier to eat.

The meals I had weren't all Michelin Star fare. There were some misses. Skyline Chili's chili in Cincinnati was nearly inedible. Funny, since a couple of people steered me there, raving it was the best chili they had ever experienced. It was a famous diner in the Queen City, but after trying to eat their staple menu item, I thought the paste they served at any Waffle House was superior, a distinction any restaurant should strive to avoid.

The biggest thrill for me was lobster rolls in the New England states. How I managed to live more than forty years on this earth and never experience this slice of heaven was a wrong that I was glad I was able to right. I don't know who invented these, but after my first bite, I was ready to nominate them for a Nobel Prize—or at least lobby to award them a Presidential Medal of Freedom.

Its brilliance was in its simplicity: chunks of Atlantic Ocean lobster blended with mayonnaise and a touch of dill. The bread was often nothing more than a hot dog bun. How it was prepared was the key. The bun was butterflied open and slathered with butter, then placed facedown on a grill until lightly toasted. Finally, the lobster mix was crammed into the bread until it burst out of the top. Any remaining melted butter was drizzled over the crustacean. I must have had twenty of them in the seventy-two hours I was there. It was a sad day when I left the area, as I could no longer find them.

Recalling those memories of past meals made a lot of miles go by much quicker as I slogged through the Oklahoma panhandle on my way to Amarillo, Texas, where I was anticipating another familiar and sumptuous meal. The elements were not my friend on this day. The sky was as black as my leather jacket, and with a stern wind, I knew nasty rain would be greeting me momentarily. Menacing thunder and lightning were already bearing down. It loudly tried to intimidate me into retreating into the motel room, and I probably would have relented if I weren't so stubborn. Besides, I had already packed Libertad, putting the waterproof tarp over the duffel bag. I slipped on my raingear—pants and a jacket that were designed to repel even the most severe downpour. The biggest hindrance was my helmet. I had a half-face shield that snapped onto the front. It kept the water out of my eyes, but I still had to use the forefinger on my left glove to wipe away the rain that accumulated on my face shield so I could see somewhat clearly.

As the thunder and lightning set off nearby car alarms, I knew travel was going to be a challenge. I wasn't sure how many of the 278 miles I would battle through rain, but I was mentally prepared to be in this storm for most of the next four hours.

A drizzle began immediately as I got on Interstate 35 and headed the twenty-six miles north to Oklahoma City. Just before I reached Oklahoma's capital, the clouds unleashed their fury. Sheets of water pummeled me, and I found refuge off the interstate under a steel canopy at a gas station.

There I sat on Libertad, deciding whether to wait out the elements. The Harley had powered through the downpour admirably, but I felt like we both needed a respite. The break was more for me than her. It only took an hour for the squall to downgrade to a sprinkle, and I decided that my upcoming dinner at The Big Texan Steak Ranch once I got settled in Amarillo would be worth the suffering.

The clouds retreated by Clinton, Oklahoma, a good sign since I still had 200 miles until I reached my destination. Three hours was what it should have taken me to reach Amarillo, but with a smooth interstate and a heavy hand on the accelerator, it would be more like two and a half, even with a quick stop to fuel up.

As I pulled into the city limits, it was just past five o'clock. Shortly after I arrived, I could see the wooden cowboy at the top of the Big Texan's sixty-foot sign. I smiled as I passed the restaurant, thinking, *I'll see you soon, my friend.* My motel was another five miles down the road, and I checked in as fast as I could. I was a carnivore on a mission, and nothing was going to delay my red-meat orgy.

The Big Texan had been around since 1960, opened as part steakhouse, part tourist attraction. Travelers viewing it first from Route 66, and later Interstate 40, provided the necessary traffic to allow the restaurant to thrive. A large gift shop allowed diners to commemorate their meal with all kinds of tchotchkes, including shot glasses, coffee mugs, and T-shirts.

One attraction that drew clientele was the seventy-two-ounce steak dinner challenge. It began soon after the facility opened, but initially was a contest featuring twelve people. The fastest eater gobbled up a sixty-dollar prize. From that contest, Big Texan owner Bob "RJ" Lee got an idea two years later. He stood on a chair in the middle of the dining room one night and proclaimed, "From this day forward, anyone who can eat the entire seventy-two-ounce dinner in one hour gets it for free."

Many have tried, and more have failed than succeeded. It was an expensive gamble. Consuming four and a half pounds of steak, as well as a shrimp cocktail, salad, baked potato, and a dinner roll can slay the heartiest of eaters. There was an elevated stage in the middle of the dining room where those who took the dare sat and were timed as all the other patrons cheered. On the wall in the lobby was the Hall of Fame of those who successfully downed the dinner, their name living on in infamy.

I did not have the gastronomic fortitude to undergo such a feat. I don't think I could eat seventy-two ounces of steak in a week, much less an hour. I was content with my twelve-ounce ribeye. As I was savoring my meal, a young man decided to take the seventy-two-ounce steak challenge. His name was announced over the speakers, and everyone clapped in support. Alas, like many before him, he lost, walking off the stage with only half his dinner eaten. His stomach was full and wallet $100 lighter. I had succeeded in polishing off my food, which included a slice of chocolate cake. There was no freebie for doing so, but I still felt like a winner as I walked out of the restaurant.

CHAPTER 41

Anxious to reach Colorado, I awoke two hours earlier than usual and departed from Amarillo early in the morning. I had long held the opinion that Colorado and Utah were two of the prettiest states in the Union, and I would be traveling through a good portion of both over the next two days.

It had been a while since I saw a mountain. The flat portion of this country was a stretch that offered little visual stimulation, and I wanted to pass through it rapidly. That was certainly the case for the first 100 miles of today's ride. I departed Amarillo on US Highway 87, and as soon as I got out of town, I was cocooned by prairie land. The two-lane road was dry, dusty, and mostly barren. The eighty-five-degree temperature didn't help much. The only highlights were small towns I could blow through. Places like Masterson, Dumas, and Cactus confirmed that the Texas panhandle was some of the most desolate road I had ever had the displeasure of being on.

When I arrived in Stratford an hour after leaving Amarillo, there was a sense of relief. The little Texas town had hints of mountains in the distance, though they were more like small hills. Still, it was a vertical dimension to the topography, and I welcomed it. I also was appreciative of the town's size. Though the population was barely 2,000, it made the previous three places I passed through look like New York City.

Deep in Tornado Alley of the Texas Panhandle, there was a wind strong enough to blow me into oncoming traffic or off the highway, making me even more eager to reach Colorado, though I still had to go through a piece of New Mexico to get there. It was encouraging that at Stratford, I made a left that signaled a westerly direction rather than going northward. It only took another hour to get out of Texas, and I sighed with relief when I saw the sign welcoming me to New Mexico. The horizon was still devoid of mountains, but I knew that soon enough, I would be in the middle of them.

That welcoming sight was in the small community of Capulin. By this point, I was at 6,800 feet in elevation, and the famous Capulin Volcano came into view. I thought I had seen its tip when I was at the tail end of Texas but wasn't quite sure. I confirmed its existence when I was in Grenville, New Mexico, spying it thirty miles out on Highway 87. When I reached Capulin, I was at the ride's halfway point. Even though I was climbing and still had about three hours of riding remaining, I knew the rest of my jaunt was downhill from there.

By the time I reached Monte Vista, Colorado, it was late in the afternoon. I had read about a unique motel and was curious to meet the owner, George Kelloff. I was staying there, so after getting situated, I walked over to the office and introduced myself.

Kelloff was the second-generation owner of the Movie Manor Motel and the Star Drive-in Theater. He took them over from his father, George Kelloff Sr., who came up with the idea to merge a motel with a drive-in movie theater.

Kelloff Sr. caused quite a stir when he constructed the single-screen drive-in theater in 1955, a novelty the sleepy town was eager to embrace. He had gotten in during the boom and parlayed the love of movies his mother had instilled in him when, as a boy, he worked the player piano at his mother's silent movie theater.

Monte Vista's population was approximately 3,000 at that time, but there were other towns in the San Luis Valley that could attract the many working-class families who, like the rest of the country, embraced the car culture.

"My dad was a visionary and a risk-taker," George Jr. recalled. "He had the ability to see what others couldn't. He knew this would work."

The concept of a drive-in theater experienced severe growing pains until finally catching on with the public in the 1950s, owing its popularity to improvements in technology, after being invented in 1932 by Richard Hollingshead Jr., who worked for his father's auto parts store. He was reportedly looking for a way for his obese mother to watch a movie comfortably.

Hollingshead hung a large white sheet between two trees in the family's Riverton, New Jersey, backyard and put an old Kodak projector on the hood of his car. He tinkered with car positions, sound systems, and weather conditions, going as far as using the sprinklers to simulate rainfall.

The first drive-in was in Pennsauken Township, New Jersey. On June 6, 1933, the second-run movie *Wives Beware* made history.

Though the drive-in proved popular initially, it languished for two decades. Hollingshead's drive-in closed three years after it opened, and the combination of a poor sound system and a lack of new movie releases hampered any chance for progress.

What saved the drive-in was the invention of the in-car speaker. When the sound came from behind the screen, the audience in their cars had a hard time hearing the movie. With the new invention, each car had a speaker. In the early 1940s, there were approximately fifty theaters in the United States, but ten years later, more than 2,000 were open.

"There were four drive-ins in the valley," Kelloff explained. "We all did well There was nothing else to do. It was their heyday. People had love affairs with their cars, and gas was cheap. They did everything in their cars, conceived babies, probably a few at this drive-in."

The drive-in for the Kelloffs was a living but not an extravagant one. The family lived in a one-bedroom house on the drive-in property, where George Jr. and his other sibling slept in bunk beds in their parents' closet until they were teenagers.

"It was cool growing up here," Kelloff remembered. "This [the drive-in] was my front yard. There was always activity going on. It was neat. Of course, my parents worked every night, so I didn't see a lot of them."

By the time Kelloff was eleven years old, he was immersed in the family business, manning the projection room, making sure the movies ran flawlessly.

"There were some tough times when I got to be a teenager. My buddies were like, 'Come on, let's go.' I couldn't because I had to work," Kelloff said. "It was seven nights a week. In those days we did double features, so we were working until midnight, one o'clock. In the heyday, we were going until one, one-thirty."

The season started around May 1, and Kelloff Sr. pushed it to late fall to get as much income before the Midwestern winter took hold over Colorado and made outdoor activity most uncomfortable, if not near impossible.

"When it was Dad's sole source of income, we were running a longer season," Kelloff explained.

That money had to be stretched through six months of closure, and Kelloff Sr. knew he was going to need something else to support his family. He got his inspiration one night in the early sixties when his in-laws came to visit. His wife's parents got the bedroom, and Kelloff Sr. and his wife slept on a fold-out couch in the living room. He looked out the window and saw the movie screen and thought it would be a great way to watch a movie.

"The following day, Dad went to the back row with a lawn chair and a speaker in his lap," Kelloff recalled. "He ran the movie and watched it from there and thought this could work. That was when he decided he was going to build the motel. He went to the bank and tried to borrow the money and got lucky with the loan."

Soon, the Movie Manor Motel opened, and the rooms facing out had a view of the movie screen. Kelloff Sr. ran speakers into those rooms, giving tourists a reason to spend more than a few hours on his property. Soon, travelers were coming from Colorado,

Arizona, and even California for a long weekend or a mini vacation. The notoriety of the motel helped with the drive-in's attendance.

"We did well, but when Dad built the motel, there was this curiosity," Kelloff declared. "People wanted to see this. I can remember when this drive-in couldn't get cars in here. It was filled up all the way back to the motel."

The secondary revenue source almost instantly outpaced the primary funds from the drive-in and allowed Kelloff Sr. to buy the town's lone movie theater in 1967. It was another smart business move from a man who had little formal education.

"The people who go to the downtown theater were a totally different clientele," Kelloff explained. "Dad recognized that. The drive-in crowd were more the working-class crowd and families."

Kelloff Sr. was building the legacy for Junior to inherit, but ironically, the son wasn't certain he wanted it.

"My wife and I got out of college, and we ran the motel's restaurant," Kelloff said. "I got to thirty, and I took a risk. I left town and did some other things. Some of the happiest times in my life were when I took some risks."

Kelloff had been a good collegiate golfer and decided to get in the golf business at one of the sport's epicenters, Phoenix.

"I took an entry-level, minimum wage job at a golf course development company," Kelloff added. "It was menial work, but at thirty, I had more maturity and got promoted quickly."

The ties of a small town were binding. Kelloff's wife missed her family and George probably did, as well, more than he wanted to admit. The two returned to Monte Vista and got work at a local golf course. It was soon after they returned that Kelloff Sr.'s health prevented him from working daily at the drive-in and motel.

"He told us if we wanted it, we could have it," Kelloff remarked. "Otherwise, he was going to sell it and retire."

Kelloff Jr. didn't share the same passion for the movies as

his dad, but he did love what his father built and wanted to continue the legacy. Romance and reality, however, were often bitter enemies, as the latter tries to squelch the former.

The battle George Kelloff Jr. waged to preserve his slice of Americana was largely successful, though he was not certain if what he had been fighting for was still there. The gradual demise of drive-in movie theaters was a sad part of this country's history, but Kelloff managed to keep his place profitable with some innovative marketing and a lot of hard work.

The idea was to do what his father did—bequeath the family business to his son. The only problem was that the son wasn't sure he wanted it, and there might not be that much left of it even if he did.

"I would like to pass it on to my son," Kelloff revealed. "Hollywood was fickle, and they were very money-oriented. Now everything was the window between film and DVD. For example, *Toy Story 3* came out last week, and they want to get it into the theaters and get it out as fast as they can because they get more revenue when it goes to DVD. The window keeps shortening. The National Association of Theater Owners, which we were a member of, has a lobby, and we fight to keep it a five-month window or a four-month window. That allows us to make a living. So far, we have been successful, but that window was shortening. It's all driven by money."

The percentage the movie distributors take from theater owners had been steadily increasing. Kelloff noted that for blockbusters, they could demand as much as 70 percent of the ticket sales.

"It is really tough for independents," Kelloff lamented. "The big chains have the power to negotiate, but the little guys were kind of on their own. It's hard to meet your overhead and make a living. That's why small theaters went away."

It was a fate that Kelloff feared might happen to him, though he intended to fight off that destiny.

"I don't know if it will survive," Kelloff shared. "My dad told me a long time ago—he was in the movie business since the thirties—

when television came out, movies were going to die. Then when VCRs came along, people predicted movie theaters were going to die, but they didn't. They took a hit, but they survived. There were always people who want to get out of the house and have an experience. Will that continue? I don't know. I hope so. All we can do was offer the best experience."

CHAPTER 42

If I was in a hurry to get home, there were certainly routes to accomplish that goal for the day's ride, but no, I had no inclination to rush. I thought a little dawdling would be beneficial for my soul. And there was no better place to procrastinate than southwest Colorado and northeast Utah.

In thirty-four miles on US 160, I was at the entrance of the Rio Grande National Forest, where it split into Highway 149. Almost immediately, the Rio Grande River greeted me on the left, while the jagged mountainside was on my right. The two-lane Highway 149 was one of those roads that one wished lasted forever. It had elevation, twists, turns, plenty of beautiful landscape, and sparse traffic. Mature pines and spruces dotted the hillside, mixed with prairie grass and large rocks, not quite big enough to be boulders but still menacing. Every so often, there would be a house nestled by the river, and I wondered how the property came to be. I assumed the land was claimed by some smart settler and then positioned the dwelling with water views from several rooms.

As I continued to go north and west, the Rio Grande would occasionally disappear, making me wonder when or if I would see it again. A few miles would pass, and it would reappear, playing a sort of highway hide-and-seek with me. We undertook this entertaining game for thirty-five miles until the river finally disappeared just past Freemon's General Store in Creede, Colorado, making a left while I continued north. It was a sad goodbye.

The next forty-two miles meandered through the Rio Grande National Forest, climbing in elevation until I reached Windy Point Observation Site. There, I could look south toward Black Mountain. It was hard to fully enjoy the views, however. My gas gauge was hovering around empty. Fortunately, Lake City, Colorado, was just eight miles up US 149, and I found a place to fill up.

The road began to get redundant after Lake City. Mounds desiring to be hills and burnt brown grass were with me for the next hour, and it got tough to not be bored. My yearning for water was rewarded after fifty miles with the Gunnison River. It led me to Highway 50, where I headed west, following the backside of the river. It took a while, but by lunch, I was out of the hills and in the flatlands of Grand Junction, Colorado.

As I was eating a patty melt at a local diner in Grand Junction, I had a decision to make. I had come from US 50 to I-70 and would be on the interstate for a hundred miles until I reached Green River, Utah. The strategy was to break away from the comfort of the national highway and head north on US 191/US 6. Or I could stay on I-70 until it reached I-15 and go straight up to Salt Lake City. It was the classic traveler conundrum of convenience over scenery. I weighed the merits of both. As I was polishing off my fries, I decided to go with US 191/ US 6. It would add some time to my ride, but I gambled that I would be paid off with more breathtaking views.

My bet paid off handsomely. US 191/ US 6 was mostly flat but with mesas to my right. The clouds encased the landscape and gave the area a more expansive feel. The highway had a scant number of cars, and the isolation was calming. It was the type of road where one could easily get lost in thought, and that was what happened to me. I was alone in a state of meditation, though a sign for the town of Woodside interrupted my feeling of Zen. Three cars approached, the only automobiles I had seen in the last half-hour. It was a sign that more civilization was on the way. The farther north

I progressed, the more traffic increased. Then the towns started to appear like weeds. Wellington was the first, followed in close succession by Price, Wood Hill, Carbonville, Spring Glen, Helper, and, finally, Castle Gate, all in the span of eighteen miles. Though nondescript, the towns did allow me to get a full tank of gas before speeding away from humanity. US 6 split from US 191, and I headed up into Price Canyon. I had just under fifty-five miles before this two-lane highway ended and I ran into Interstate 15. I enjoyed it as much as I could, knowing that I would soon be in Spanish Fork and the beginning of a cavalcade of cars.

By the time I reached I-15, it was four o'clock, and now I was in commuter mode like the accompanying cars that surrounded me. I had an hour until I reached Salt Lake City, and I had gone from being one with the road to trying to survive the concrete jungle. I jockeyed for the best position on the four lanes, all while avoiding the occasional motorist swerving into my lane without turning to see if there was another vehicle there.

I reached Salt Lake City and was trying to regain the sereneness I had felt back on Highway 191. I had heard of a little bistro that might just get it back for me, so I trekked over to the One World Café. The Bohemian-style restaurant was on the street level of a two-story brownstone building. The owner of One World Café, Denise Cerreta, lived on the second floor. On this evening, she was toggling back and forth between business and residence. She was upstairs when I arrived, but I hoped she would pop back in so I could ask her how she came up with the idea for this unique type of business.

What made One World Café so special was that Cerreta didn't have menu prices. A customer ordered food, seconds were permitted if hungry enough, and then a patron paid what they believed the meal was worth. There was a decorated box that sat on a small table next to a water jug and mugs, and the tab was settled there. No one monitored the box, so diners were on the honor system. If patrons didn't have money, Cerreta allowed them to work for their meal, washing dishes or any other type of odd job she might have.

As I devoured my Swedish meatballs and penne pasta, Cerreta appeared and went to the kitchen. With a mouth full of food, I complimented her on my dinner and asked her how she came up with this business.

"I was in the café one day and this big energy came in, and I got this message of doing donations and having people price their own food," Cerreta recalled. "It sounds crazy; I had told no one of my vision, nobody the story. Only I knew, but I did it. The next person who walked through the door, I said, 'No more pricing; price your own.' That was a huge thing for me. That's how it happened."

Opening a restaurant was a monumental risk for Cerreta. Her original vocation was acupuncture, and she had a successful practice in the same building, but she knew she wanted something more. The restaurant began as a small coffee house, then expanded.

"I had no restaurant experience except for waiting tables when I was an undergrad," Cerreta remarked. "I had no knowledge of running a kitchen or any part of a restaurant. I ended up putting up this little sandwich shop thinking that would round out my practice."

As the responsibilities of the sandwich shop grew, Cerreta started to reassess her other job.

"I realized there were people who weren't sick, they were lonely," Cerreta surmised. "Also around the same time, I felt like I had hit my spiritual glass ceiling in acupuncture. My intuition was, in order to grow, I needed to close it up. That was the biggest leap for me."

The restaurant expanded to full meals, and Cerreta was a one-woman operation, purchasing food, cooking it, washing the dishes, and cleaning the dining area and bathrooms.

"I started to cook family style," Cerreta explained. "I asked people how much they wanted and not to waste food. I did all local organic because I didn't want to serve anything I wouldn't eat myself."

It was about two months into the operation that she started the concept of having people pay what they wanted. The revelation

Cerreta had was one she wasn't going to ignore.

"You know, sometimes, when you are used to working with your intuition and trusting what needs to happen . . ." she said. "I had to learn a lot as I went along, and it was a struggle. I remember waking up in the morning, crying, thinking I couldn't do this one more day."

Still, she kept at it, and friends would come along and help, though they did question if Cerreta was doing the right thing.

"I was totally committed after this really *Field of Dreams* moment." Cerreta laughed. "I could have talked myself out of it, but I was going to keep my word. I think there were people who were thinking, 'When do we call the funny farm to come pick her up?'"

The local newspaper heard about her venture and did a story that was picked up nationally. Suddenly, locals and tourists started to show up at her place, intrigued by this funky restaurant and its unusual pricing structure.

The idea caught on, and Cerreta has been asked to help similar businesses with this idea. She has had a hand in several places and started a foundation called One World, Everybody Eats, which not only helps other like-minded restaurants but was committed to combating hunger around the world.

When I finished my meal, I put twenty dollars in the box and then went to the sink to wash some dishes that had piled up. The peace I had felt on the road earlier returned. My meal had no price I could put on it.

CHAPTER 43

There were more picturesque ways to get to Las Vegas from Salt Lake City than my chosen route, but I wasn't interested in taking them. On this day, I was far more interested in speed.

I wanted to get to the mecca of all things excess as soon as possible and selected Interstate 15, the main artery between Salt Lake City and Las Vegas. My one day in Sin City was going to be a truncated weekend of debauchery that so many millions of visitors undertake weekly. My only caution was not to get caught speeding to the city nicknamed "Lost Wages." I was eager to have a drink in one hand and a pair of dice in the other.

It was quite the dichotomy, considering my starting point for the day's ride, and that may have been one of the reasons for wanting to depart in such a hurry. The beauty of Salt Lake City is unmistakable. The city was framed by the Wasatch Mountains that jut above the city's skyline. The country's epicenter for Latter-day Saints featured a temple that was not the oldest one in Utah but the most majestic. The wholesomeness of the town permeated everywhere. No hard alcohol in the grocery stores. Instead, drinkers had to go to a state-run liquor center that had all the characteristics of an adult bookstore. No one looked at one another there, and the purchases were made hastily, so the customers may flee the parking lot before their car was spotted by a neighbor.

The entire city used to be shut down on Sundays, a byproduct of the church's influence. Now, however, most stores stay open on the Lord's Day, a change that doesn't please some of the more conservative citizens. I noticed some tattoo shops and massage parlors at one end of Salt Lake City, something that was unheard of twenty years ago. Even though certain dubious businesses had chipped away at the moral fabric of the town, its purity was still mostly intact for the time being.

I knew that would not be the case in Las Vegas, where one could throw a rock and hit an adult-oriented business. It was just the visual stimulation I sought; even if I didn't want to patronize those types of facilities, it was still oddly comforting to have them around. My enthusiasm to arrive was palpable, even though I had to travel 421 miles through the desert to get there.

Surprisingly (well, maybe not so much), since I was speeding for most of the ride, it took me only five hours to arrive. I even gained an hour with the switch from Mountain time to Pacific. Another hour to see what kind of trouble I could find.

Trying to procure a reasonably priced motel in Las Vegas used to be quite easy. Years ago, when my friends and I wanted to come up from Los Angeles, we could leave on a Friday afternoon with no reservation and just drive up to places on the Las Vegas Strip. Between the El Rancho, Circus Circus, Frontier, and even the Sahara, a cheapskate like me could find a bargain room on the weekend. Those days were gone now. The resorts did their level best to extract every nickel out of guests even before they hit a blackjack table. Discovering a reasonably priced place to stay now entailed going to the run-down motels at the north end of Las Vegas Boulevard.

I located one across from the Stratosphere, and the woman running the counter was surprised I wanted the room for more than an hour. It was thirty dollars, which was about twenty-five bucks too much. The décor was from the '50s, when it was built. The wallpaper was faded and smoky, the bed lumpy, with a piece of cheap wood acting as the headboard. The television had adult channels to set the mood for those utilizing this establishment as a temporary love nest. The room reminded me of where former child actors would go to overdose as a troubled adult—some guy facedown in nothing but tighty-whities, a bottle of cheap vodka near his left hand, and a bottle of prescription barbiturates clutched in his right fist.

It didn't matter to me, however. I wasn't going to be in the room that much anyway. I figured the only requirements I demanded were a bed and a shower, and this place had both. My desire was to be either at a craps table or in a poker game, with as much free alcohol as they would give me. That would keep me occupied for most of the evening

Before that, though, I wanted to take a little walk. It was nice outside, as the afternoon sun wasn't too aggressive. I headed toward downtown and walked past a bunch of local shops and restaurants. They weren't of much interest, but one intrigued me. A Little White Chapel was one of the many places those in love could formalize their union. The marriage business was huge in Las Vegas.

Most chapels had some sort of gimmick. One had a medieval theme, where a guy dressed as a sorcerer performed the ceremony. Some had a minister who would marry couples in front of the *Welcome to Las Vegas* sign. Still, another rented out movie star outfits and couples could do the deed dressed like Dorothy and the Tin Man from *The Wizard of Oz*.

Charolette Richards would never allow any of that. The owner of A Little White Chapel was an intensely religious woman, and, when I met her that day, she was very adamant about the sanctity of marriage, even though she was credited with the Elvis-themed wedding.

"Elvis might come to your wedding," she exclaimed, "but he won't marry you . . . I will."

Richards had performed more than 50,000 marriages, and it was ironic that for all the joy she had brought to so many people, her own love life had largely been devoid of happiness.

Richards's life was hard almost from the beginning. She married young and had three small children by the time she was twenty-one. Her husband, Willy, moved her from her parents' home in Oregon to Kentucky, then promptly abandoned her to go to Las Vegas to try to catch the economic boom of the late '50s. He wired money and told her to drive a car with no air-conditioning across the country in the sweltering summer to be a family again. Along the way, in Arkansas, a dog bit her baby's face, the wound requiring fifty-four stitches. That only delayed an already arduous journey, and, when she arrived in Las Vegas, she was eager to be reunited with her husband.

He told her he worked at the newly built Stardust. She asked where he was, but management said they had never heard of him. She went to the Domino Motel where he said he was staying. He had never checked in.

"I walked up and down Las Vegas Boulevard, thinking he'd see me and the kids and stop," Richards recalled. "The first day was unsuccessful, the second day was unsuccessful, and the third day unsuccessful. I left the car parked on the street outside the motel so he could recognize it, but he never came."

The following day, she met a man named Merle Richards, who had seen her walking up and down the Strip and asked her what she was doing. When she told him she was looking for her husband, Richards conveyed to her that he was probably never coming back.

Merle got her a job at the Little Church of the West Wedding Chapel inside the Last Frontier Hotel. She worked as a secretary, calling the minister when a couple came in to get married, filling out the marriage license, and playing the 78-rpm record of, "The Wedding March." Richards even made side money by constructing floral arrangements in her kitchen and selling them at the chapel.

She got her first marriage annulled and, shortly after, married Merle. Life with Merle wasn't perfect, but it was as close to normal as Richards had experienced. Merle was an alcoholic, and he was at the bar more than at home, but Richards made it work.

"He definitely rescued us," she recalled. "He was a terrible alcoholic, but I loved him so much."

Richards had stability with her job at the chapel, and that was enough to distract her from a bad marriage. Still, something was missing. Richards didn't know what it was but believed her life had a hole in it. She had a revelation one night in the most unlikely of places. She was in a bar, looking for her wayward husband, when she met a young man named Jeremiah who was estranged from his parents. She called his father, who was a pastor, and agreed to fly back to Oklahoma to return their son.

When Richards arrived in Oklahoma with Jeremiah, his father invited her to a tent revival he hosted. Richards was not a religious woman and didn't get much out of the experience.

"I wasn't making any headway as far as God was concerned," she noted. "I was kind of bitter. I didn't know who I was or who I was going to be."

Richards kept taking trips back to Oklahoma, however. Part of the reason was to take a break from her husband, whose drinking had worsened.

"I enjoyed it; I just didn't know why," Richards said of her travels. "I wasn't ready to give my all to the Lord."

On her ninth trip, the moment grasped her and wouldn't let go.

"I was in the church, and it hit me," Richards recalled. "Whatever it was, I wanted it. I felt the touch of God, and my whole life changed in that church."

When she came back to Las Vegas, she wanted to share her life-altering change with her husband but found news that immediately tested her faith. Merle had met another woman, admitting his infidelity.

"I had just given my heart to the Lord, and now this was what God was going to do with me?" Richards questioned. "I sat and thought about it, and thought if this was the work of God, he sure isn't very good. I really felt that way. I realized later that was God's will. Everything happens for a reason."

The two stayed together but lived apart. A few months after his confession, Merle succumbed to his disease. Richards was devastated. While she was grieving over Merle's death, A Little White Chapel went up for auction. With the help of some friends, Richards was able to buy the business. It became her new love and, along with her unwavering faith, the foundation of her life.

The early '60s was a golden era for Las Vegas. The town attracted celebrities like Frank Sinatra and Judy Garland, both of whom utilized the services of the chapel. Other notables who got married there over the years have included actors Joan Collins, Bruce Willis, and Demi Moore, and NBA superstar Michael Jordan.

The chapel was one of more than forty in the city known for easy and quick nuptials. Richards knew early on that she had to stand out if she wanted to survive. She put her floral business there, allowing brides to pick out arrangements on the property. She also had tux and bridal gown rentals, as well as a pink Cadillac that customers could get married in.

One of her biggest innovations was the drive-thru wedding kiosk. Richards had disabled clients who sought her services, and when she saw them struggle to get out of their vehicles, she came up with the idea to put a stand in the parking lot under a covered roof so they could easily say their "I dos." It became so popular that other nondisabled couples took advantage of the drive-thru wedding.

Over the years, the area changed. It lost its glamour, and the little motels families stayed at in the sixties and seventies became dens for drug addicts and prostitutes. Richards didn't bemoan her new reality, instead, seeing an opportunity. She reached out to her transitory neighbors and tried to talk to as many as would listen. To Richards, they represented the lost souls God instructed his followers to help.

"I have prostitutes walk by all the time," Richards said. "I try to talk to them about the Lord. I tell them there's another way."

She shared with them resources they can use, such as drug treatment centers, women's shelters, and crisis centers. She had served on several boards of nonprofits designed to help the people she encounters every day.

"I would like to help them all, but I am so busy with my business," Richards explained. "I have to take care of that first."

An ordained minister for more than forty years, Richards visited with couples before the ceremony to make sure they were committed to other By law, she was not allowed to marry anyone who was intoxicated, but that was about the only city restriction. Richards had a much more stringent set of rules she imposed. Before the proceedings, she distributed her "Recipe for a Happy Marriage," which included two heaping cups of kindness, four armfuls of gentleness, and one lifetime of togetherness. She will not tolerate disruptions during the ceremony and often offered to pray over the couple afterward.

"I know some places don't take weddings seriously," Richards stated. "But I do. This was a serious commitment you are making with God."

Richards, who was in her seventies, gave up on love in her life years ago, instead devoting herself to a higher calling.

"It wasn't meant to be for me," Richards declared with a touch of sadness in her voice. "I dedicated myself to God."

She then looked at me, and her eyes softened. She took my hand and asked, "What about you? Are you married?"

"No," I replied.

"Well, don't give up. It will happen for you," she said, smiling. "I will pray that you find someone special."

Funny, I thought as I hugged her goodbye, *I believed I just did.*

CHAPTER 44

This was it. There were no other side highways or detours to take. Nor were there any other possibilities to delay coming home, other than taking the little money I had remaining and sitting in some casino's dusty keno parlor, sucking on secondhand smoke, and listening to colorful language from little old ladies who failed to hit their ten-spot for the millionth time. I never knew someone could get so enraged over losing a dollar. I had lost 200 times more money in five minutes at a craps table in Las Vegas and didn't exhibit the ire or spew the profanities that these senior citizens managed to emit.

So, as glamorous as that lifestyle seemed to be, I decided to grab some breakfast and then head south the remaining 242 miles to my apartment in Sunset Beach, California. I chose for my last meal on the road the quintessential fare that Sin City was famous for and, in many ways, epitomized America. I went to an all-you-can-eat buffet. The breakfast version was just as gaudy as the lunch and dinner offerings. Of course, if a veteran of eating at the buffet, one went late in the shift to maximize one's food-eating dollar. For example, show up close to 11 a.m., and one paid the breakfast price but was going to get lunch items as well. Grab a late lunch and stall, and dinner choices started to appear.

It didn't matter to the casino. They charged less than ten bucks at the Sahara for breakfast, and it was probably a loss-leader for the resort, another attraction to get people in to gamble. That was the original intent when the buffet was established in 1941 at the El Rancho Vegas. The theme was a Western chuck wagon, and twenty-four hours a day, gamblers could pay a dollar and feast on a variety of cold cuts, salad, and some hot dishes. The excess of Vegas was born in the advertising, which said, "Every possible hot and cold entree to appease the howling coyote in your innards in the late-night, pre-dawn hours. Everything you can eat, and you'll want it all!"

The buffet had evolved since then, but the concept remained the same and was on display when I swung by the Sahara. There was an omelet bar, with a chef making the custom entrée for an eager line of people. Next to it was a carving station with ham, pork loin, and sausage. There was a row of food on each side of those stations. Scrambled eggs, eggs benedict, chorizo and eggs, ham scrambles, breakfast-link sausage, sausage patties, bacon, ham patties, shrimp, biscuits and gravy, cheese blintzes, fried chicken, baked chicken, chicken fried steak, pancakes, blueberry pancakes, French toast, waffles, chicken hash, bagels, smoked salmon, toast, cinnamon rolls, apple Danish, muffins, and croissants were all on display, and, by the look of some of the patrons, it appeared they had been here many times. It certainly made me feel better about the bulge around my midsection, smaller in comparison. I would be lying if I didn't admit to getting my money's worth, however, though I justified my gluttony by thinking I needed the extra food for the day's excursion.

Shortly after breakfast, I was loading my duffel bag onto the back of the Harley and securing it with bungee cords. Part of me was content with returning to Sunset Beach and falling back into some pattern of normalcy. My job was waiting for me, but I had already decided somewhere in the Midwest that I was quitting. There were people who needed me. There would be other jobs; there wouldn't be another mother or best friend. I had pushed my luck long enough and wanted to get back and be with them as much as they would let me. I knew Heather would be happy to see me. I wasn't sure what my mom's reaction would be.

Then, there was the other half of me who thought maybe I should head north and try to find a new adventure. Fall was here, and winter would come soon enough. I could find work at one of the ski resorts in Utah or Colorado, make enough money, and then head out in the spring when the weather got nice again. It didn't take me long to rule out that career choice, however. I was certain that my ski-bunny days were over, middle-age getting in the way and all. I would be the oldest guy in the ski lodge, with people half my age looking at me with a mixture of pity and contempt.

No, it was time. I knew it. My body was the swing vote. It was time to go home and recover from 11,265 miles and forty states. *Not bad*, I thought, *for a little more than two months.* I had seen over two-thirds of this country on a motorcycle and met more people in seventy-three days than most encountered in a lifetime. What I needed more than anything was a chiropractor and a gym membership. I was convinced my spine was completely out of alignment after riding on a motorcycle for so long and then rewarding myself with lumpy motel mattresses. The food I ate was not good for me, as well. Diner food, while delicious, was a sin I was going to have to cleanse on a treadmill and stationary bicycle for double the time I was on the road.

Going to Southern California from Las Vegas was a trip I had taken countless times. The journey home was usually done with a lighter wallet. I had lost my rent money on several occasions before I started taking gambling much more seriously. I came up to Southern Nevada two years before I could legally gamble. A couple of places either didn't know or didn't care that I was under twenty-one. Sometimes the jaunts north were with friends, but several outings were solo.

My early years of gambling were when all the mistakes were made, and I was certain I committed just about every error possible. The biggest faux pas was downing all the free alcohol the cocktail waitresses served me while I was playing. A great strategy for the casino, not so much for the customer. If I did manage to stay sober for more than fifteen minutes, I might get lucky and win a few hands of blackjack. Then the adult beverages would kick in, and my chip stack would disappear as fast as my vodka.

It was a costly education, and those long car trips back to Los Angeles gave me time to contemplate what had transpired in the prior forty-eight hours. In a beat-up car with no radio, I had plenty of time to think, traversing through the middle of the desert, wondering what excuse I could tell my landlord so he wouldn't evict me. After determining what I thought was a plausible reason to warrant why the rent wasn't coming, I could move on to why my gambling skills were so unsatisfactory. It took a lot of trial and error, but I improved exponentially by the time I turned thirty.

This ride home came with a stuffed wallet. I hit a streak of luck on the craps table the previous evening and was $500 richer. It would certainly make the dull descent through the desert more pleasant.

Still, the uncertainty of what the future held at home was foremost in my mind when I crossed the Nevada-California border. I had grown fond of the free will I had experienced the last two-plus months. I could wake up when I wanted, knowing I could do anything I desired or go anyplace I chose. It was a prospect that many claim to yearn for but were terrified of after a taste of it. Most people inherently need routines. They want to wake up at the same time, go to a secure job, and leave that job at a certain hour. That was what comforted them.

I never did like being boxed in. I had a suspicion that was my mindset, and it was only reinforced on the trip. It was perfectly acceptable to be who I was. I was done apologizing for being different. If I didn't want to conform to society or believe wholeheartily in the American Dream, then those who loved me would accept that, and those who didn't would be exiled from my life.

I had my own dream that I had formulated in my mind from the people I met as I rode across the country. The truck-stop dentist showed me I could follow a career in an unconventional but satisfying way. The traveling preacher taught me that leaving behind everything that was comfortable was a destiny that can't be controlled. Even Patsy Cline had influenced me into believing that those who ostracized me for following my dreams were only scared of pursuing their own.

I would be my own person, beholden to no one. I remembered a family friend who didn't care for my lifestyle and, in her passive-aggressive manner, tried to insult me.

"You don't miss many meals do you," she said.

"I don't miss much of anything," I shot back.

And that was the key to my happiness. It just took thousands of miles of road therapy to finally figure it out. I knew there would be coworkers who would question my decision to quit. I didn't even know if I was going to waste my breath trying to explain why. They wouldn't understand, and they certainly wouldn't accept it. Much easier to smile and walk away. My family had been used to my quirkiness since I was a little boy, so they might not even notice.

As I rolled through Barstow, I felt contentment that only someone who was at peace with himself can possess. I did have one issue. How was I going to fund my lifestyle and escape the machine? I had two hours left to devise a strategy, and, if nothing else, racking my brain for a solution would pass the time.

I was no closer to an answer when I got off the freeway exit for my apartment, but the excitement of being less than five miles from the end of my journey distracted me from my conundrum. As I neared the beach, I began to see the familiar landmarks of my town. I crossed the bridge that dissected the Seal Beach Naval Weapons Shipyard, and then I descended into Sunset Beach.

My hometown looked the same, and my apartment was a welcome sight. I parked Libertad and opened my garage, pulling her inside. I took off my duffel bag and went up the stairs to my front door. I got inside and plopped my luggage down in the living room.

I stripped off my clothes, thankful I wouldn't have to wear jeans for a while. I put on a bathing suit, T-shirt, and sandals, and made my way to the beach.

The sun was shining, but fall was near, and the Pacific Ocean was already chilly. The waves bounced me around the gentle surf as I just swam and floated, enjoying the water. I started to come ashore, and, when I reached the border of the surf and the sand, I looked out to my right and saw the Queen Mary in the distance. To the left, farther out on the horizon, there were massive cargo ships and a cruise ship, waiting to get into the Port of San Pedro. They were the typical vessels that I would see daily, and they made me smile. A comforting regularity slowly returned.

Closer to me, there were a couple of fishing boats, the people on board going after calico bass, yellowtail, perch, and halibut. One boat was beyond the fishing vessels. It looked like a yacht and seemed slightly out of place. It was larger than several of the ones I had seen in Huntington Harbour, the main dock for luxury craft across the street from my dwelling. The yacht left the harbor, going through the channel and under the bridge I had crossed thirty minutes earlier, making its way to Anaheim Bay and finally out to the Pacific Ocean.

The yacht was now barely in view, and its size told me it was going somewhere farther than an afternoon pleasure cruise. It gradually disappeared from my sight, but even though I couldn't see it any longer, I still pondered where it might be headed. *Mexico, perhaps or maybe Hawaii, or even Alaska.* While the water from the ocean nipped at my feet, I fantasized about what it would be like to ride to Alaska on my motorcycle.

ACKNOWLEDGMENTS

As are most books, this one was an odyssey, and though the writing is mine alone, it was not a solo endeavor. So many people encouraged and assisted me at the beginning of my journey, during it, and after it was over.

Valuable insights on what to expect on the road came selflessly from Mark Montgomery, Bob Hutton, George Reiter, Ken Skolyan, David Jewell, Ken Steinhardt, Eric Goldberg, and Ron Stewart. Their collective years of riding numbered in the hundreds, and they prepared me for every possible scenario. The logistics of the trip went nearly flawlessly because of them.

Along the way, friends and family provided meals, lodging, moral support, and a loving ear to bend. Jeff Donlin, Warren Harkins, Brian Robin, Michael Miller, Louie Steinkirchner, Bernie Steinkirchner, Carolyn Steinkirchner, Paul Steinkirchner, Chris Aguilar, Michael Conyers, Michelle Brugman, Tom Reger, and Diane Montgomery.

My quirks as a writer are many. One is practicing my craft in public places. I usually write in bars or open spaces where I am graciously allowed by management to occupy a table and smoke a cigar. At the table with me is a yellow legal pad, pen, and a drink.

Finding places that would break the smoking law in California and let me smoke in their establishment was a challenge. A few did in Sunset Beach, Huntington Beach, Buena Park, and Trabuco Canyon.

Moving to Las Vegas made the task easier. The employees at the Chevron Snow Mountain Smoke Shop let me sit for hours outside, smoking and writing, and buying only a diet Coke. A large portion of the book was written there, and thank them for indulging me.

This book would not have been possible without three people. The first is Judi Hoelderlin. I spent countless hours with this amazing woman whose expertise helped me get my life straightened out.

The second is Jordan Fabish. Her mastery and love of the English language were evident in her thorough editing. The attention to detail and proficiency with grammar made me a better writer. Her graceful touches are sprinkled throughout, and I am forever in her debt.

Lastly, I want to thank my wife, Brenda. She, more than anyone else, knew how much I labored over this book. I asked for more solitude to write than any husband should demand, but Brenda never balked at my requests. Without her understanding, the book would not have been completed. She is a woman I don't deserve, but I am thankful every day that she accepted my proposal.

CPSIA information can be obtained
at www.ICGtesting.com
Printed in the USA
BVHW042009060223
657986BV00004B/14